What Your Colleagues Are Saying . . .

"Jim Burke and Barry Gilmore's *Academic Moves for College and Career Readiness* provides clarity and structure for teachers who seek to help their students become more competent and confident thinkers, and does so without compromising the critical role of a teacher's content knowledge and creativity in a dynamic classroom. Its economy of expression makes complex ideas accessible, while annotated student work provides a window into learner application. Most significantly, the book is written in the voice of teachers, who live what they recommend."

—CAROL ANN TOMLINSON,
William Clay Parrish, Jr., Professor, University of Virginia,
and Author of *The Differentiated Classroom*, Second Edition

"Burke and Gilmore present a powerful and practical synthesis of the highest-leverage thinking moves that students—especially linguistically diverse students—need to develop for school, work, and life. They provide what teachers want: clear and concise descriptions of each thinking move, analyses of student work samples, and innovative classroom practices and scaffolds that can be used to develop the moves in a variety of contexts. Fifteen stars!"

—JEFF ZWIERS,
Senior Researcher at Stanford University

"Jim Burke's books need to be on the 'must-read' list of—at the very least—all English teachers! *Academic Moves for College and Career Readiness* is a worthy addition to that list with the 'academic and thinking' moves he and his coauthor, Barry Gilmore, describe critical for any of us who want to 'up our game' in the classroom."

—LARRY FERLAZZO,
Teacher, *Education Week* Advice Columnist, and
Author of *Helping Students Motivate Themselves*

"What sets *Academic Moves for College and Career Readiness* apart is its emphasis on student practice and practical application of exemplary instruction. This book speaks to teachers in *their* language across curriculum areas. Burke and Gilmore have hit the mark on what our students need for college and career readiness."

—JAYNE ELLSPERMANN,
National Principal of the Year (2014)

ACADEMIC MOVES

for College and Career Readiness

Grades 6–12

....

15 MUST-HAVE SKILLS EVERY STUDENT NEEDS TO ACHIEVE

....

JIM BURKE & BARRY GILMORE

www.resources.corwin.com/burkeacademicmoves

CORWIN LITERACY

FOR INFORMATION:

Corwin

A SAGE Company

2455 Teller Road

Thousand Oaks, California 91320

(800) 233-9936

www.corwin.com

SAGE Publications Ltd.

1 Oliver's Yard

55 City Road

London EC1Y 1SP

United Kingdom

SAGE Publications India Pvt. Ltd.

B 1/I 1 Mohan Cooperative Industrial Area

Mathura Road, New Delhi 110 044

India

SAGE Publications Asia-Pacific Pte. Ltd.

3 Church Street

#10-04 Samsung Hub

Singapore 049483

Publisher: Lisa Luedeke

Editorial Development Manager: Julie Nemer

Editorial Assistant: Emeli Warren

Production Editor: Melanie Birdsall

Copy Editor: Patrice Sutton

Typesetter: C&M Digitals (P) Ltd.

Proofreader: Scott Oney

Indexer: Amy Murphy

Interior Designer: Gail Buschman

Cover Designer: Rose Storey

Director of Marketing Strategy: Maura Sullivan

Printed in the United States of America

Library of Congress Cataloging-in-Publication Data

Burke, Jim, 1961-

Academic moves for college and career readiness, grades 6-12 : 15 must-have skills every student needs to achieve / Jim Burke, Barry Gilmore.

pages cm
Includes bibliographical references and index.

ISBN 978-1-4833-7980-7 (pbk.: alk. paper)

1. Thought and thinking—Study and teaching—United States.
2. College preparation programs—United States.
3. Education—Standards—United States. I. Gilmore, Barry. II. Title.

LB1590.3.B87 2015
370.15′2—dc23   2014045597

This book is printed on acid-free paper.

16 17 18 19 10 9 8 7 6 5 4 3 2

CONTENTS with list of student samples

15. Transform

Visit the companion website at
www.resources.corwin.com/burkeacademicmoves
for downloadable resources, including reproducible
annotated student essays, Mental Moves, Rubrics,
Planning Pages, and more.

Detailed definitions clearly break down each concept

Bold headings foreground each term and highlight related keywords

The Main Idea gets at the gist of each skill

Before: Preparing Students to Analyze sections set the stage for successful instruction

Shaded boxes provide guidance on introducing students to each move

1

Analyze

break something down methodically into its parts

break down · deconstruct · examine

Analyze: break something down methodically into its parts to understand how it is made, what it is, how it works; look at something critically in order to grasp its essence

CORE CONNECTIONS

- Determine central ideas or themes of a text and **analyze** their development (RL2)
- **Analyze** how and why individuals, events, and ideas develop and interact over the course of a text (RL3)
- **Analyze** how specific word choices shape meaning or tone (RL4)
- **Analyze** the structure of texts (RL5)
- **Analyze** how two or more texts address similar themes or topics (RL9)
- **Analyze** and interpret data to determine similarities and differences in findings (NGSS, MS-PS1-2)

The Main Idea

Analysis is such a pervasive goal of teachers in all disciplines that it may even seem difficult, at first, to define the concept or to frame it as a clear process. Indeed, the term *analyze* appears so often in prompts and academic instructions that it's easy to assume that this is a skill students already possess. Yet analyzing a painting, a current event, a passage of **text**, or a conversation, each requires similar steps that may not be intuitive to all students.

Underlying Skills:

- **Understand genres and conventions.** What comprises a novel? What are the elements of a science experiment, a primary source, or a poem?
- **Recognize *tools or elements*.** In order to analyze, students must be able to pick out pieces of a text such as rhetorical devices, elements of design, or types of **argument**.
- **Recognize *patterns and structures*.** Students must develop the habit of watching for repetition or other structural elements.

Before: Preparing Students to Analyze

Students may bring misconceptions to the task of analysis. As you practice analysis for your subject area, be sure to clarify the need for the following with your students:

Suspend your judgment.	**Do more than summarize.**
Analysis should be based on evidence. You can use analysis to form an academic argument, but analysis differs from an opinion.	Too often, students who are asked to analyze fall back on recounting only what happens. Analysis involves critical thinking and examination.
Example: Imagine you're asked to analyze the effectiveness of a speech by the mayor of your town. Whether or not you voted for the mayor or agree with his/ her platform is not the point; your analysis must be based on the tools used to convey meaning within the speech itself.	*Example: An essay prompt asks you to analyze a character in a novel. Rather than merely describing what the character does, you must look at how the author uses tools such as description or dialogue to build the character in a way that creates meaning.*

Before you teach students to analyze a text, issue, situation, or work, try these four things:

- **Model:** Save student work so that you can show a class a successful example of a piece broken down into its component parts (see example, page 9). Have students practice the task of analysis on the piece in pairs or groups.
- **Define Expectations:** What does a successful analysis in your discipline look like? If it's presented in an essay, do you expect to see specific types of **evidence**, a particular type of thesis statement, or a particular conclusion?
- **Build Content Knowledge:** Give students the academic language and understanding they need to look for evidence effectively. Do they need to understand terms such as *diction* or *tone*? Do they need to know *how* to read a political cartoon or a data chart? Prepare students for success by giving them the tools to analyze in your content area.
- **Practice Mental Moves:** Assign short texts to small groups or pairs and have students practice making the mental moves and answering the questions described in the Mental Moves feature in the side bar. As you introduce skills such as analyzing, post the moves on the wall and keep circling back to them so that students internalize them and **transfer** them to new learning situations.

Core Connections provides an at-a-glance view of related national and state standards

Underlying Skills showcases the objective of the lessons in each section

Sidebars
distill the
intellectual
process behind
each academic
move

During:
Practicing
sections get
straight to
the heart of
modeling
usage and
giving students
practice

- **Practice Mental Moves:** As students prepare to construct academic arguments, have them research ideas and then discuss those ideas in small groups or pairs by answering the questions listed in the Mental Moves feature in the sidebar. Post these questions on the wall and keep circling back to them so that students internalize them and can **transfer** them to new learning situations.

Obstacles to the Moves

When teaching students to argue, watch out for these areas of difficulty:

- **Faulty Logic.** Basing an argument on a mistaken assumption (such as a misunderstanding of a plot point, for instance) can undermine a strong argument. Help students avoid such missteps by asking them to research carefully.

- **Lack of Clarity.** Academic arguments often reside in formal papers. Sometimes, students will be so convinced that their audience wants a certain level of formality in writing that they overdo it and lose clarity and precision.

- **Hasty Assumptions.** As with faulty logic, overgeneralizing (say, about a historical era) can lead to a weak argument. Help students be precise.

Mental Moves

Argue

1. Make a Claim
What is my position?

2. Support the Claim
What evidence best supports this position?

3. Anticipate Opposition
What might an opponent of my position claim?

4. Consider Your Audience
What type of appeal will best convince my audience?

5. Integrate
How will I structure my discussion of claim and counterclaims?

During: Practicing Analysis

Students get better at analysis with practice. Whether they're trying to make sense of a football play or the design of a football stadium, repetition is a key to developing analytical skill.

In approaching texts—whether the "text" is a paragraph, a poem, an advertisement, or a video—the key skill in analysis is **close reading** and observation. Close reading doesn't come naturally to many students; practice helps move students past a "read and done" mentality to a habit of rereading and digging deeper.

To give students practice in close reading, try this:

- Present a short text to the class—for instance, a magazine ad, an opening paragraph, or a commercial

- Have students work in small group to select key details—word from a text, literal descriptions of a picture, or patterns—that they think *might* be meaningful. Each group should list around ten.

- Combine the words from all groups on the board. Then, ask students to work with a partner to draw an inference from the list. What overarching emotions or ideas emerge from the list as a whole?

- As a class, share and discuss the inferences. Could you create a thesis statement about the meaning of the piece from these insights? If so, what might it be?

ELL Focus: Do This One Thing to Help

Inference is likely to be harder for English language learners (ELL) students than others when dealing with verbal texts, but pictures bridge language. Try an inference activity that begins with the visual and allow students to write down important details in their own languages before composing their conclusive statements in English.

Discussion, Presentation, Technology, and Multimedia

- **Discuss.** Analysis can occur on many levels. Close reading takes place microscopically; students must practice **zooming in** to the level of words in order to make sense of a text. But macroscopic, or "zooming out," exercises are also valuable activities. Discussion is a critical vehicle for this level of comprehension and analysis Small group discussion should happen frequently and can also take place at the end of a unit, novel study, or grading period.

- **Role Play.** Consider role play as a means of asking students to analyze. Assign each student a character or historical figure, for instance, to represent in a discussion—students will have to use the same process of gathering evidence and drawing conclusions to portray a figure accurately.

ELL Focus:
Do This One
Thing to Help
sections give
quick-tips for
differentiating
instruction

Discussion,
Presentation,
Technology,
and Multimedia
sections cover
important
classroom
considerations

After: Producing sections spotlight students making their academic moves

The task describes a sample student assignment

Scaffolding With Webb's DOK pages demonstrate how to strategically lead instruction for each skill to drive deeper understanding

---

After: **Producing Analysis**

Student Example 1: The Analytical Essay

By the end of his tenth grade year, Spencer was one of the top writers in his class. Naturally insightful about literature and abstract ideas to begin with, Spencer acquired skills during tenth grade that improved his ability to construct an essay—the ability to incorporate quotes more smoothly, for instance, and the ability to construct more complex sentences.

Nonetheless, the assignment to analyze a nonfiction text, William Faulkner's short but thorny Nobel Prize acceptance speech, proved challenging. After grappling with some of the complicated ideas in the speech and discussing the historical context with his teacher, however, Spencer wrote a typically strong essay.

A key step in Spencer's approach to the text was his annotation of the speech. Spencer's teacher helped him move beyond simple highlighting to careful zooming in by suggesting he mark the following then conferencing with him about his notes on the speech:

- Words and phrases that convey more than a literal meaning
- Shifts and transition words
- Phrases that seem to sum up a big idea
- Examples of unusual syntax, such as fragments or rhetorical questions

Here is one paragraph from Spencer's final draft:

> Faulkner speaks to future writers more than he thanks the givers of the award, which is generally what an award-receiving speech might concern, inspiring them to prevail and reminding them of the worth of the poet in mankind's existence. In the second paragraph, for instance, Faulkner begins to speak of mankind's fears, and how they can affect his spirit—this then leads to the benefits of letting go of these fears: good writing based on universal "truths of the heart." In this middle section of the speech, Faulkner uses diction: "sweat," "heart," "bones," "scars," and "glands" to produce a very natural image of the human body, expressing the toil that man must labor through to create good universal stories. Faulkner does not write this off as an easy task but one that takes courage to forget all one's fears, lest they end up writing empty stories, ones that leave no mark on any "universal bones." He uses body imagery as a window to describe.

The Task

William Faulkner's Nobel Prize acceptance speech consists of five paragraphs delivered in 1950, shortly after World War II. As you read it, pay attention to rhetorical tools, such as imagery, metaphor, and diction. Then, write an essay in which you analyze Faulkner's point of view.

1. Look Closely
Spencer homes in on a single paragraph to illustrate his point.

2. Select Details
Spencer collects a series of specific words that serve as evidence for his argument.

3. Find Patterns
Spencer has broken the speech into three parts for his essay, noting the structural transitions between each section of Faulkner's argument.

4. Infer
Throughout his paper, Spencer looks for more than the literal level of Faulkner's message.

Scaffolding Analysis With Webb's DOK

HOW SPENCER WORKED

Level One (Recall)
- *Sample Task:* Annotate or make notes in order to identify and remember appropriate evidence for your analysis.
- *What Spencer Did:* Read through the speech, marking phrases he thought he might quote with particular attention to inferences.

Level Two (Skill)
- *Sample Task:* Organize the details you have found into categories that will contribute to your understanding of the bigger picture. *How do details x and y differ from z?*
- *What Spencer Did:* Analyzed each paragraph of the speech, honing in on the main point and how it contributed to overall meaning.

Level Three (Strategic Thinking)
- *Sample Task:* Plan your argument by considering an overall point and how to support it. *Which groups of evidence can support _____, and how should they be presented?*
- *What Spencer Did:* Developed a thesis statement and wrote the essay by integrating quotations, paraphrasing, and his own interpretations.

Level Four (Extended Thinking)
- *Sample Task:* Compare this piece to others of similar or different genres and, using research and knowledge built over time, analyze it in the context of other speeches and its historical time.
- *What Spencer Might Have Done:* Spencer might have gone on to compare Faulkner's speech to another Nobel acceptance speech, such as Toni Morrison's, researching context and applying knowledge built from other units of study or even from other classes in his comparison.

Student examples focus on a range of genres and illustrate the product to look for and the process to get there

Shaded boxes highlight the mental moves as they appear in a student work

Reproducible rubrics simplify the assessment process

Planning Pages provide space for recording lesson objectives

Rubric for Analytical Responses

SCORE	THESIS AND OVERALL ANALYSIS	USE OF EVIDENCE	ORGANIZATION	STYLE, VOICE, AND CLARITY	CONVENTIONS AND MECHANICS
5 Outstanding	A well-developed thesis introduces a sophisticated interpretation that goes beyond a literal level with nuanced and interesting insights	Ample and appropriately selected details effectively support the analysis throughout the response	Clear and consistent organization with well-executed transitions excellently supports the analysis, including an excellent introduction and conclusion	The response is clear and original and employs appropriate stylistic elements for effect in an exceptional manner	Syntax, grammar, and conventions are correct and add to the effectiveness of the response
4 Exceeds Expectations	The thesis is clear and introduces an interpretation that goes beyond a literal level	Appropriately selected details support the analysis throughout the response	The organization is clear and supports analysis; the introduction and conclusion are well-executed	The response is clear and employs appropriate stylistic elements for effect	Few or no errors are present in usage or syntax
3 Meets Expectations	The thesis is clear; interpretation may not reach beyond literal or obvious levels	Details adequately support the analysis but may demonstrate some inconsistencies in execution or application	The organization, including introduction and conclusion, are adequate to support the analysis	The response is mostly clear and adequately employs stylistic elements	Minor errors in usage may be present, but without repetition or undermining overall effectiveness
2 Approaching Expectations	The thesis is vague or unclear; the analysis may not accurately interpret the work	There is insufficient evidence to support the analysis or details are not always adequate to support analytical points	Some flaws in organization or lack of clarity and transitions make the analysis hard to follow	The response may be unclear or misuses stylistic elements in ways that interfere with voice and meaning	Patterns of errors in usage or syntax undermine the effectiveness of the response
1 Well Below Expectations	The thesis is vague or absent, and analysis is inaccurate	Evidence and details are missing or insufficient to support the analysis	The organization lacks focus and clarity; transitions may be unclear	The response is vague or lacks clarity; stylistic choices may confuse rather than enhance meaning	Significant errors in usage or syntax obscure the meaning and effectiveness of the response

Planning Page: Analyze

Analyze: break something down methodically into its parts to understand how it is made, what it is, how it works; look at something critically in order to grasp its essence

Learning Goal
What will your students analyze? What learning outcomes or assessments do you wish to see?

Before How will you prepare students to analyze texts, issues, situations, or works?	**During** What activities will you use to model, scaffold, and engage students in analysis?	**After** How will you measure the effectiveness of your lesson?

Notes From This Chapter
What ideas or activities from this chapter do you wish to remember as you teach students to analyze?

Introduction

The genesis of this book stems from something most of us do nearly every day at work: waiting to get on the copy machine to run off a few handouts for class. One day as I (Jim) waited impatiently to get my turn, I began surveying the stacks of handouts that waited to be retrieved and distributed to students. I found myself reflexively drawn to the language of the directions, problems, and prompts.

While the machines whirred out my colleagues' copies (and I wondered if I would get mine made in time for class!), I became fascinated with the handouts—the words, sentences, and general demands that such language makes on students' minds. I realized that these simple photocopies were what teachers are really putting in students' hands and telling them to do. Writing about the challenges and needs of English learners (ELs), Heritage, Silva, and Pierce (2007) insist that the challenge for teachers of ELs is to "plan instruction that meets the language learning needs of students to ensure that their ability to speak, listen, read, and write in academic subjects across the curriculum does not lag behind that of their peers" (p. 171).

The thing is, such "challenges" are by no means limited to ELs, for as these authors subsequently note, borrowing from Vygotsky, "language and thinking develop simultaneously through everyday sociocultural experiences, and [such] thinking occurs through scaffolded interaction . . . that takes place [during] more structured experiences" (p. 182). Nor, for that matter, are these challenges matters of vocabulary alone; rather, these obstacles to entering the academic world are as much about the cognitive or mental "moves" students need to be able to make when thinking and doing the work required by our different disciplines.

As if they had heard my thoughts, the teachers gathered around the copy machine began lamenting their struggles to get students to read, to write, to speak about—in short, to *think* in—their discipline. By this time, I had discovered and begun flipping through extra copies of textbooks stored in the copy room, finding in their directions and prompts the same words asking for the same mental moves and processes that the teachers around me complained their students could not do. There was, in other words, what Graff and Birkenstein call a "deep, underlying structure, [an] internal DNA" common to the academic and cognitive moves these various disciplines—and teachers—were asking students to make (2014, p. xxi).

At the word level, my colleagues were frustrated by students' lack of familiarity and fluency with "Tier Two" words, which are those words of "high utility for mature language users . . . found across a variety of domains" (Beck, McKeown, & Kucan, 2013, p. 9). It is facility with these "mortar words" that allows students to connect the "bricks" of the larger ideas we are trying to convey in our classes and teach our students to understand. The hope is that students can *do* these things— for example, *analyze, argue, determine*—with some fluency when reading, writing, or thinking about the complex, abstract, and higher-order ideas they encounter as they move from grade to grade (Zwiers, 2008, p. 24). These academic moves, captured in the fifteen words that compose the chapters in this book, are at the center of new SAT changes. As Cyndie Schmeiser, chief of assessments for the College Board, reported: "Gone from the SAT are words like *turgid, sagacious,* (and probably, *umbrage*!) and instead, words that gain their meaning from context. . . . Words kids will use in college and the world . . . *synthesize, analyze*" (2014).

From the start, we asked how we might address the need to teach students these academic and mental moves crucial not only to English but also to all core academic subjects. After much discussion and many e-mails, we arrived at what seemed a concise but useful list of fifteen words that we immediately realized were, as mentioned above, not merely words but essential *moves* in the classroom as well as on assessments, such as the Common Core and the SAT and ACT. We also took the extra step of checking these words against such standards documents as the Common Core State Standards so as to ensure these were the words most commonly used to describe what students should know how to do. Some years back, in his book *To Think*, Frank Smith grappled with the same question, eventually arriving at 77 "thinking words" (1990, p. 2). Smith's list includes all the words discussed here, but many more than any of us have time to use (or teach!) when designing lessons, assessments, or writing prompts.

The fifteen "academic moves" presented here, along with the second list of alternative moves that are not so easily tested but nonetheless vital to more innovative and ambitious thinking, emerged over time through conversations we had with colleagues and each other, typically anchored in our own experiences in the classroom and Barry's insights as a former teacher and now principal who spends much of his time observing and evaluating teachers' instructional moves across a variety of subjects. It is this cross curricular integration that we hope you will agree is an especially powerful element of this book, for as Barry himself has written elsewhere, "Students must learn how to use literacy skills unique to science, social studies, English, and math and, at the same time, understand how such skills are related" (Lent & Gilmore, 2013, p. xxv).

Though every discipline comes with its own set of what many call "thinking moves" (see Dombek & Herndon, 2003; Ritchhart, Church, & Morrison, 2011), our aim (and hope) here is to help address what we might think of as a sort of Tower of Babel effect in which students go from class to class, within and across disciplines, hearing different words used to describe the same actions. On occasion, for example, students may hear a teacher say they want the class to "analyze" a text or set of data when, in fact, they meant "evaluate." This confusion is related to what Graff and Birkenstein have called "the Volleyball Effect," which they describe thus:

> Students are batted from one course and set of expectations to another as the rules mysteriously change without notice. Thus one instructor wants students to develop arguments and interpretations of their own, while another discourages it, wanting only evidence that the students grasp a body of information.... Making matters even more confusing, instructors are often not explicit about these expectations and prohibitions, leaving students to guess them, if they can, on their own. No wonder students often approach us with questions like "Do you want my ideas in this paper or just a summary of the reading?" (2009, p. 4)

Thus, another of our goals, one very important to us both and reflected in all our previous work, is that the words and the ideas in this book should be used to bring some consistency and clarity to the language we all use when teaching or designing assignments within and across disciplines. To that end, Jim's school has made the list of words with definitions into a poster that hangs in classrooms throughout the school and provided copies to teachers to keep handy for reference when planning lessons or meeting to assess or develop curriculum and assessments. Only through such integrated, sustained efforts within and across departments and grade levels can students achieve the sort of depth of knowledge and intellectual agility called for by models such as **Webb's Depth of Knowledge** (2002) and Wiggins's and McTighe's *Understanding by Design* (2011, 2013).

Ultimately, what we have done here is conduct a sort of cognitive audit of our own work and others' to see what we would find. This is exactly the sort of inquiry that Ritchhart, Church, and Morrison call for based on their work at Harvard's Project Zero and discussed in depth in their book *Making Thinking Visible*:

> To help you identify the possible discrepancy between students' classroom activity and teaching that is likely to lead to understanding, [b]egin by making a list of all the actions and activities with which your students are engaged in [a given] subject.... You might want to brainstorm the list with a couple of colleagues or teammates. Now, working from this list, create three new lists:
>
> 1. The actions students in your class spend most of their time doing. What actions account for 75% of what students do in your class on a regular basis?
>
> 2. The actions most authentic to the discipline, that is, those things that real scientists, writers, artists, and so on actually do as they go about their work.
>
> 3. The actions you remember doing yourself from a time when you were actively engaged in developing some new understanding of something within the discipline or subject area.

They summarize their emphasis on thinking within various subject areas by emphasizing the importance of not just "learning *about* the subject . . . [but] learning *to do* the subject, [which] means solving problems, making decisions, and developing new understanding using the methods and tools [and language] of the discipline" (2011, p. 10).

Findings by Ritchhart, Perkins, Tishman, and Palmer (as cited in Ritchhart, Church, et al., 2011) offer a useful complement to our central argument and core ideas discussed in this book. Seeking to identify the essential "thinking moves that are integral to understanding and

without which it would be difficult to say we had developed understanding" (p. 11), they identified a total of eight thinking moves, the last two of which align closely with our alternative list of words, which you will find in the appendices:

1. Observing closely and describing what's there

2. Building explanations and interpretations

3. Reasoning with evidence

4. Making connections

5. Considering different viewpoints and perspectives

6. Capturing the heart and forming conclusions

7. Wondering and asking questions

8. Uncovering complexity and going below the surface of things (Ritchhart, Perkins, et al., as cited in Ritchhart, Church, and Morrison, 2011, p. 11).

Despite the various challenges to and criticisms of the Common Core State Standards, one principle the CCSS framework has rightfully brought back into focus is the role of deep, sustained, analytical thinking across subject areas and grade levels. What we have endeavored to show here, above all, is what students can do when taught these academic moves and the means to use them in any subject area. You will see throughout this book middle and high school students designing and doing work that challenges us all to challenge our students—and ourselves—to do not just *more* but also better work. The ideas and lessons, assignments, and activities presented through and across all disciplines embody in powerful ways the "13 Habits of a Systems Thinker" recently introduced by Daniel Goleman and Peter Senge (2014).

Archimedes, who as a Greek mathematician, philosopher, scientist, and engineer provides a succinct model of the cross disciplinary mind and systems thinker, famously said that if given a long enough lever, he could move the world. Our hope here is that we have given you a list of words and ideas you and your students can use to move the world if given the chance to show what they know and can do thanks to the time they spent in your school, your department, and your classroom.

Works Cited

Beck, I. L., McKeown, M. G., & Kucan, L. (2013). *Bringing words to life: Robust vocabulary instruction* (2nd ed.). New York, NY: Guilford Press.

Dombek, K., & Herndon, S. (2003). *Critical passages: Teaching the transition to college composition.* New York, NY: Teachers College.

Graff, G., & Birkenstein, C. (2009, September). Exploring the continuum . . . between high school and college writing: An immodest proposal for connecting high school and college [Special issue, CCC Special Symposium]. *College Composition and Communication, 61*(1), 1–4.

Graff, G., & Birkenstein, C. (2014). *They say/I say: The moves that matter in academic writing* (High School ed.). New York, NY: Norton.

Heritage, M., Silva, N., & Pierce, M. (2007). Academic English: A view from the classroom. In A. L. Bailey (Ed.), *The language demands of school: Putting academic language to the test* (pp. 171–210). New Haven, CT: Yale.

Lent, R. C., & Gilmore, B. (2013). *Common Core CPR: What about the adolescents who struggle or just don't care?* Thousand Oaks, CA: Corwin.

Ritchhart, R., Church, M., & Morrison, K. (2011). *Making thinking visible.* San Francisco, CA: Wiley & Sons.

Schmeiser, C. (2014, March 6). Why the SAT won't penalize you for wrong answers. WYNC's *Brian Lehrer Show.* Retrieved from http://www.wnyc.org/shows/bl/

Smith, F. (1990). *To think.* New York, NY: Teachers College.

Zwiers, J. (2008). *Building academic language: Essential practices for content classrooms.* San Francisco, CA: Jossey-Bass.

Acknowledgments

A book such as this is the result of many people sharing with us their own ideas and discussing openly and in some detail their teaching practices to help us understand just what these essential academic moves are and how people teach them. We are particularly grateful to those teachers and colleagues who were willing to share and respond to our ideas from the earliest stages. These include Steve Mills, Di Yim, Melissa Murphy, and Morgan Hallabrin from Jim's school, as well as Corey Brown and all the teachers with whom Jim worked in the Fremont Unified School District.

Special thanks to the many teachers at Hutchison School and elsewhere who contributed to this work, including, in particular, Jennifer Futrell, Ivy Phillips, Donna Budynas, John Reynolds, Becky Deehr, and Sue Gilmore. These teachers shared not only their own ideas, but also provided offered the examples of student work used throughout the book to illustrate the ideas in practice. In addition, we thank the host of current and former students who allowed us to showcase particular assignments and products here.

Collaborations always come with challenges unique to the work and those involved in doing it. Yet on this project, the usual obstacles of time, distance, and differences of opinion were never anything but opportunities for us to dig deeper into our own experiences and learning. Throughout our efforts to write the book, people at Corwin were remarkable in their insights and support. Lisa Luedeke, our editor, "got it" from the moment we discussed the idea for the book with her; her guidance from the beginning helped to improve the book and our own understanding of what we were creating, and we're grateful for the help from Maura Sullivan, marketing manager; Julie Nemer, editorial development manager; Emeli Warren, editorial assistant; Melanie Birdsall, production editor; Rose Storey, cover designer; and Gail Buschman, interior designer.

As with any book we write, our deepest gratitude is always for our students, who remain our most important teachers when it comes to what is possible, and our families, who inevitably are called on to support us and make sacrifices of their own during the time we wrote this book.

Jim: As ever, my sincere gratitude to my wife Susan and daughter Nora for their patient support while I worked on the book. Most of all, however, this time around my deepest thanks must go to Barry Gilmore for agreeing to work with me on this project, and to Lisa Luedeke for bringing us together. I have long respected and admired Barry's work, and after working with him on this book, that regard has only deepened and matured.

Barry: My first thanks are extended to Katy and Zoe, my daughters, who not only show remarkable patience while I write but are sometimes even forced to test out ideas as well. I am also deeply grateful for the opportunity to collaborate with Jim, an educator whom I've considered a model of insight, thoughtfulness, and expertise for many years, and once again with Lisa, the best editor in this business.

Analyze

break something down methodically into its parts

break down • deconstruct • examine

Analyze: break something down methodically into its parts to understand how it is made, what it is, how it works; look at something critically in order to grasp its essence

CORE CONNECTIONS

- Determine central ideas or themes of a text and **analyze** their development (R2)

- **Analyze** how and why individuals, events, and ideas develop and interact over the course of a text (R3)

- **Analyze** how specific word choices shape meaning or tone (R4)

- **Analyze** the structure of texts (R5)

- **Analyze** how two or more texts address similar themes or topics (R9)

- **Analyze** and interpret data to determine similarities and differences in findings (NGSS, MS-PS1–2)

The Main Idea

Analysis is such a pervasive goal of teachers in all disciplines that it may even seem difficult, at first, to define the concept or to frame it as a clear process. Indeed, the term *analyze* appears so often in prompts and academic instructions that it's easy to assume that this is a skill students already possess. Yet whether students analyze a painting, a current event, a passage of **text**, or a conversation, they must use similar steps that may not be intuitive.

Underlying Skills:

- **Understand *genres* and *conventions*.** What comprises a novel? What are the elements of a science experiment, a primary source, or a poem?

- **Recognize *tools* or *elements*.** In order to analyze, students must be able to pick out pieces of a text such as rhetorical devices, elements of design, or types of **argument**.

- **Recognize *patterns* and *structures*.** Students must develop the habit of watching for repetition or other structural elements.

Before: Preparing Students to Analyze

Students may bring misconceptions to the task of analysis. As you practice analysis for your subject area, be sure to clarify the need for the following with your students:

Suspend your judgment. Analysis should be based on evidence. You can use analysis to form an academic argument, but analysis differs from an opinion. *Example: Imagine you're asked to analyze the effectiveness of a speech by the mayor of your town. Whether or not you voted for the mayor or agree with his/ her platform is not the point; your analysis must be based on the tools used to convey meaning within the speech itself.*	**Do more than summarize.** Too often, students who are asked to analyze fall back on recounting only what happens. Analysis involves critical thinking and examination. *Example: An essay prompt asks you to analyze a character in a novel. Rather than merely describing what the character does, you must look at how the author uses tools such as description or dialogue to build the character in a way that creates meaning.*

Before you teach students to analyze a text, issue, situation, or work, try these four things:

- **Model:** Save student work so that you can show a class a successful example of a piece broken down into its component parts (see example, page 9). Have students practice the task of analysis on the piece in pairs or groups.

- **Define Expectations:** What does a successful analysis in your discipline look like? If it's presented in an essay, do you expect to see specific types of **evidence**, a particular type of thesis statement, or a particular conclusion?

- **Build Content Knowledge:** Give students the academic language and understanding they need to look for evidence effectively. Do they need to understand terms such as *diction* or *tone?* Do they need to know *how* to read a political cartoon or a data chart? Prepare students for success by giving them the tools to analyze in your content area.

- **Practice Mental Moves:** Assign short texts to small groups or pairs and have students practice making the mental moves and answering the questions described in the Mental Moves feature in the sidebar. As you introduce skills such as analyzing, post the moves on the wall and keep circling back to them so that students internalize them and **transfer** them to new learning situations.

Obstacles to the Moves

When teaching students to analyze, watch out for these areas of difficulty:

- **Projection.** Students sometimes create an analysis based on what they want a work to say rather than on what the evidence supports.

- **A Point, but Not *the* Point.** In some cases, it's fine to analyze a minor theme or aspect of a work, but make sure students do this on purpose and not because they're missing core ideas.

- **Incorrect Inferences.** By nature, **inference** is tricky. When students get symbolic or inferential thinking wrong, their analysis can go downhill quickly.

Mental Moves

Analyze

1. Look Closely

How is it made? What are the key elements?

2. Select Details

Which elements contribute most to overall meaning?

3. Find Patterns

What repeats? What is the structure and how does it support key ideas?

4. Infer

What is going on beneath the surface? What is implied, symbolic, or metaphorical?

5. Draw Conclusions

How can I clearly explain the overall meaning?

During: Practicing Analysis

Students get better at analysis with practice. Whether they're trying to make sense of a football play or the design of a football stadium, repetition is a key to developing analytical skill.

In approaching texts—whether the "text" is a paragraph, a poem, an advertisement, or a video—key skills in analysis are **close reading** and observation. Close reading doesn't come naturally to many students; practice helps move students past a "read and done" mentality to a habit of rereading and digging deeper.

To give students practice in close reading, try this:

- Present a short text to the class—for instance, a magazine ad, an opening paragraph, or a commercial.

- Have students work in small groups to select key details—words from a text, literal descriptions of a picture, or patterns—that they think *might* be meaningful. Each group should list around ten.

- Combine the words from all groups on the board. Then, ask students to work with a partner to draw an inference from the list. What overarching emotions or ideas emerge from the list as a whole?

- As a class, share and discuss the inferences. Could you create a thesis statement about the meaning of the piece from these insights? If so, what might it be?

ELL Focus: Do This One Thing to Help

Inference is likely to be harder for English language learners (ELL) than others when dealing with verbal texts, but pictures bridge language. Try an inference activity that begins with the visual and allow students to write down important details in their own languages before composing their conclusive statements in English.

Discussion, Presentation, Technology, and Multimedia

- **Discuss.** Analysis can occur on many levels. Close reading takes place microscopically; students must practice **zooming in** to the level of words in order to make sense of a text. But macroscopic, or "zooming out," exercises are also valuable activities. Discussion is a critical vehicle for this level of comprehension and analysis. Small group discussion should happen frequently and can also take place at the end of a unit, novel study, or grading period.

- **Role Play.** Consider role play as a means of asking students to analyze. Assign each student a character or historical figure, for instance, to represent in a discussion—students will have to use the same process of gathering evidence and drawing conclusions to portray a figure accurately.

- **Present.** Presentation is often used for **summative assessment**, but consider using it as a **formative assessment** tool to spur on analysis. Have students present their initial selection of details and evidence (they might even make a slide presentation of these) and use the presentation to spark discussion with the class about possible conclusions.

- **Surf.** Incorporate technology by having students analyze a website, paying particular attention to component parts, such as Frequently Asked Questions (FAQ) pages, menus, and screen layout.

YouTube Moment: To use presentation as a formative tool for analysis, begin by having students work in pairs or groups and search for an important speech from American history on YouTube; include searches such as "MLK I Have a Dream speech," "FDR Day of Infamy speech," or "JFK Inaugural Address." Conference with students or have them research online to give context to the speeches and **scaffold** their understanding. Then, have each group analyze the rhetoric and imagery of a speech and then present its findings to the class. After the presentations and any discussion they provoke, have students complete individual analyses of the speeches in the form of an essay, PowerPoint, or other written response.

After: Producing Analysis

Student Example 1: The Analytical Essay

The Task

William Faulkner's Nobel Prize acceptance speech consists of five paragraphs delivered in 1950, shortly after World War II. As you read it, pay attention to rhetorical tools, such as imagery, metaphor, and diction. Then, write an essay in which you analyze Faulkner's point of view.

By the end of his tenth grade year, Spencer was one of the top writers in his class. Naturally insightful about literature and abstract ideas to begin with, Spencer acquired skills during tenth grade that improved his ability to construct an essay—the ability to incorporate quotes more smoothly, for instance, and the ability to construct more complex sentences.

Nonetheless, the assignment to analyze a nonfiction text, William Faulkner's short but thorny Nobel Prize acceptance speech, proved challenging. After grappling with some of the complicated ideas in the speech and discussing the historical context with his teacher, however, Spencer wrote a typically strong essay.

A key step in Spencer's approach to the text was his annotation of the speech. Spencer's teacher helped him move beyond simple highlighting to careful zooming in by suggesting he mark the following and then conferencing with him about his notes on the speech:

- Words and phrases that convey more than a literal meaning
- Shifts and transition words
- Phrases that seem to sum up a big idea
- Examples of unusual syntax, such as fragments or rhetorical questions

Here is one paragraph from Spencer's final draft:

Faulkner speaks to future writers more than he thanks the givers of the award, which is generally what an award-receiving speech might concern, inspiring them to prevail and reminding them of the worth of the poet in mankind's existence. In the second paragraph, for instance, Faulkner begins to speak of mankind's fears, and how they can affect his spirit—this then leads to the benefits of letting go of these fears: good writing based on universal "truths of the heart." In this middle section of the speech, Faulkner uses diction: "sweat," "heart," "bones," "scars," and "glands" to produce a very natural image of the human body, expressing the toil that man must labor through to create good universal stories. Faulkner does not write this off as an easy task but one that takes courage to forget all one's fears, lest they end up writing empty stories, ones that leave no mark on any "universal bones." He uses body imagery as a window to describe to future writers what to include in their stories if they plan to write well (an idea central to his argument); themes at the very core of humankind—love, pity, honor, pride, compassion, and sacrifice. Faulkner's message is a crucial one to the future writers of the world: carry on through the struggle of making good literature, for it is an invaluable job that cannot be done without.

1. Look Closely

Spencer homes in on a single paragraph to illustrate his point.

2. Select Details

Spencer collects a series of specific words that serve as evidence for his argument.

3. Find Patterns

Spencer has broken the speech into three parts for his essay, noting the structural transitions between each section of Faulkner's argument.

4. Infer

Throughout his paper, Spencer looks for more than the literal level of Faulkner's message.

5. Draw Conclusions

The final sentence of the paragraph sums up Faulkner's idea as well as Spencer's own analysis.

Student Example 2: Analyzing Visual Text

It was the 2005 movie version of *Pride and Prejudice* that helped ninth grade student Gaby decide to read the book with a literature circle group in her English class. Once she did, however, she found the novel itself equally rewarding.

The Task

With your reading group, choose one key scene from the book you read. Watch the same scene in any movie version. Then, write an analysis of the movie scene in which you draw a conclusion about the effect of the scene on the audience. Refer to specific details from the movie, such as the use of props, camera angles, characterization, or the movement or placement of actors, in your response.

Gaby's English teacher had planned the group reading selections to be sure that each book had an easy-to-find movie interpretation available. The assignment she gave—to watch a key scene and analyze it—could easily have been framed as a compare-and-contrast exercise (and would still have addressed the seventh common core reading standard). As a starting place, however, the teacher wanted Gaby and her peers to focus closely on the craft of the video itself, not merely on plot differences.

After modeling a "close reading" of a movie scene with her students and discussing choices made by the director and actors, Gaby's teacher made an **anchor chart**—a reference tool for the class that could be posted on the wall as an ongoing reminder—of video techniques and tools and placed it on her wall.

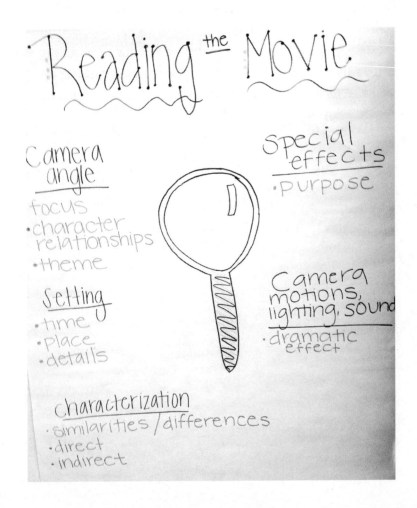

Then, she had the students get to work. Here is Gaby's response:

The movie exaggerates Lizzy's resistance to Mr. Collins in the scene where he proposes. The actress holds onto Jane's arms and begs her not to go, and she mouths "please" to her father as her final plea before they all leave her alone with Mr. Collins. Mr. Collins also gives Lizzy a wildflower in the movie, which symbolizes his simple love for her; however, Lizzy does not want simple love; she wants a complex and deep connection. In the novel, Lizzy sits patiently and listens to the proposal, but in the movie, she constantly tries to interrupt. The camera frames Lizzy awkwardly in the center of the shot for the first part of the scene and then cuts to an over-the-shoulder view when Mr. Collins kneels to propose—she freaks out when he kneels in front of her; then she cuts him short and storms out of the room. Because of the assertiveness and anger that the movie Lizzy portrays, the audience is supposed to understand all of the forcefulness of her character. Through the novel, readers interpret Lizzy's refusal however they want to, but the movie makes her sound very forceful, strong, and independent. I think the directors/producers wanted the audience to know that Lizzy is not the typical "I want to get married and have a steady life with an okay husband," but she really wants love and connection in her marriage, and that sets her apart from the rest of her family and the girls of that era.

Works Cited

Faulkner, W. (1950). *Nobel Prize acceptance speech.* Stockholm, Sweden.

Universal Studios Home Entertainment. (Producer). (2006). *Pride & prejudice* [Motion picture on DVD]. Universal City, CA: Universal Studios Home Entertainment.

Scaffolding Analysis With Webb's DOK
HOW SPENCER WORKED

Level One (Recall)

- *Sample Task:* Annotate or make notes in order to identify and remember appropriate evidence for your analysis.

- *What Spencer Did:* Read through the speech, marking phrases he thought he might quote, with particular attention to inferences.

Level Two (Skills)

- *Sample Task:* Organize the details you have found into categories that will contribute to your understanding of the bigger picture. *How do details x and y differ from z?*

- *What Spencer Did:* Analyzed each paragraph of the speech, homing in on the main point and how it contributed to overall meaning.

Level Three (Strategic Thinking)

- *Sample Task:* Plan your argument by considering an overall point and how to support it. *Which groups of evidence can support _____, and how should they be presented?*

- *What Spencer Did:* Developed a thesis statement and wrote the essay by integrating quotations, paraphrasing, and his own interpretations.

Level Four (Extended Thinking)

- *Sample Task:* Compare this piece to others of similar or different genres and, using research and knowledge built over time, analyze it in the context of other speeches and its historical time.

- *What Spencer Might Have Done:* Spencer might have gone on to compare Faulkner's speech to another Nobel acceptance speech, such as Toni Morrison's, researching context and applying knowledge built from other units of study or even from other classes in his comparison.

Rubric for Analytical Responses

SCORE	THESIS AND OVERALL ANALYSIS	USE OF EVIDENCE	ORGANIZATION	STYLE, VOICE, AND CLARITY	CONVENTIONS AND MECHANICS
5 Outstanding	A well-developed thesis introduces a sophisticated interpretation that goes beyond a literal level with nuanced and interesting insights	Ample and appropriately selected details effectively support the analysis throughout the response	Clear and consistent organization with well-executed transitions excellently supports the analysis, including an excellent introduction and conclusion	The response is clear and original and employs appropriate stylistic elements for effect in an exceptional manner	Syntax, grammar, and conventions are correct and add to the effectiveness of the response
4 Exceeds Expectations	The thesis is clear and introduces an interpretation that goes beyond a literal level	Appropriately selected details support the analysis throughout the response	The organization is clear and supports analysis; the introduction and conclusion are well-executed	The response is clear and employs appropriate stylistic elements for effect	Few or no errors are present in usage or syntax
3 Meets Expectations	The thesis is clear; interpretation may not reach beyond literal or obvious levels	Details adequately support the analysis but may demonstrate some inconsistencies in execution or application	The organization, including introduction and conclusion, are adequate to support the analysis	The response is mostly clear and adequately employs stylistic elements	Minor errors in usage or syntax may be present, but without repetition or undermining overall effectiveness
2 Approaching Expectations	The thesis is vague or unclear; the analysis may not accurately interpret the work	There is insufficient evidence to support the analysis or details are not always adequate to support analytical points	Some flaws in organization or lack of clarity and transitions make the analysis hard to follow	The response may be unclear or misuses stylistic elements in ways that interfere with voice and meaning	Patterns of errors in usage or syntax undermine the effectiveness of the response
1 Well Below Expectations	The thesis is vague or absent, and analysis is inaccurate	Evidence and details are missing or insufficient to support the analysis	The organization lacks focus and clarity; transitions may be unclear	The response is vague or lacks clarity; stylistic choices may confuse rather than enhance meaning	Significant errors in usage or syntax obscure the meaning and effectiveness of the response

Planning Page: Analyze

Analyze: break something down methodically into its parts to understand how it is made, what it is, how it works; look at something critically in order to grasp its essence

Learning Goal
What will your students analyze? What learning outcomes or assessments do you wish to see?

Before	During	After
How will you prepare students to analyze texts, issues, situations, or works?	What activities will you use to model, scaffold, and engage students in analysis?	How will you measure the effectiveness of your lesson?

Notes From This Chapter
What ideas or activities from this chapter do you wish to remember as you teach students to analyze?

2

Argue

provide reasons or evidence to support or oppose

claim • persuade • propose

Argue: provide reasons or evidence in order to support or oppose something; persuade another by reason or evidence; contend or maintain that something is true

CORE CONNECTIONS

- Delineate and evaluate the **argument** and specific claims in a text, including the validity of the reasoning as well as the relevance and sufficiency of the evidence (R8)
- Write **arguments** to support claims in an analysis of substantive topics or texts, using valid reasoning and relevant and sufficient evidence (W1)
- Construct and present oral and written **arguments** supported by empirical evidence and scientific reasoning to support or refute an explanation or a model for a phenomenon or a solution to a problem (NGSS, MS-PS2–4)

The Main Idea

Students argue every day. But arguing with your parents about cleaning your room is not the same as constructing an intellectual argument. In the latter case, the word *argument* describes the process of stating and supporting a claim, as well as taking into account possible counterclaims. An *academic argument* is not one you win or lose, and it's not simply an opinion; it's a balanced and reasoned process that requires accountability.

Underlying Skills:

- **Engage ideas critically.** Passive learning is not an option when students write even the simplest pieces, much less sophisticated arguments. Students must approach topics and texts with critical thinking in order to argue effectively.

- **Consider multiple sides of an issue or idea.** An ability to consider counterarguments (easily represented by a **Venn diagram**) is crucial to structuring a solid argument.

- **Support an idea.** Arguments demand evidence tied thoughtfully to statements of position (such as a thesis statement or hypothesis). You can illustrate a point when describing something ("The cups in the cafeteria are all red"), but *arguing* a point requires more nuanced detail ("The cups in the cafeteria *should* be blue") and demands reasons and evidence.

Before: Preparing Students to Argue

As you introduce students to the concept of argument, it's important to discuss the related but not synonymous term *persuade*. Keep in mind that an argument is always an attempt to persuade, but a piece of persuasive writing may not be an academic argument; it may simply be an opinion and an attempt to win.

Argue	Persuade
An argument relies on the careful examination of evidence. It takes all points of view and perspectives into account and assumes a scholarly audience.	Persuasive essays or speeches attempt to win the audience over. They may appeal to emotions as much as to logic or the weight of evidence.
Example lead sentence: While some might argue that students should be expelled for the complaints they make about their teachers online, the law supports their freedom of speech in the digital arena as well as the real world.	*Example lead sentences: Should schools allow students to post negative comments about their teachers online? Absolutely not; recognizing the potential damage of posts to real human beings is a vital component of any student's education.*

We include both of these terms in this section, but students need to learn to recognize them in assignments and prompts and answer accordingly.

Before you teach students to analyze a text, issue, situation, or work, try these four things:

- **Model:** Gather several articles from a local newspaper, including those from the front page and the editorial section. Ask students to discuss which present an argument and which merely report information. Then, for any articles that argue, analyze the components of that argument. To whom do they appeal and how?

- **Define Expectations:** You may wish to develop a rubric and discuss it with students before they write or speak. Are you requiring a **claim and counterclaim**? How much and what kinds of evidence must be used?

- **Build Content Knowledge:** As you will with other terms in this book, discuss the nature and conventions of *evidence* in your subject area. What type of details might a student use to support an argument in a history class, a science discussion, or a literary analysis?

- **Practice Mental Moves:** As students prepare to construct academic arguments, have them research ideas and then discuss those ideas in small groups or pairs by answering the questions listed in the Mental Moves feature in the sidebar. Post these questions on the wall and keep circling back to them so that students internalize them and can **transfer** them to new learning situations.

Obstacles to the Moves

When teaching students to argue, watch out for these areas of difficulty:

- **Faulty Logic.** Basing an argument on a mistaken assumption (such as a misunderstanding of a plot point, for instance) can undermine a strong argument. Help students avoid such missteps by asking them to research carefully.

- **Lack of Clarity.** Academic arguments often reside in formal papers. Sometimes, students will be so convinced that their audience wants a certain level of formality in writing that they overdo it and lose clarity and precision.

- **Hasty Assumptions.** As with faulty logic, overgeneralizing (say, about a historical era) can lead to a weak argument. Help students be precise.

Mental Moves

Argue

1. **Make a Claim**

   What is my position?

2. **Support the Claim**

   What evidence best supports this position?

3. **Anticipate Opposition**

   What might an opponent of my position claim?

4. **Consider Your Audience**

   What type of appeal will best convince my audience?

5. **Integrate**

   How will I structure my discussion of claim and counterclaims?

During: Practicing Argumentation

For younger students, use a modified Venn diagram to introduce the concept of argument, using the labels below ("agree" and "disagree") or similar labels such as "pro" and "con" for the two sides:

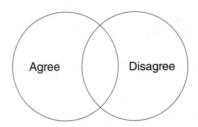

You might try using hula hoops on the floor and allowing students to present oral claims and counterclaims while standing inside one; then ask what someone in the overlapping section might say. Alternatively, you could use the middle section as an "undecided" section in which students can stand until they are forced to make a choice and explain why (see the "get off the fence" activity in the section on discussion that follows).

For older students, you may wish to discuss the importance of audience and Aristotle's triangle of persuasive appeals, including *ethos* (trust and authority), *logos* (reason and logic), and *pathos* (emotion and values). Make it clear to students that pathos is a tool more often reserved for persuasive argumentation, while academic arguments generally rest on ethos (e.g., quotes from a text) or logos (e.g., a reasoned line of thinking).

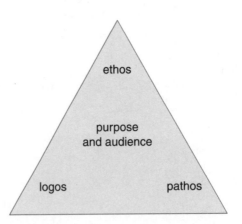

ELL Focus: Do This One Thing to Help

Ferlazzo and Hull-Sypnieski (2014) suggest having ELL students translate key words, such as *problem, cause, effect, solution,* and *reason,* into their native languages. Then ask the students to find key details or evidence related to each of those concepts. They also used sentence starters—in English—to help the students get going: "The main problem is that . . ." Once students have begun in this way, structuring an argument may be a less overwhelming task.

Discussion, Presentation, Technology, and Multimedia

- **Discuss.** To get students thinking about claims and counterclaims, try a get-off-the-fence discussion.

  - → First, come up with a series of arguable statements or questions about a text or topic. *Example: Romeo and Juliet are not truly in love; they're infatuated only with one another.*

  - → Have students who agree with the statement move to one side of the room and students who disagree move to the other. Balance discussion by calling on each side in turn.

  - → Students who are undecided may stand in the middle of the room but may not speak. At the end of the discussion, have these students choose a side and explain why.

  - → After you've discussed several statements, have students write down their thoughts, including noting any convincing arguments made by other students, places they changed their minds, or new ideas about the topic. Use these notes to come up with a claim and counterclaim as a class.

- **Track.** Once students have practiced identifying claims and counterclaims, teach them to create a table in Microsoft (MS) Word or to use columns in MS Excel in order to create **T charts**. This use of technology not only allows students to catalog pros and cons, for instance, but also provides them a tool for organizing and reorganizing that material to find the most effective argument.

- **Present.** When students share material with the class, ask them to include a counterclaim as part of the presentation, perhaps devoting one slide to this task. Encourage them to use this moment in a presentation as a chance to involve the audience by asking for feedback or discussion on a point.

YouTube Moment: The online world is robust with argumentation, from political speeches on YouTube to blogs to posts and comments in online forums. Students need to learn to navigate these arguments. Choose a video with user comments (you will probably wish to screen the comments for appropriate content before using them with students) and ask students to look at those user comments for appeals to logos, pathos, and ethos and to evaluate the effectiveness of each. Ask if each is an argument or a persuasive/opinion piece. How do they know? Present their findings to the class.

After: Producing Arguments

Student Example 1: Argumentative Writing

The Task

Does an individual have the right to violate an unjust law? If so, under what circumstances? Write an essay in which you argue that individuals do or do not have this right. Use examples from history or from our reading to support your argument.

The ninth grade reading list at Anton's school included a number of canonical texts with a common motif: Sophocles' *Antigone*, Arthur Miller's *The Crucible*, and Robert Bolt's *A Man for All Seasons*. At the same time, Anton's social studies class discussed the civil rights movement and, specifically, Martin Luther King Jr.'s "Letter From a Birmingham Jail." Because the idea of resisting laws cut across their disciplines, Anton's English and American History teachers decided to assign a cross disciplinary assignment focused on an argumentative task. The assignment unfolded in three steps.

Step One: Discussion

In social studies class, Anton and his peers participated in a fishbowl discussion focusing on the question "What makes a law just or unjust?" The fishbowl procedure worked this way:

- Four to five students sat in an inner circle and discussed their answer to the question.

- The other students sat in an outer circle and took notes on points raised in the discussion.

- When an outer circle student wanted to contribute a point, he or she would tap one of the inner circle students on the shoulder and take that place, while the speaker returned to the outer circle.

- The teacher monitored the discussion, encouraging new speakers to add points by asking if anyone could add a different point of view.

Step Two: Claim and Counterclaim

The next day, Anton's English teacher took students to the computer lab and allowed them access to online versions of all three of the plays they'd read that grading period. He had them work in pairs to find two lines in the texts, one that supported the idea that citizens should obey laws and one that supported the idea that citizens should resist unjust laws. When several of the pairs struggled to come up with lines, the teacher offered two suggestions: first, the students were allowed to summarize actions or scenes in the play instead of writing down a specific line of text, and second, they could use the search function to look for specific words in the online texts.

Anton and his partner searched the online text for the word *law* in all three plays. From those, they chose the following two lines from *Antigone*:

- **Citizens should obey:** "I will obey those in control. That's what I'm forced to do." (Ismene)

- **Citizens should resist:** "I'll lie down there forever. As for you, well, if you wish, you can show contempt for those laws the gods all hold in honour." (Antigone)

Anton and his partner wrote each line on a sticky note and put it on the board in the room along with those from the rest of the class. The teacher then gave each student five minutes to read each group of sticky notes silently and, individually, come up with a statement that summarized the lines. When the students returned to their seats, he called on volunteers to share their statements and, as a class, the students came up with a claim and counterclaim:

- **Claim:** Because laws represent the collective wisdom of a society, no one individual has the right to violate those laws.

- **Counterclaim:** Because the majority group in a society can overlook the rights of minorities or can be misled by a powerful view, individuals have the right to violate laws that are clearly unjust.

Step Three: Individual Writing

In preparation for writing a full essay in answer to the prompt above, Anton's teacher asked each student to write a single paragraph in class. Students were allowed to use their notes from the discussion and to refer to the sticky notes on the board in order to express their initial thoughts.

Anton's teacher was clear about the expectations for the assignment. Following the mental moves for argument, students were expected to both take a stand (make a claim) and recognize alternate points of view (counterclaim). The teacher also emphasized the importance of evidence in establishing these claims.

Here is Anton's first draft, written in class:

1. Make a Claim

Anton states his position—his argument—clearly.

2. Support the Claim

Anton draws on an example from his social studies class.

3. Anticipate Opposition

Anton clearly engages one possible counterclaim and works to disprove it.

4. Consider Audience

Anton will write a formal essay; he uses appropriate language and evidence for this task.

5. Integrate

Anton's essay will likely include three body paragraphs. Alternatively, he could have argued his claim first and then engaged a counterclaim.

Laws shape and define the structure of any group of people by setting boundaries, justly or unjustly. However, at a certain point, laws might infringe upon the basic universal human rights of any individual if the law is not carefully thought out and planned. Unjust laws are broken in modern society quite often, and not only are there points at which individuals may break a law but should break it. An example of this is the civil rights movement, in which individuals such as Martin Luther King Jr. violated laws through civil disobedience in order to fight injustice. One might claim that such disobedience creates chaos and incites others to break the law, but without the ability to protest such laws, how will change ever occur? Examples from history (civil rights) and two plays (*Antigone* and *The Crucible*) demonstrate this fact. If humans can't violate a clearly unjust law, any government could oppress its people without fear of consequences—there must be a way to stop bad government and bad laws.

Student Example 2: Class Discussion

In John Reynolds's eighth grade Global Studies class, there's no simple multiple choice exam at the end of the semester. Instead, each student is expected to research the position of a nation involved in the tension between North Korea and the rest of the world. Students write individual "white papers" summarizing the position of the countries they're assigned and then work in teams of three to prepare arguments for a solution to the conflict that draws on factual information and represents the actual positions of the countries they represent. On the day of the exam, the students gather around a large table and conduct six-party talks while Mr. Reynolds plays the role of facilitator and takes notes on each student's contributions.

Because this is an exam, Mr. Reynolds needs to assess each student. The final grade includes several components, each of which has its own rubric: a score for the white paper, a score for contributions to the discussion, an individual self-assessment, and a reflection written by each student that discusses the effectiveness of his or her contributions.

Here is the reflection written by Sam, who took on the role of South Korea. While Sam never uses the words *claim* or *counterclaim* in this reflection, those ideas are clearly present:

> **The Task**
>
> *Using your research, represent your assigned country in our classroom's six-party talks concerning the North Korean border. Be prepared to use evidence to propose a solution to the disputes over the border's military conflict and to persuade other countries to see your point of view.*

In order to positively contribute to the group, I knew that I had to have a goal and understanding of what South Korea, my assigned country, would desire. The first day of deliberation, I brought forth several points, but specifically a main issue in North Korea that their population is starving. The response to my point was surprising; argumentative debate and disorder broke out. I realize now that the tone and accusation I made came out incorrectly; I was intending on bringing up a way to show that North Korea needs other countries' help. The following day, I made sure to react to comments with a calmer and less aggressive manner, and I used my notes to prepare to respond to other views to reach a compromise. I proposed that North Korea should rejoin the six-party talks and start to denuclearize their weapons, and as more trust is gained, South Korea would take action in removing the United States troops from their border. While discussing in small groups on the first day, I found out that each country had different objectives and main concerns, which made forming a solution harder, but after talking and presenting evidence, overall, all of the countries contributed to making a final, peaceful compromise.

By allowing his students to work together and discover the consequences of argument, evidence, and counterclaims in action, Mr. Reynolds creates a sense of relevancy and practicality. He also gives students a valuable discussion experience with enough structure to ensure learning.

"When the girls do a project with several assessment pieces, as Sam did in her reflection," John told us, "they deconstruct their learning, and this, to me as a teacher, is the essence of creating and nurturing exemplary students. The written piece of argument as content is important, but the self-assessments, reflections, and peer evaluations demonstrate how students learn where their arguments succeeded, failed, and could be improved."

Works Cited

Ferlazzo, L., & Hull-Sypnieski, K. (2014, April). Teaching argument writing to ELLs. *Educational Leadership*, 71(7). Retrieved from http://www.ascd .org/publications/educational-leadership/apr14/vol71/num07/Teaching-Argument-Writing-to-ELLs.aspx

Orwell, G. (2013). *1984*. New York, NY: HarperCollins.

Scaffolding Argument With Webb's DOK
HOW ARGUMENT WORKS IN JIM'S CLASSROOM

The following examples come from a recent unit Jim taught on Orwell's *1984*.

Level One (Recall)

- *Sample Task:* Define *ironic* (1) as it appears in the dictionary and (2) as you understand it in your own words.

- *What Jim's Students Did:* Looked online for simple definitions and then composed their own, setting Jim's students up to think more deeply about uses of irony in the novel.

Level Two (Skills)

- *Sample Task:* Explain how Orwell's (2013) use of the word *victory* (e.g., Victory Mansions, Victory Gin) is ironic, supporting your answer with details or examples from the text.

- *What Jim's Students Did:* Applied this key literary term and their knowledge of how to analyze and find evidence to this novel.

Level Three (Strategic Thinking)

- *Sample Task:* A *conditioned response* is defined as the learned response to a previously neutral stimulus. For example, let's suppose that the smell of food is an unconditioned stimulus, a feeling of hunger in response to the smell is an unconditioned response, and the sound of a whistle is the conditioned stimulus. The conditioned response would cause you to feel hungry when you heard the sound of the whistle.

  Respond to the claim that everyone's behavior during the Two Minutes Hate (2013, pp. 11–17) is a conditioned response. In your response, you should agree, disagree, or do both (agree *and* disagree). Explain your reasoning, supporting your explanation with examples from the text.

- *What Jim's Students Did:* Drew together a number of skills—*analysis, organization,* and *support,* for instance—to produce a synthesized piece that made a clear argument.

Level Four (Extended Thinking)

- *Sample Task:* Think back to the lessons from your history class earlier this year concerning behavior during the 1950s and the McCarthy era. What do you think Orwell would have said about the reactions of US citizens to the House Un-American Activities Committee trials? Using evidence from your notes or research, argue that Orwell would or would not have characterized these reactions as conditioned responses.

- *What Jim's Students Did:* Linked their current study to another discipline and unit, prompting thinking that required making connections and revisiting material.

Rubric for Argument

SCORE	THESIS AND ARGUMENT	USE OF EVIDENCE	ORGANIZATION	STYLE, VOICE, AND CLARITY	CONVENTIONS AND MECHANICS
5 Outstanding	A well-developed thesis introduces a clear argument that includes a strongly developed claim and addresses counterclaims	Ample and appropriately selected details effectively support the argument throughout the response	Clear and consistent organization with well-executed transitions excellently supports the argument, including an excellent introduction and conclusion	The response is clear and original and employs appropriate stylistic elements for effect in an exceptional manner	Syntax, grammar, and conventions are correct and add to the effectiveness of the response
4 Exceeds Expectations	The thesis is clear and introduces a claim as well as counterclaims	Appropriately selected details support the argument throughout the response	The organization is clear and supports the argument; the introduction and conclusion are well-executed	The response is clear and employs appropriate stylistic elements for effect	Few or no errors are present in usage or syntax
3 Meets Expectations	The thesis is clear; claims and counterclaims are addressed in an adequate manner	Details adequately support the argument but may demonstrate some inconsistencies in execution or application	The organization, including introduction and conclusion, are adequate to support the argument	The response is mostly clear and adequately employs stylistic elements	Minor errors in usage or syntax may be present, but without repetition or undermining overall effectiveness
2 Approaching Expectations	The thesis is vague or unclear; claims may be unclear, and counterclaims may be absent or vaguely addressed	There is insufficient evidence to support the argument, or details are not always adequate to support points	Some flaws in organization or lack of clarity and transitions make the argument hard to follow	The response may be unclear or misuses stylistic elements in ways that interfere with voice and meaning	Patterns of errors in usage or syntax undermine the effectiveness of the response
1 Well Below Expectations	The thesis is vague or absent, and claims are unclear	Evidence and details are missing or insufficient to support the argument	The organization lacks focus and clarity; transitions may be unclear	The response is vague or lacks clarity; stylistic choices may confuse rather than enhance meaning	Significant errors in usage or syntax obscure the meaning and effectiveness of the response

Planning Page: Argue

Argue: provide reasons or evidence in order to support or oppose something; persuade another by reason or evidence; contend or maintain that something is true

Learning Goal
What will your students argue? What learning outcomes or assessments do you wish to see?

Before	During	After
How will you prepare students to construct arguments about texts, issues, situations, or works?	What activities will you use to model, scaffold, and engage students in creating argument?	How will you measure the effectiveness of your lesson?

Notes From This Chapter
What ideas or activities from this chapter do you wish to remember as you teach students to argue?

3

Compare/Contrast

identify similarities or differences between items

delineate • differentiate • distinguish

Compare/Contrast: identify similarities or differences between two or more items in order to understand how they are alike, equal, or analogous to each other

CORE CONNECTIONS

- Analyze how two or more texts address similar themes or topics in order to build knowledge or to **compare** the approaches the authors take (R9)
- **Compare and contrast** the structure of two or more texts and analyze how the differing structure of each text contributes to its meaning and style (RL5)
- **Compare and contrast** a written story, drama, or poem to its audio, filmed, staged, or multimedia version, analyzing the effects of techniques unique to each medium (RL7)
- Analyze displays of pictorial data to **compare** patterns of similarities (NGSS, MS-LS4–3)

The Main Idea

The ability to compare and contrast works effectively has always been a staple of academic argument. Initially, most students learn to compare and contrast in the style of a Venn diagram (see the preceding chapter on argument), isolating similarities and differences in two ideas, texts, or objects. But a sophisticated comparison requires more nuance; it demands that we *organize* and look for subtleties in differences and qualify similarities. As a result, strong compare/contrast exercises can prompt very deep thinking and lively discussion.

Underlying Skills:

- **Recognize similarities and differences.** Sometimes, similarities and differences are obvious to students (how one school dress code differs from another), but content-specific comparisons may require discussion and practice (how does the process of passing a law differ in the United States and United Kingdom?).
- **Organize.** Is it better to present one side and then the other or to examine each point through multiple lenses? What about how to organize similarities or difference into categories and groups? Students need guidance and practice in organizational decisions.
- **Transition smoothly.** A balanced compare/contrast paper or presentation requires the careful use of transitional words and phrases.

Before: Preparing Students to Compare and Contrast

It's not unusual for instructions to compare, contrast, *differentiate*, or *distinguish* to appear in writing-on-demand prompts as well as instructions across all disciplines. Because students will encounter these words frequently in a variety of tasks, it's important that they be able to identify exactly what they're being asked to do.

Compare Only

Example: Read the following two poems and then write an essay in which you compare the authors' use of point of view.

The student must choose, based on the context of the question and task, whether this comparison includes discussing only similarities or also differences. In this case, it is likely that both should be addressed.

Contrast Only

Example: Contrast George W. Bush's address to the nation after 9/11 with Franklin D. Roosevelt's (FDR's) address after Pearl Harbor.

The student should focus on key differences. The structure of the response should allow for three or four essential distinctions and draw a conclusion based on those dissimilarities.

Compare and Contrast

Example: Read the following editorials; then write a response in which you compare and contrast the techniques employed by the writers.

The student must consider and discuss both similarities and differences. The response may discuss similarities and differences in turn or may discuss the two pieces point by point.

Before you teach students to compare and contrast texts, issues, situations, or works, try these four things:

- **Model:** Have students find similarities and differences in a work, issue, or process and write them on two different colors of sticky notes;

Mental Moves

Compare and Contrast

1. Identify the Task

Am I being asked to compare, contrast, or both?

2. Gather Evidence

What are the key elements I should compare?

3. Organize

Should I discuss one text and then another or compare point by point?

4. Check Transitions

Is each point clearly introduced?

5. Draw Conclusions

What does this comparison reveal?

then put these on the board. Give everyone a few minutes to read through both sets of notes. Then, have students work in small groups to *organize* and *draw conclusions* from all they've read. When groups are done, invite them to write their conclusions as a single sentence on the board. Discuss these as a class.

- **Define Expectations:** Make it clear to students whether they will be evaluated on the structure of the comparison, the content of the comparison, or both. In some formal settings, students are expected to name the points in the introductory paragraph. Be clear about your expectations for how the comparison is introduced and developed.

- **Build Content Knowledge:** Quite often, a comparison and contrast task can raise as many questions as it answers. Gather these questions from your class and use them to build **content knowledge** about an event or text before students write a second draft. Encourage research as necessary.

- **Practice Mental Moves:** In small groups or pairs, have students practice with a sample task, making the mental moves and answering the questions listed in the Mental Moves feature in the sidebar. Post these moves on the wall and keep circling back to them so that students internalize them and can *transfer* them to new learning situations.

Obstacles to the Moves

When teaching students to compare and contrast, watch out for these areas of difficulty:

- **Shallow Differences.** Texts can be different in many ways, not all of which matter—make sure comparisons are not just correct but relevant.

- **Weak Transitions.** Because organization matters so much in comparison and contrast tasks, weak transitions can confuse the reader and rob the product of its power and clarity.

During: Practicing Comparison and Contrast

It's fine to introduce students to compare-and-contrast tasks with a Venn diagram or T chart—these are useful tools for *identifying* similarities and differences. Ultimately, however, students will need to go beyond gathering comparisons to *categorize* and *draw conclusions* from the comparisons they make.

Key to this practice is organization. Consider the following three models for organizing a compare-and-contrast paper:

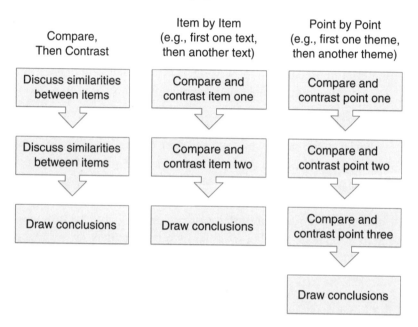

Rather than requiring a specific approach, consider modeling all three organizational strategies for students using the same information. Then, let each student choose how to organize his or her own paper. The process of grappling with organization is likely to deepen student thinking about texts or topics and may even lead to unanticipated conclusions or lines of thought.

ELL Focus: Do This One Thing to Help

Consider providing your ELL students with a Venn diagram or T chart in which you have already included headings or examples for guided practice. Keep in mind that ELL students may bring a wealth of knowledge to a compare-and-contrast task but may get sidetracked by unfamiliar words. You may even suggest to ELL students that they first fill out a Venn diagram in their native languages and then translate them into English for discussion, presentation, and writing.

Discussion, Presentation, Technology, and Multimedia

- **Debate.** Compare-and-contrast assignments lend themselves to debate: Have pairs of students present similarities (student one) and differences (student two) to the class, and then respond to one another to explain why the similarities or differences are more important to an understanding of the two items. Such debate can be structured as a formal exercise, with time limits, guidelines, and patterns of response, or as an informal, on-the-spot activity during a class period.

- **Evaluate.** An excellent tool for teaching reliability and credibility of sources is to have students compare and contrast web source material. Find two pages on the same topic (or have students find the pages on assigned topics) and do a comparison and contrast: which is more reliable, trustworthy, and scholarly and why?

- **Track.** As with *argument*, students can set up an online tracking tool, such as a table in MS Word, to catalog similarities and differences as they read. Then, when they need to organize and reorganize this material in preparation for writing, they can click and drag chunks of text or notes to form their own organized method of presentation.

YouTube Moment: Having students compare and contrast two scenes from two movie versions of the same work is always an interesting exercise (and easy to do with commonly filmed works like Shakespeare plays). For other works, however, your students can easily find student-generated "trailers" online with a simple search. Have them find two trailers—official or unofficial—for a book or text and compare and contrast the ideas, images, and techniques used. Then have them create—and post—their own book trailers.

After: Producing Work That Compares and Contrasts

Student Example 1: The Analytical Essay

Peter, an eleventh grade student, read Gilman's *Herland* in a literature circle with four or five fellow students. A key component of the literature circle was the element of choice:

> **The Task**
>
> *The novel* Herland, *by Charlotte Perkins Gilman, includes six main characters, three males and three females. In a well-written essay, contrast Gilman's presentation of males and females in the novel. What point does Gilman hope to make by presenting the two genders differently?*

1. Students ranked books that interested them from a short list provided by the teacher. The teacher gave a **book talk** about each of the books before students made their rankings.

2. Based on their rankings, the teacher placed the students in groups of four or five and assigned them to a book.

3. Groups worked together to compose a reading schedule (within a specified time frame) and a contract that outlined expectations for the group members.

4. On specified class days, the group met, discussed the book so far, generated questions, and took notes (which they also turned in to their teacher).

5. At three unannounced times during the reading unit, the teacher had group members fill out anonymous evaluations of group members and self-evaluations, which were used as part of the assessment for the reading project.

6. Toward the end of their reading, each student presented a possible essay topic to the group. The group discussed the topics; then, each person in the group chose one of the topics to respond to.

The topic Peter chose was not the one he invented, nor one others in his group chose to address, but he liked the idea: *Compare and contrast the male and female characters in the novel.* Peter decided he could structure a strong essay with two layers of comparison and contrast, making connections not just between the two genders but between the characters within each gender, as well.

Here is an excerpt from Peter's paper:

Peter's Essay Excerpt

1. Identify the Task

Following the wording of the assignment, Peter plans primarily to identify differences in this essay.

While the male characters in *Herland* possess individual characteristics, each man represents an archetype of masculine nature. <u>By contrast, the female characters Celis, Alima, and Ellador are more individual and are not broken into exclusive types.</u> Each of these women changes in the novel from being confused and amused upon first meeting the men to loving the men. However, each woman loves her man in a distinct way. This raises another question: Are the women of Herland distinct because of their different reactions to the men, or are they distinct and therefore react differently to the men? There may be insufficient evidence in *Herland* to answer this question one way or the other because the novel is written exclusively from a male's perspective. Whatever the cause, Celis, Alima, and Ellador, though similar to each other in ways, are more individual than Jeffrey, Terry, and Vandyke because the girls are portrayed with more depth, whereas the men are portrayed as stereotypes.

2. Gather Evidence

Peter incorporates textual evidence to support each claim.

3. Organize

Peter has decided to discuss the characters as pairs: each male and a corresponding female in the following paragraph.

<u>Terry, for instance, representing the overly aggressive male,</u> is unfit for Herland because his only desire is to meet and court the girls of the country. <u>Even after staying for some time in Herland, Terry insists that because Herland is civilized, "there must be men" (p. 66).</u> Terry's concept of Herland is incorrect and is the source of his incompatibility with the society. Upon realizing that the girls are not the ignorant, submissive girls he was looking for, Terry shows his overwhelming masculinity more than ever by refusing to admit that the girls are indeed female. Terry's fundamental misconception is that to be feminine, one must be inferior, obey, and be impressed by males, as shown by Terry's failed attempt to impress the girls with jewels.

4. Check Transitions

The transitional phrases allow the reader to follow Peter's argument easily.

5. Draw Conclusions

Following on his thesis from the introduction, Peter will compare not only males to females but also females to each other, thus, firming up his point that female characters in the work are more individualized.

Alima, <u>by contrast,</u> is distinct from her fellow females; she "had a more stormy temperament than either of the others" (p. 106). Furthermore, Van characterizes Alima as strong: "She never gave an inch. A big, handsome creature, rather exceptionally strong even in that race of strong women" (p. 75). <u>These descriptions prove that Alima is not who she is because of Terry; rather, she is an individual suited to Terry because she is strong and stubborn</u> . . .

Student Example 2: Historical Writing

Compare-and-contrast assignments are a staple of many history assignments; comparing how one event unfolds to another prompts students to think both globally and specifically and to examine broad historical movement as well as specific *evidence*. As a tenth grade Advanced Placement (AP) World History student, John encountered these tasks frequently, but with a new twist: the challenge of **writing on demand** in a limited period of time. His teacher encouraged him to be, above all, clear and to the point. For a history paper written in a limited time frame, she also suggested some specific guidelines:

The Task

Compare and contrast the influence of North America and Latin America on global networks from 1750 to the present.

- Write a one-sentence introduction that clearly states the comparison
- Write about one item first and then the other
- Include details with clear transitions
- Include at least one point of comparison and one of contrast

The task to which John responded here was similar to actual AP questions, but his teacher simplified the prompt to help students focus on the task of comparison. Here is John's first draft:

Both Latin America and North America had major influence on global networks starting in 1750 while they were colonies supporting Europe up until the present, where they trade for their own benefit and wealth as independent nations.

Starting in 1750, Latin America was a group of European colonies, mostly Spanish and Portuguese, and they contributed to new agricultural products that were shipped to Europe in order to enhance trade for their country. They also contributed to the countries' wealth because they had to continually keep up trade with them in order to sustain and grow its economy. Another way these colonies affected the global trade was the European countries would buy the goods and then resell the goods to other neighboring countries or colonies in another region. The Latin American colonies did eventually gain independence and begin their own countries, but these countries continued to trade with the European countries, but they also put the "middleman" out of the equation and traded directly with the countries that Europe had resold the goods to.

The North American region has a similar story. It was a group of colonies owned mainly by Britain. These North American colonies produced goods mainly for Britain and had introduced new crops and goods to the European marketplace. The peoples in this area soon also gained independence, but continued to maintain trade with the European countries. They were also able to take the European power out of the picture and trade with other countries whereas they had had to go through European countries first. North America was slightly different from much of Latin America, however, in that it had a large amount of imported slaves that were relied on for a majority of labor, and when slavery was abolished, the production rate dropped dramatically, but then they began to receive a lot of indentured servants that took on a lot of labor and increased production again and became the trading and economic powers that are present today.

Work Cited

Gilman, C. (2014). *Herland*. Newburyport, MA: Open Road Media.

Scaffolding Comparison With Webb's DOK
WHAT PETER'S GROUP DID

When Peter's teacher wanted each group in the class to construct useful prompts for possible essays, she created a series of instructions that helped each group develop their questions:

Level One (Recall)

- *Sample Task:* Identify all central characters in the work.

- *What Peter's Group Did:* Discussed the meaning of "central" and then made a list that included the six most obvious characters, three men and three women.

Level Two (Skills)

- *Sample Task:* For each character, choose phrases or words from the text or identify moments that help define that character and explain the character's behavior.

- *What Peter's Group Did:* Assigned each group member a character and looked for key words and phrases; they then worked together on the last character and added to others as a group.

Level Three (Strategic Thinking)

- *Sample Task:* Choose three ways in which the characters in the novel could be compared and contrasted and, for each, compose a question that could generate possible discussion or writing.

- *What Peter's Group Did:* Realized that the most obvious comparison in this novel would be to compare males to females, but each member thought of other possible comparisons: characters who wind up happy to those who wind up unhappy, for instance, or characters who follow the rules and those who break the rules. In the end, the group wound up with several questions, including the one Peter answered.

Level Four (Extended Thinking)

- *Sample Task:* Imagine that your group has been asked to write the preface to a new edition of your group novel, including an assessment of the work's historical importance, literary merits, and effects on other authors over time. As a group, investigate and present your plan for this preface with appropriate citations.

- *What Peter's Group Did:* Peter's group assigned each group member research tasks and then compiled the information and worked together to create an outline for the preface. After discovering that the novel had originally appeared only in magazines and was first published in book form in 1979, they decided in particular to research the genre of utopias and dystopias written by women in the 20th century and the effect Gilman had on those writers.

Rubric for Comparison and Contrast

SCORE	THESIS AND DISCUSSION	USE OF EVIDENCE	ORGANIZATION	STYLE, VOICE, AND CLARITY	CONVENTIONS AND MECHANICS
5 Outstanding	A well-developed thesis clearly sets up a comparison and/or contrast and expertly lays out both the goals and organization of the response	Ample and appropriately selected details effectively support comparisons and contrasts throughout the response	Clear and consistent organization with well-executed transitions excellently supports the discussion, including an excellent introduction and conclusion	The response is clear and original and employs appropriate stylistic elements for effect in an exceptional manner	Syntax, grammar, and conventions are correct and add to the effectiveness of the response
4 Exceeds Expectations	The thesis clearly addresses both goals and organization of the comparison and/or contrast	Appropriately selected details support the comparisons and contrasts throughout the response	The organization is clear and supports the discussion; the introduction and conclusion are well-executed	The response is clear and employs appropriate stylistic elements for effect	Few or no errors are present in usage or syntax
3 Meets Expectations	The thesis is clear; the comparison and contrast is addressed in an adequate manner	Details adequately support comparisons and contrasts but may demonstrate some inconsistencies in execution or application	The organization, including introduction and conclusion, are adequate to support the discussion	The response is mostly clear and adequately employs stylistic elements	Minor errors in usage or syntax may be present, but without repetition or undermining overall effectiveness
2 Approaching Expectations	The thesis is vague or unclear; the organization or goals of the comparison and/or contrast may be uncertain	There is insufficient evidence to support comparisons and contrasts, or details are not always adequate to support points	Some flaws in organization or lack of clarity and transitions make the discussion hard to follow	The response may be unclear or misuses stylistic elements in ways that interfere with voice and meaning	Patterns of errors in usage or syntax undermine the effectiveness of the response
1 Well Below Expectations	The thesis is vague or absent, and organization and goals of the comparison and/or contrast are unclear	Evidence and details are missing or insufficient to support comparisons and contrasts	The organization lacks focus and clarity; transitions may be unclear	The response is vague or lacks clarity; stylistic choices may confuse rather than enhance meaning	Significant errors in usage or syntax obscure the meaning and effectiveness of the response

Planning Page: Compare and Contrast

Compare/Contrast: identify similarities or differences between two or more items in order to understand how they are alike, equal, or analogous to each other

Learning Goal
What will your students compare/contrast? What learning outcomes or assessments do you wish to see?

Before	During	After
How will you prepare students to compare and contrast texts, issues, situations, or works?	What activities will you use to model, scaffold, and engage students in this compare/contrast activity?	How will you measure the effectiveness of your lesson?

Notes From This Chapter
What ideas or activities from this chapter do you wish to remember as you teach students to compare and contrast?

4

Describe

report what one observes or does

Describe: report what one observes or does in order to capture and convey to others a process, impression, or a sequence of events in a narrative

CORE CONNECTIONS

- **Describe** how a particular story's or drama's plot unfolds in a series of episodes as well as how the characters respond or change as the plot moves toward a resolution (RL3)

- **Describe** how a text presents information (e.g., sequentially, comparatively, causally) (RH5.6–8)

- Use narrative techniques, such as dialogue, pacing, and **description,** to develop experiences, events, and/or characters (W3b.6–8)

- Construct an explanation that includes qualitative or quantitative relationships between variables that **describe** phenomena (NGSS, MS-LS4–4)

The Main Idea

Telling what we see and experience is a key piece of learning, so much so that students usually begin learning to write description at a fairly young age. Yet both narrative and informative writing require descriptive skills that must be honed and practiced. What's more, the same tools of description apply whether a student is setting the scene for a story to take place, creating a piece of objective journalism, or describing a scientific event.

Underlying Skills:

- **Observe closely.** Description relies on details. Noticing, documenting, and creatively relating those details are elements that can separate a prosaic description from a memorable one. Younger students will benefit from writing exercises that focus on all five senses.

- **Research.** Whether a student is describing a scene set in another country or interviewing a firsthand witness of an account, accurately relating the truth in a way that conveys a full picture can require painstaking background research.

- **Write clearly and succinctly.** While descriptive text can certainly be complex, it requires specificity and clarity to communicate atmosphere and mood (or, in history or scientific disciplines, to communicate exactly what occurred in a process, test, or event).

Before: Preparing Students to Write Description

Elementary teachers often do a good job of teaching students to describe using all of their senses. This skill (as well as recognizing which sense to use at different times) is important, but it isn't the only component of strong descriptive writing or oral presentation. Before you teach description, be sure your students have familiarity with some key components of language:

Sensory Images As obvious as using all five senses to describe may be, it's an easy lesson to forget.	**Imagery** Metaphor, simile, analogy, and other rhetorical strategies are key to creating a vivid description.
Specificity Instead of *tree*, a student might use *oak* or *elm*. Avoiding words such as *thing* or *it* can lend force to description.	**Vocabulary** Is the villain of a story evil, or is he odious? Is the hero good or stalwart? Look for such examples in **mentor texts** to drive home the value of vocabulary in description.
Syntax Varied syntax—including both sentence length and a variety of sentence starts—can add power and liveliness to a description. In revision, take time to have students review the number of words and sentence starts in their writing to consider their use of syntactical variety.	**Strong Verbs** It's worth separating out verbs from other vocabulary for students who might not otherwise consider them. Verbs can do much of the heavy lifting in description; think, for instance, of *"the students clamored"* instead of *"the students were noisy."*

Before you teach students to develop a text, issue, situation, or work, pay attention to these four areas:

- **Model:** Find a passage of strong descriptive text and look for one element at a time—first adjectives, then verbs, then imagery, for instance. Discuss how these elements combine to develop mood, setting, or process. Then, have students practice in small groups with an additional descriptive text.

- **Define Expectations:** Be specific about elements of writing or language in a rubric. It can be tempting to include a category such as "strong description" in a rubric, but such designations may seem

Mental Moves

Describe

1. Observe and Research

What details do I need to include?

2. Visualize and Plan

What sensory information do I wish to convey?

3. Consider Your Audience

Who are my readers and what do they need to know?

4. Organize

In what order should the details be presented?

5. Revise

Does my language convey as strong and clear an impression as possible?

subjective to students and thus difficult to understand. Instead, focus on clarity, sentence types, or verb strength.

- **Build Content Knowledge:** The language in the boxes above helps students build not just descriptive ability but reading ability as well (in any discipline). Use them to direct focus on specific content and processes. In a scientific description, for instance, precision of verbs (*dissolve* instead of *disappear*) can make all the difference.

- **Practice Mental Moves:** When students are ready to begin writing, have them discuss with a partner the questions listed in the Mental Moves feature in the sidebar. Post the mental moves chart on the wall and keep circling back to the questions so that students internalize them and can *transfer* them to new learning situations.

Obstacles to the Moves

When teaching students to describe, watch out for these areas of difficulty:

- **Flowery Prose.** We want details in description, but not too many— an overabundance of vocabulary words or flowery images can have the opposite of the desired effect. Help students focus on the quality, not the quantity, of descriptive phrases and passages.

- **Focusing on the Wrong Parts of Speech.** Students often turn to adjectives to spice up description, but verbs tend to do the real heavy lifting in descriptive passages.

During: Practicing Description

Despite what students may think, strong descriptive writing rarely just happens—it's the result of *brainstorming, planning,* and *revision.* Teaching students to describe, therefore, also means teaching them to prepare.

Consider, for instance, an assignment made by Emily's ninth grade teacher. He asked Emily to describe a visit to a relative (in this case, Emily chose her grandmother). Before writing, however, Emily was instructed to

A. Draw a picture or floor plan of the scene

B. Label things in the picture you could touch, taste, see, smell, or hear

C. Write one strong adjective or verb on the picture for each item she'd labeled

For the last instruction, Emily was allowed to use a thesaurus or consult with friends. Here is an excerpt of Emily's resulting rough draft:

> Sunlight streaming through the blinds in my bedroom beckons me awake, but soft sheets and promises of breakfast in bed hold me steadfast for a little longer. My eyes slowly flutter open, and my six-year-old self looks around and smiles at the realization of where she is. The robin egg colored walls and chandelier allude [to the certainty] that I'm in Kitty's house and that if I spend a little more time in bed, I may get a breakfast fit for a king served to me on a tray. Gleefully, I slip beneath the covers and patiently wait.
>
> From the kitchen, maple syrup and sizzling sausage perfume the air, and I hear Earnestine, Kitty's maid, loudly conversing and laughing with Kitty that "Missy sleeps mighty late this morning." After fifteen minutes or so, Kitty opens the bedroom door and slowly makes her way towards my bed with her and Earnestine's labor of love in hand. In my lap, she sets down a tray splayed with homemade silver-dollar pancakes, juicy Jimmy Dean sausage, genuine maple syrup, hot melted butter, and a tall glass of fresh-squeezed orange juice. It's no wonder why I loved my sleepovers at Kitty's house, or why my waistline was always a few inches ahead of my friends'.

For narrative and other descriptive assignments such as this one, try using peer editing to have students focus on imagery, sensory details, and language. Rather than focusing on simple error finding (as too much peer editing tends to do), make the editing sessions collaborative, inviting partners to help make scenes vivid and communicate mood, atmosphere, and tone.

ELL Focus: Do This One Thing to Help

Your ELL students may need more help with vocabulary than others in the class. Allow them to draw, if possible, and help them learn to find words in English using a thesaurus or other sources that enliven their writing. It's important, however, not to let such exercises go astray—the end result is both for the writing to sound genuine and for students to learn meanings of the words they use, so focus on a few key terms and be sure to discuss the connotations of those words with the writers.

Discussion, Presentation, Technology, and Multimedia

- **Partner.** Have students practice describing objects or events in class out loud to one other student. This may be particularly helpful in science or math classes: Students should describe a process orally and then see if their partner can rewrite or re-create it based on their description. In language arts, try having students describe doing or making something to someone who tries to do it as the student speaks as an exercise in the importance of clarity and specificity.

- **View.** Descriptive tools are as important to visual media as they are to writers. Filmmakers, painters, and other artists all use tools of description in their work. When you show film clips for your class—no matter the discipline—consider having students discuss the elements of description that go into making a scene. How do tools such as lighting, camera angle, and choice of shot create mood and atmosphere? How do these elements contribute to overall meaning? Also, consider comparing the descriptive elements of a passage of fiction and the same elements in a movie version of the story.

- **Track.** When reading or planning descriptions, have students use software such as Inspiration to make digital **concept maps** (or use a table with columns in MS Word or Excel for a simpler version of the same idea). Track specific elements of description—different senses of different tools of language, such as those described in the *Before* section of this chapter.

YouTube Moment: Search YouTube for "Book Talks" and browse talks conducted by students or teachers and share one with your class. In a book talk, a presenter describes a book, including the basics of its plot and characterization, to an audience in an attempt to entice them to read the work. After students study the descriptions in a few samples, including how much of the plot is revealed and how much is not, invite them to film or present their own book talks for your class.

After: Producing Descriptive Writing

Student Example 1: Description in Journalism

In a weekly meeting of the seventh grade team at Barry's school, the teachers discussed the need for a cross curricular project that would teach the students the value of service and citizenship. They decided to center activities in every class around an upcoming visit to a nonprofit food bank. In social studies, the students would learn about food deserts and food insecurity in the city. In math, they'd work with sample budgets and learn how difficult it can be to feed a family fresh, healthy food. The science teacher volunteered to introduce a lab on food preservation techniques.

> **The Task**
>
> *You will be assigned a short article that reflects some aspect of our study of food deserts and food insecurity. Write your articles by describing the program, process, or problem you are assigned.*

Ivy Phillips, the seventh grade English teacher, saw the project as a chance to offer a culminating assessment that would also help her introduce **informational writing (informative/explanatory writing)**, one of the three genres emphasized in the CCSS, to her students. She decided to have each class create a newspaper documenting the experience across all of the course and the field trip. Students would have a chance to work on describing, reporting, and developing an informational piece of text; at the same time, the newspaper would serve to help students both reflect on the experience and document it for others. Each class selected editors and designers and assigned articles to students. As Ms. Phillips described it,

> One of the first activities the class participated in was finding out who works at a newspaper; each student had a role. My students were required to check in with one another rather than depending on me. Editors, photographers, data analysts, and others were constantly milling about the room to be sure all pieces of the newspaper were accurate and cohesive. The process of creating the paper was organized chaos; I imagine the newsroom feels that way too!

Seventh graders Catherine and Ansley were assigned to cover the growth of community gardens in the city. Ms. Phillips wanted to impart to her students the need for journalism both to engage and to inform; description was needed, but so was objectivity and information. Catherine and Ansley had limited space in which to convey their information, so clarity and precise description were vital.

Gardens for Good

By Catherine and Ansley

1. Observe and Research

Ansley and Catherine collected information on their topic from several sources before writing.

In areas where it is hard to access fresh produce, people are creating a new way to access fresh fruits and vegetables. The nearest grocery store could be 10 miles away, and the people in need of fresh foods may not own a car. According to the USDA Agricultural Marketing Service, food deserts are "defined as urban neighborhoods and rural towns without ready access to fresh, healthy, and affordable food."

2. Visualize

The girls use appropriate adjectives for this informative purpose.

A way people in these areas are preventing this problem is by creating food gardens. A food garden is a community garden.

3. Consider Audience

This article uses the short paragraphs and direct sentences common to newspapers for readers who want information.

Community gardens are gardens where residents can grow fresh, raw food in the surrounding neighborhoods. These gardens help people who only have access to fast and processed foods to get the nutrients needed. These fresh foods can improve people's life span and decrease the risk of many diseases. Raised beds growing fresh food are occurring more often throughout Memphis. These gardens not only help those struggling financially to get fresh food, but they also bring the community closer. They work together to attend this shared garden space to keep it living and healthy. Everyone has to pitch in; furthermore, if they help with the garden, they get the fruits and vegetables.

4. Organize

The article is logical in its presentation of information and definitions.

A lack of access to food is not the only characteristic of food deserts; food deserts also have a surplus of convenience stores and fast-food restaurants. The end result is obesity and other diseases.

5. Revise

Class editors read the girls' article to make sure it flowed, was grammatically correct, and fit the allotted space. They determined there was room for this short conclusion.

Food gardens are helping people in food deserts. People who live in food deserts can benefit from learning to grow and to preserve food and then preserve it to make it last longer.

Student Example 2: Description in Science

The cooperative nature of the above assignment allowed students to see how writing functions across disciplines. In particular, the science teacher had students write scientific descriptions of their study of food preservation; Ms. Phillips then offered to include some of these descriptions in the class newspaper.

Once again, students needed to know their audience for this material; they needed to understand that a *retelling*, not an embellishment, was the most important goal. Josephine wrote the following piece for publication in the class newspaper.

> A recent study on food preservatives was completed in our school. Common preservatives used in the study included sugar, which reduces the amount of free water available for bacterial growth. Sodium chloride, which absorbs water from foods, was also used in the study. Sodium chloride makes the environment too dry to support harmful mold or bacteria. Acids, such as vinegar, are another preservative that was used.
>
> Peas were put in a jar with water. Peas were also put in different test tubes, some with water and some with nothing. In the experiment, the vinegar solution was the only preservative that prevented microbe growth in the peas. After a few days, the peas were observed. The peas with no preservatives and peas with sugar as a preservative were the ones that looked like they had the most bacterial growth.
>
> In the study, agar plates, which held the peas, were streaked with the solutions. After 48 hours, they were observed, and the two agar plates with the most bacterial growth were the ones with no preservative and the one with water. The acids, the sugar, and the sodium chloride were the ones that preserved the peas the most.

Students need help to understand that when the word *description* appears in instructions, the purpose of that description provides important information about how it should be written. Underscore with your students that *scientific description*, *narrative description*, and *journalism* draw on the same mental moves but may nonetheless lead to different products.

Scaffolding Description With Webb's DOK

HOW CATHERINE AND ANSLEY WORKED

Always remember that in using Webb's model, what comes after the verb is ultimately more important than the verb itself. Consider these examples:

Level One (Recall)

- *Sample Task:* Describe the features of a newspaper.

- *What the Girls Did:* Based on their study of newspapers, they listed features in class as preparation for choosing a kind of article to write.

Level Two (Skills)

- *Sample Task:* Describe how a food garden works.

- *What the Girls Did:* Made a list of notes on the basic nature and function of food gardens and organized those notes for their article.

Level Three (Strategic Thinking)

- *Sample Task:* Describe the effects of food gardens on your community, using your notes, research, and analysis.

- *What the Girls Did:* Wrote their article, revised it, and submitted it for the class newspaper.

Level Four (Extended Thinking)

- *Sample Task:* Using evidence from your research, describe how you might design a food garden for your neighborhood and how you might raise money and awareness in order to make it a reality.

- *What the Girls Might Have Done:* In a later class discussion, they might have used all they had learned to debate the merits of and plan for a possible food garden in their own communities.

Rubric for Description

SCORE	DEVELOPMENT AND OVERALL EFFECT	USE OF DETAILS AND RESEARCH	DESCRIPTIVE ELEMENTS AND STYLE	VOICE AND CLARITY	CONVENTIONS AND MECHANICS
5 Outstanding	The description is compelling in depth and tone; the approach demonstrates creativity and sophistication	Ample and appropriately selected details effectively build the description throughout the response	Elements such as imagery, word choice, and vocabulary strongly enhance the description throughout the response	The response is clear and original	Syntax, grammar, and conventions are correct and add to the effectiveness of the response
4 Exceeds Expectations	The description is appropriate in depth and tone; the approach is somewhat creative	Appropriately selected details support the description throughout the response	Elements such as imagery, word choice, and vocabulary contribute to the description throughout the response	The response is clear and somewhat original	Few or no errors are present in usage or syntax
3 Meets Expectations	The description is adequate to the task; depth and tone are sufficient, and the approach may be straightforward but adequate	Details adequately support the description but may demonstrate some inconsistencies in execution or application	Elements such as imagery, word choice, and vocabulary adequately support the description throughout the response	The response is mostly clear and adequate to the task	Minor errors in usage or syntax may be present, but without repetition or undermining overall effectiveness
2 Approaching Expectations	The description is vague or weak in tone and depth; the approach may be conventional or difficult to understand	There is insufficient detail, or details are not always adequate to support points	Elements such as imagery, word choice, and vocabulary may be weak, missing, or inappropriately used in the response	The response may be unclear or may not strive for originality	Patterns of errors in usage or syntax undermine the effectiveness of the response
1 Well Below Expectations	The description is insufficient in tone or depth and lacks creativity or sophistication	Details are shallow or are insufficient to support the description	Elements such as imagery, word choice, and vocabulary are missing from the description	The response is vague or does not present an original approach	Significant errors in usage or syntax obscure the meaning and effectiveness of the response

Planning Page: Describe

Describe: report what one observes or does in order to capture and convey to others a process, impression, or a sequence of events in a narrative

Learning Goal
What will your students describe? What learning outcomes or assessments do you wish to see?

Before	During	After
How will you prepare students to describe texts, issues, situations, or works?	What activities will you use to model, scaffold, and engage students in description?	How will you measure the effectiveness of your lesson?

Notes From This Chapter
What ideas or activities from this chapter do you wish to remember as you teach students to describe?

Determine

make a decision or arrive at a conclusion after considering all possible options, perspectives, or results

establish • identify • define

Determine: consider all possible options, perspectives, results, or answers in order to arrive at a decision; provide guidance by establishing what is most important or relevant

CORE CONNECTIONS

- Read closely to **determine** what the text says explicitly and to make logical inferences from it; cite specific textual evidence when writing or speaking to support conclusions drawn from the text (R1)

- **Determine** central ideas or themes of a text and analyze their development (R2)

- **Determine** the meaning of words and phrases as they are used in the text, including figurative and connotative meanings; analyze the cumulative impact of specific word choices on meaning and

The Main Idea

More often than not, when the word *determine* appears in an academic task, it does not imply a simple choice. Rather, the term generally assumes an underlying understanding; the instruction to determine a theme, for instance, assumes that students understand themes and how they work, while the instruction to determine the best process for solving a math problem assumes that students can perform the required computations. Teaching students to determine, therefore, means teaching them to harness knowledge they already possess and apply it with critical thinking to a decision-making process.

Underlying Skills:

- **Identify main ideas.** Recognizing what's important—and what is not as important—is a crucial step in making determinations about texts, words, or data.

- **Consider alternatives.** By nature, the task to determine which of many ideas or approaches to use requires critical decision making.

- **Apply prior knowledge.** Understanding discipline-specific elements is a necessity in making choices between options.

CORE CONNECTIONS

Continued

tone (e.g., how the language evokes a sense of time and place; how it sets a formal or informal tone) (RL4.9–10)

- **Determine** an author's point of view or purpose in a text and analyze how an author uses rhetoric to advance that point of view or purpose (RI6.9–10)

- **Determine** or clarify the meaning of unknown and multiple-meaning words and phrases by using context clues, analyzing meaningful word parts, and consulting general and specialized reference materials, as appropriate (L4)

- Analyze and interpret data to **determine** similarities and differences in findings (NGSS, MS-LS4–1)

Before: Preparing Students to Determine Choices

The task of *determining* in academic activities ranges from simple choice to broad reflection. Make sure you and your students recognize various applications of the word so that when they see it in prompts, they will be prepared to complete the task appropriately.

A choice between stated alternatives.

Example: Determine which definition of the word fits this context better.

Dichotomous choices, such as defining a word one way instead of another, can be helpful to prompt critical thinking. Determining the best of two or three ways to solve a math problem, for instance, may take more active thought than simply solving the problem.

A choice among unstated possibilities.

Example: Determine the central theme of this poem.

Often, students are asked to make determinations based on their understanding of the discipline (theme, process, or method, for instance). Here, the student must demonstrate an understanding of the medium and an ability to defend a choice with evidence.

A subjective decision posed as a choice.

Example: Determine which of the following ideas you think would make the best science project and explain why.

In tasks that involve opinion, the key part of the task often lies in the explanation, not the choice. Students need to understand how to make a case to defend a choice that may be partly opinion (with a basis in an understanding of evidence).

Before you teach students to make determinations, try these four things:

- **Model:** Walk students through determinations as you would make them. Begin by demonstrating word meaning determinations in your discipline. What do you do when you come across an unfamiliar word in a text? What resources are available? How do you apply word meanings to context?

- **Define Expectations:** Be clear with students about whether the choice or the explanation is the most important piece on which they will be assessed in a response. Some tasks that students consider subjective, such as determining themes in a novel, teachers approach as more objective, with a right and wrong answer. Let students know what a strong response will include.

- **Build Content Knowledge:** When determinations involve a choice from a large or infinite number of options, content knowledge becomes key. It's also important when students must back up and defend determinations. Make sure your students understand the discipline-specific information they will be expected to apply.

- **Practice Mental Moves:** In small groups or pairs, have students practice, with sample tasks, answering the questions listed in the Mental Moves feature in the sidebar. Post these on the wall and keep circling back to them throughout the unit so that students internalize them and can *transfer* them to new learning situations.

Obstacles to the Moves

When teaching students to determine, watch out for these areas of difficulty:

- **Ignoring Context.** Whether they are determining a word meaning or the meaning of a data set, students must use context clues to help guide their understanding.

- **Hasty Organization.** Sophisticated determinations, such as the central idea of a text, combine the use of analysis, support, and development of ideas, all of which must be communicated logically and with clear organizational strategy.

Mental Moves

Determine

1. Identify Choices

What am I being asked to determine? Am I being given choices or is the question open-ended?

2. Identify the Task

What is the takeaway or product of this determination? What am I being asked to produce or decide?

3. Find Support

What evidence will help me make this determination?

4. Organize

How can I explain my choice through the use of argument and counterargument or a structured presentation of evidence?

5. Draw Conclusions

What is the central meaning, idea, or message of this text, these data, or this information? What is my determination?

During: **Practicing Determination Tasks**

As students work to determine meanings of text, both at the level of a single word or phrase and at the more global level of main ideas and themes—a **dialectical journal** can be a useful tool. The term *dialectical* indicates the idea behind such a journal: It is a conversation between the reader and text. In the left-hand column (of two, usually), students list quotes from the text, and in the right-hand column, they respond to those quotes with reactions, questions, links, or interpretations.

Here is a sample page of such a journal from Clare, an eleventh grade student studying *The Great Gatsby* (Fitzgerald, 2013). Notice that Clare uses the journal to bridge the distance between the text and academic statements of theme by relating the work to her own life and then summarizing. There are two items worth noting here: one is that using a dialectical journal only for text-to-self connections without using it to reach deeper themes and make more academic connections may limit students' text comprehension; the other is that such journals, if overused, may seem overwhelming to students and slow down reading.

Clare's Journal Page

Chapter V	I can't speak for everyone, but there have definitely been
Key quotation:	times in my life where I was so excited for something, so enthralled by the anticipation of an occurrence that I'd built up an idea of what it would be like in my head. And often, that imaginative idea far exceeded reality. Although I'm not saying that this is what is happening to Gatsby, I think Nick is onto something when he reflects on Gatsby's obsession with the green light on Daisy's dock. The simile, "as close as a star to the moon," expresses the almost unfathomableness of their reconnection. A star is light-years away from the moon, although they sit just beside each other in the sky from Earth's view. And even though Daisy's house was visible across the water, Gatsby was full of awe and wonder at the fact that that insurmountable distance had been closed at last. Jay Gatsby is the type of man to put great faith in others, and great faith in ideas of himself. From his youth, he believed that he was "a son of God," and that that meant something other than being James Gatz from Minnesota. His idealistic mentality was always driven further by something—inheriting a seaman's legacy, accumulating wealth, getting the girl, getting the girl all for himself, erasing the past five years of her life, and so on. Each of those goals had been accompanied by some "enchanted" idea. And when he achieved it, the enchantment broke.
"Possibly it had occurred to him that the colossal significance of that light had now vanished forever. Compared to the great distance that had separated him from Daisy it had seemed very near to her, almost touching her. It had seemed as close as a star to the moon. Now it was again a green light on a dock. His count of enchanted objects had diminished by one." (p. 93)	
Motif	Five years struggled on Daisy's lips, five years of regret and lost conversations and love. But she didn't say any of this. She lied, quite blatantly in fact, about the beauty of the shirts. The subtleties and dishonesty motif continues.
"Suddenly, with a strained sound, Daisy bent her head into the shirts and began to cry stormily. 'They're such beautiful shirts,' she sobbed, her voice muffled in the thick folds. 'It makes me sad because I've never seen such—such beautiful shirts before.'" (p. 92)	

ELL Focus: Do This One Thing to Help

Journaling as a practice offers ELL students the opportunity to practice fluency in a nonthreatening manner and to connect academic language to informal language. Consider mechanisms to keep ELL students from being too hampered by language limitations as they work on journals; you may allow them to write individual words in their native languages when the English word is hard to find (and then review the journal and translate later on) or to draw pictures in the right-hand column and then describe the picture in English.

Discussion, Presentation, Technology, and Multimedia

- **Discuss.** In order to prepare for class discussions, have students collect information that will help them determine answers, and collect this information on poster paper or sticky notes. Consider, for instance, this example in which a social studies class prepares to discuss the prologue from Chaucer's *Canterbury Tales*.

    → The teacher began with reminders of a discussion from the day before about the three estates of society in Chaucer's time—the clergy, the nobility, and the commoners.

    → Students found one example of a character in the prologue who reflected the ideals of his or her social class and wrote about it on a sheet of poster paper.

    → Students found one example of a character in the prologue who did *not* reflect the ideals of his or her class and wrote about it on a separate sheet.

    → On a third sheet, students wrote one question or puzzle they had about a character in the prologue.

    → Students gathered in groups of four or five to determine their response to this statement: *Overall, Chaucer condemns the system of the three estates through his descriptions in the General Prologue.*

    → Students then participated in a whole-class discussion on the same topic in which each speaker was required to begin with a statement he or she had determined from the group discussions.

- **Present.** In classes where students must determine correct processes (such as math), ask students to model answers for the rest of the class and focus discussion on how students determined which process to use.

- **Survey.** If you have access to computers for your students (or cell phones), use polling software, such as pollseverywhere.com or surveymonkey.com, to take stock of class determinations. Using such software, you can set up multiple choice questions in advance and have each student respond anonymously to get a picture of where the entire group stands. After each question, ask someone who got the right answer (and, if you and your students feel comfortable enough, someone who got the wrong answer) to explain how he or she made that determination. Hint: This is a good activity for test and exam review.

YouTube Moment: Pick any reality show that is appropriate for your students and for which an episode has been posted online. After setting context as needed, show students only the very end of the episode—the part where other participants or a panel of judges *determine* which contestant must leave the show. Ask students to identify and *evaluate* the criteria used to make these eliminations. How are such decisions determined? What is the role of evidence and support?

After: Producing Works That Determine

Student Example 1: Determining Through Poetry

It would have been easy for a teacher to assign Clare, the student mentioned earlier in this section, an analytical essay in which she analyzed a character in *The Great Gatsby*. Clare would likely have done a fine job on such an assignment—and possibly have been bored by it. The exercise of writing a monologue drew on the same analytical skills, including the ability to *determine* how Jordan's point of view might be expressed in the novel, and also to bring creativity to a *summative assessment* of the work.

"This is told from Jordan's perspective," Clare told us, "but we aren't supposed to mention that, it's for the reader to figure out. In this case, I explored the idea that Jordan was really in love with Nick rather than just enamored. I drew from a specific line, when Nick says something like *I could have loved her.*"

As you read the poem Clare turned in, ask yourself whether there's any doubt that she understood the novel and its themes.

> **The Task**
>
> *Read through your dialectical journal, looking for clues that will help you determine how other characters see events differently or similarly to the narrator, Nick. Then, write a monologue (you may use prose or verse) in which you express the views of that character.*

Clare's Poem

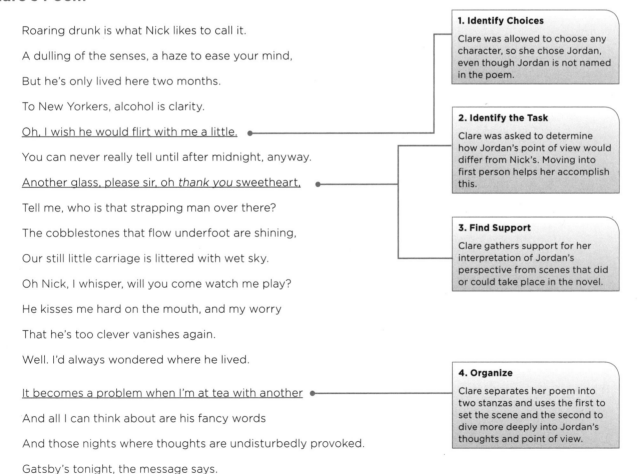

Roaring drunk is what Nick likes to call it.

A dulling of the senses, a haze to ease your mind,

But he's only lived here two months.

To New Yorkers, alcohol is clarity.

Oh, I wish he would flirt with me a little.

You can never really tell until after midnight, anyway.

Another glass, please sir, oh *thank you* sweetheart,

Tell me, who is that strapping man over there?

The cobblestones that flow underfoot are shining,

Our still little carriage is littered with wet sky.

Oh Nick, I whisper, will you come watch me play?

He kisses me hard on the mouth, and my worry

That he's too clever vanishes again.

Well. I'd always wondered where he lived.

It becomes a problem when I'm at tea with another

And all I can think about are his fancy words

And those nights where thoughts are undisturbedly provoked.

Gatsby's tonight, the message says.

1. Identify Choices

Clare was allowed to choose any character, so she chose Jordan, even though Jordan is not named in the poem.

2. Identify the Task

Clare was asked to determine how Jordan's point of view would differ from Nick's. Moving into first person helps her accomplish this.

3. Find Support

Clare gathers support for her interpretation of Jordan's perspective from scenes that did or could take place in the novel.

4. Organize

Clare separates her poem into two stanzas and uses the first to set the scene and the second to dive more deeply into Jordan's thoughts and point of view.

I laugh, and call for the car and a bottle of anything.

Well. The champagne will do, I muse.

Won't it? He asks, concerned, shrewd brows crinkling.

But I only said it to evoke that very face.

I swim in Gatsby's pool—not the one outside,

The one with bourbon-soaked memories

<u>And dark depths in which to lose yourself.</u>

<u>Nick whispers sweet nothings and replenishes me,</u>

<u>And the liquor seeps in to fill the last cracks,</u>

<u>Just as the words I love you die on my lips.</u>

5. Draw Conclusions

By the end of her poem, Clare uses metaphors to convey not just Jordan's literal experience but also her feelings.

Student Example 2: Determining Word Meanings

We include the word *define* as a subset of determination because definition means more than simply looking up a word in a dictionary; it means making choices between meanings according to context. To illustrate this idea, here is another entry from a dialectical journal, this one from a student named Isaac who was studying *Pride and Prejudice*:

Quote from the novel:	My reflection:
"Vanity and pride are different things, though the words are often used synonymously. A person may be proud without being vain. Pride relates more to our opinion of ourselves, vanity to what we would have others think of us."	I looked up the word "vanity," because I wanted to understand this better. Besides being a piece of furniture, the definitions I found actually relate it to pride. However, its root word means "empty" or "hollow." I *think* this is what Darcy is getting at—that it's okay to be proud of yourself, but not in an empty way where you just want flattery.

This sort of word study is heavily emphasized in the Common Core standards; indeed, perhaps the most prominent use of the word *determine* rests in standards related to vocabulary such as this one:

Determine the meaning of words and phrases as they are used in the text, including figurative and connotative meanings (RL4.9–10)

This practice of determining word meanings needs to begin in the early grades and needs to take place across subjects. It also offers a prime opportunity for teachers in multiple subject areas to discuss just *how* we determine word meanings and how we determine subjective material in general. Take, for example, Grace's sixth grade science fair proposal. Grace planned to study the scents of perfumes when exposed to light or darkness, but her teacher wanted her to understand not just the process of an experiment but also the background behind it. She had Grace do some research, the result of which was this paragraph:

> The word perfume comes from the Latin word *per fumum*. *Per fumum* means "through smoke." Perfume was believed to only be used by gods. After a sacrificial event, perfume was burned in order to cover the odor. Fragrance is in everything, and even if a product has no fragrance or is unscented, it actually has scent to neutralize and reduce stronger smells.

By underscoring the importance of definition and etymology as part of word study, Grace's science teacher sets a stage whereon word meanings and connotations are important. The value of this lesson resounds across disciplines, so vocabulary in Grace's grade was no longer a matter of words one *memorized* from a list, but of an ongoing *exploration* of words to determine how they contributed meaning to passages.

Works Cited

Fitzgerald, F. S. (2013). *The great Gatsby.* Rockville, MD: Wildside Press.

Hosseini, K. (2003). *The kite runner.* New York, NY: Riverhead Books.

Scaffolding Determination With Webb's DOK

HOW CLARE WORKED

Level One (Recall)

- *Sample Task:* List characters from the novel other than the narrator.

- *What Clare Did:* To prepare to write her poem, she made a list of characters that she could use to consider alternate points of view.

Level Two (Skills)

- *Sample Task:* Choose a character other than Nick and pick one scene or line that character might have interpreted differently than Nick himself does. Explain your answer.

- *What Clare Did:* Focused on a single line from Nick's narration and used it to spark her own thinking about Jordan's perspective throughout the novel.

Level Three (Strategic Thinking)

- *Sample Task:* Write a monologue from the point of view of a character other than Nick.

- *What Clare Did:* Wrote a poem exploring how Jordan's thoughts might flow differently than Nick's.

Level Four (Extended Thinking)

- *Sample Task:* In class, be prepared to compare and contrast Fitzgerald's use of first person narration to that of two others from your readings this year.

- *What Clare Might Have Done:* In thinking about this discussion prompt from her class, Clare connected the narrative style of *The Great Gatsby* to other works she read during the year, such as *The Kite Runner*.

Rubric for Determination Tasks

SCORE	OVERALL DETERMINATION	USE OF EVIDENCE	ORGANIZATION	STYLE, VOICE, AND CLARITY	CONVENTIONS AND MECHANICS
5 Outstanding	A well-developed introduction presents a clear set of choices and makes a compelling case for a determination and determining factors	Ample and appropriately selected evidence effectively supports the determination throughout the response	Clear and consistent organization with well-executed transitions excellently supports the determination, including well-developed arguments and counterarguments as appropriate	The response is clear and original and employs appropriate stylistic elements for effect in an exceptional manner	Syntax, grammar, and conventions are correct and add to the effectiveness of the response
4 Exceeds Expectations	The introduction presents a set of choices and makes a case for a determination and determining factors	Appropriately selected evidence supports the determination throughout the response	The organization is clear and supports the determination; arguments and counterarguments are present when appropriate	The response is clear and employs appropriate stylistic elements for effect	Few or no errors are present in usage or syntax
3 Meets Expectations	The introduction presents a set of choices and makes an adequate but straightforward case for a determination and determining factors	Evidence adequately supports the determination but may demonstrate some inconsistencies in execution or application	The organization is adequate to the task of the determination but may be inconsistent	The response is mostly clear and adequately employs stylistic elements	Minor errors in usage or syntax may be present, but without repetition or undermining overall effectiveness
2 Approaching Expectations	The introduction does not make choices clear or may not make a clear case for a determination and determining factors	There is insufficient evidence to support the determination, or details are not always adequate to the task	Some flaws in organization or lack of clarity and transitions make the determination hard to follow; arguments and counterarguments may be unclear	The response may be unclear or misuses stylistic elements in ways that interfere with voice and meaning	Patterns of errors in usage or syntax undermine the effectiveness of the response
1 Well Below Expectations	The introduction is vague and insufficient to the task	Evidence and details are missing or insufficient to support the determination	The organization lacks focus and clarity; required elements such as arguments and counterarguments may be absent	The response is vague or lacks clarity; stylistic choices may confuse rather than enhance meaning	Significant errors in usage or syntax obscure the meaning and effectiveness of the response

Planning Page: Determine

Determine: consider all possible options, perspectives, results, or answers in order to arrive at a decision; provide guidance by establishing what is most important or relevant

Learning Goal
What will your students determine? What learning outcomes or assessments do you wish to see?

Before	During	After
How will you prepare students to determine or define?	What activities will you use to model, scaffold, and engage students in determining or defining concepts?	How will you measure the effectiveness of your lesson?

Notes From This Chapter
What ideas or activities from this chapter do you wish to remember as you teach students to determine or define?

6

Develop

improve the quality or substance of

formulate • generate • elaborate

Develop: improve the quality or substance of; extend or elaborate upon an idea in order to give it greater form; add more complexity or strength to an idea, position, or process

CORE CONNECTIONS

- Write narratives to **develop** real or imagined experiences or events using effective technique, well-chosen *details*, and well-structured event sequences (W3)

- **Develop** the topic with well-chosen, relevant, and sufficient facts, *extended definitions*, concrete details, quotations, or other information and examples appropriate to the audience's knowledge of the topic (W2b.9–10)

- **Develop** a model to predict and/or describe phenomena (NGSS, MS-PS1-1)

The Main Idea

It's one thing to *generate* an abstract idea such as an essay topic, science project, or work of art. *Developing* that idea—carrying it from a simple conceit to a full-fledged product—is a complicated task. It usually requires both tangible research tasks, such as collecting evidence to extend and connect, and the intangible hard work of thinking through possible extensions and connections beyond the immediate text or issue.

Underlying Skills:

- **Think critically.** Development is a product of *examination* and reexamination. Students must spend some time with an idea to develop it more fully.

- **Make connections.** Using prior knowledge, students connect the core idea to others: from elsewhere in a text to other issues, to other works, or to previous activities.

- **Tolerate ambiguity.** At the core of developing ideas lies the ability to accept that mature lines of thinking are often not black and white. Students must take into account that a scientific phenomenon may have several possible causes; a text may pose multiple questions without clear answers; a historical event may be seen through different lenses by different observers.

Before: Preparing Students to Develop

Students encounter the concept of development in a wide variety of contexts. They've probably been asked to develop narratives, ideas, proposals, or essay topics. While all of these tasks share similarities—the need to **brainstorm**, for instance—the actual work of developing ideas may not cross over from one genre to another easily for students. For instance, consider the similarities and differences of the following tasks.

Narrative Writing

Write a narrative to develop real or imagined experiences (W3)

To complete this task, students must be familiar with plot models, point-of-view possibilities, and elements of descriptive writing, such as sensory images. A key question for students is, *How can I best engage my audience through imaginative thinking?*

Non-Narrative Writing

Develop a topic for an informational or analytical essay or presentation (W2)

In this task (common to English, social studies, or other disciplines), students must build upon knowledge of a text or issue as well as other texts or issues. The task requires *critical thinking* as much as imagination. A key question is, *How can I make my idea more nuanced and complex without it becoming too cumbersome?*

Scientific Thinking

Develop a model to predict and/ or describe phenomena such as the Earth-Sun-Moon relationship (NGSS, MS-ESS1-1)

In science, students often develop ideas to explain already-fixed phenomena. The task, therefore, requires *critical thinking* and *problem solving*. A key question is, *What are possible explanations or processes I could pose in studying this issue?*

Before you teach students to develop a text, issue, situation, or work, try these four things:

- **Model:** Have students read and highlight key phrases in a *mentor text*; then, discuss how these phrases help to develop the text or idea as a class. Look for moments in examples that are reproducible for students.

- **Define Expectations:** The variety of uses of the word *develop* in different disciplines means that teachers must be clear about what is expected of students and how they will be assessed.

- **Build Content Knowledge:** Each of the tasks described in the boxes on this page requires students to apply specific content knowledge: when and how often to use adjectives in **narrative writing**, how to find themes, or how to use the scientific principles that guide phenomena. Help students remember this content information through notes, *anchor charts*, and discussion.

- **Practice Mental Moves:** Once students have an assignment or topic, have them practice the mental moves in the sidebar by asking themselves these questions in pairs or individually. Post these questions and "moves" on the wall and keep circling back to them as students practice their development skills so that students internalize them.

Obstacles to the Moves

When teaching students to develop, watch out for these areas of difficulty:

- **Narrow Thinking.** Development requires looking at a problem or idea from different angles and even being willing to start over, not limiting inquiry.

- **Haste.** If students skip research steps or brainstorming processes or don't try to generate ideas, they're likely to develop an idea more weakly than if they include these steps.

Mental Moves

Develop

1. Gather Information

What has already been done? What evidence is available?

2. Ask Questions

What else do I want to know?

3. Qualify

What are the gray areas? Where are the ambiguities?

4. Make Connections

How does this topic relate to other internal or external ideas or works?

5. Organize and Discuss

How will these pieces fit together into a meaningful presentation?

During: Practicing Development

The development of an idea in academic writing is evident—and is mapped out for the writer—by the thesis statement. Thus, helping students understand how to craft a more nuanced thesis can aid them in developing more nuanced arguments.

For instance, consider the following thesis from a student paper:

Hamlet's crimes in the play lead him to lose all of those whom he loves, including Ophelia, Gertrude, and Laertes.

This thesis is serviceable; it probably sets up a five-paragraph essay that may or may not be convincing (one wonders whether Hamlet "loses" each of these characters). It does not stretch very far, however, nor challenge the student to live up to developing an idea with depth.

So how does the student enrich such a statement? One possibility is to start with diction. This student could be challenged to further consider words such as *crimes, loses,* or *loves.*

Another possibility is to teach models of syntax. Consider the following models:

Not only this, but that:

Not only do Hamlet's crimes cause the death of those close to him, but they render him unfit to be king as well, leaving a state open to outside rule.

Parallel structure (of independent clauses):

Hamlet tells himself that he is committing murder for justifiable reasons; Shakespeare tells the audience that Hamlet is committing murder to assuage his reluctance to challenge his uncle.

A series of three balanced pairs:

Hamlet's crimes in the play are motivated by love and hate, by madness and rational thinking, by both a reluctance to fail his father and a reluctance to become his uncle.

These statements are arguable—they may or may not be true. The student's task is to gather evidence and make a case for the idea presented here (and to modify the statement as needed). They also do not necessarily generate five-paragraph essays; they may lead to organizational structures that are more organic in nature.

ELL Focus: Do This One Thing to Help

For students working outside of their native languages, focusing them on one element of wording at a time may be a good starting point. Using the example above, for instance, you might consider asking a student to look more deeply at the word *crimes,* find synonyms, and discuss the meaning of those synonyms. Such pinpointing of the ideas embedded in words can help ELL students gain vocabulary and also enrich their thinking about a text or topic.

Discussion, Presentation, Technology, and Multimedia

- **Discuss.** Good discussions focus on the development of ideas. The role of the teacher is to facilitate the sharing of ideas and, importantly, to help students capture their thinking during and after discussions. A fishbowl discussion (see Chapter 2, Argue, for an example in the context of an assignment) is an excellent way to generate ideas about a thorny topic:

  → Have a few students sit in a center circle and discuss while others sit in an outer circle and take notes.

  → Allow students in the outer circle to "tap in" and replace those speaking.

  → At the end of the discussion, have students record one idea someone else shared that they found important, one thing that changed their minds about the topic, and one conclusion about the topic.

  → These notes serve both as assessment tools and as material for future writing and discussion.

- **Research.** Developing good ideas means researching. Help students learn the value of good research, including online research, by giving a purpose to their information gathering. Informational writing is important, but it's much more interesting to most students to uncover information that will help them write a piece of historical fiction, design a project (see student example two below), or create an authentic work of art.

- **Map.** Development can lead in many directions. Some students and teachers prefer to organize material in a traditional outline form, but for simply generating and teasing out the nuances of ideas, a concept map or webbing strategy may generate useful material. You might also direct students to look at the SmartArt feature of Microsoft Word to get ideas for possible models and visual ways to organize material—sometimes, thinking of material in a different way (as a circle instead of a hierarchy, for instance) can help prompt new directions for development.

YouTube Moment: Search YouTube for "Where Good Ideas Come From," and you'll find a short video by author Steven Johnson about how ideas are developed. Show this video to your students and then discuss the points Johnson makes about hunches and ideas colliding. How do these ideas apply to writing an essay, creating a science project, or designing a set for a play, for instance? You can find this video directly at https://www.youtube.com/watch?v=NugRZGDbPFU.

After: Producing Developed Work

Student Example 1: The Analytical Essay

> ### The Task
>
> *Choose a single image or motif from* Romeo and Juliet. *After working with your group in class, write an essay in which you link this image or motif to themes of the work. Be sure to develop your essay with examples from throughout the play.*

Barry's ninth grade English class read *Romeo and Juliet* late in the year, after they had already practiced a variety of forms of writing. Barry had noticed a trend with this class; they tended to fall back on thesis statements that produced simple five-paragraph essays. The papers were clear and often well written, but he worried that the students avoided deep thinking in their essays. His planned essay prompt on symbolism in the play could easily have fed into more of the same.

Instead of simply assigning the writing task, therefore, Barry developed a process to get the students thinking more complexly. Here is the process with specific examples from one student, Carter.

Step One: Group—Whole-Group Brainstorming

Barry assigned students to groups of four or five (using his knowledge of particular student strengths and weaknesses). Then, he gave each group a few minutes to brainstorm symbols from the play—images, motifs, objects, or references that occurred throughout *Romeo and Juliet*. When each group had a short list, he asked them in turn for one symbol at a time, which he would write on the board and discuss as necessary. As other groups noted that they had come up with items close to one on the board already, a discussion of the complexities of certain symbols already began to emerge.

Here is the list from Carter's class:

Poison	Flowers and herbs	Churches and tombs
Sun, Moon, and stars	Weather: rain, storms, sunshine	Disguises and masks
Animals (especially birds)	Blood	Eyes and ears (sight, etc.)
Weapons	Names	Light and dark
Gestures (thumb biting)	Mythology and allusions	Natural and civil laws

Step Two: Group Research

With the list complete, each group chose one item; Carter's group chose to examine images of celestial bodies, including the Sun, Moon, and stars. As a group, they looked for lines throughout the play that included these words or images. Barry gave a few instructions to each group:

- *Your group must find at least seven to ten different lines or scenes that include the word or concept. If it's a struggle to find the words, choose a different symbol.*

- *You may look up the text online and search for a word electronically. Remember to use synonyms and specific terms (lark as well as bird).*

- *Record each line with an appropriate citation (act, scene, line number) so that you or others can find the line later.*

- *It's okay to refer to scenes where the concept is discussed without the specific word being mentioned. (For instance, there may be a discussion of someone's name that never includes the word* name.*)*

Step Three: Group Conversation

The conversation that followed could have easily been done in class, but because all of Barry's students had access to computers in the school or at home, he had them conduct a written, digital conversation about the symbols and images. Most groups chose to do this through a shared online document or instant message site, though some used e-mail. One group used cell phones and conducted a group text session. The assignment was to try to come up with commonalities between the quotes and see what themes emerged. Barry also instructed the groups to consider connections to other symbols, themes, and ideas that had been raised in class discussions of the play. For instance, here is a snippet of the conversation in Carter's group just as the students typed it:

Sarah: Romeo vows to Juliet "by the moon" in act two scene two.

Jasmine: Is that the balcony scene:

Sarah: end of it

Carter: But Juliet he shouldn't swear that way cause the moon is inconstant

Jasmine: why is the moon inconstant

Carter: I guess cause it changes not like the sun.

Sarah: So this is about whether or not love lasts.

A nice benefit of these online conversations is that Barry was able to read through them and briefly respond to the groups before the next step of the assignment.

Step Four: Group "Thesis" Construction

Following the conversations, Barry gave each group time in class to work on a single PowerPoint slide that summed up the ideas of the group. The groups then presented to the class and answered questions (the entire activity took one class period). Groups were instructed to use bullet points. Here is the slide Carter presented on behalf of his group:

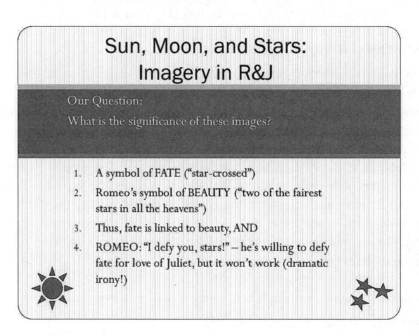

Step Five: Individual Essay Writing

Barry threw in a wrinkle before assigning individual essays: If any student liked another group's image and ideas better than her or his own, that student could piggyback and use the ideas and evidence to write on a different topic. A few students took this option, though most were so invested in their own work by this point that they, like Carter, chose to write on their group's original topic.

Here is the introduction of Carter's final essay. Notice the development of the topic. While Carter was a good writer, had he simply been assigned to write about celestial bodies as symbols, his thesis would likely have been very simple. Here, though, he explores fairly sophisticated ideas.

Carter's Introduction

In *Romeo and Juliet,* Shakespeare uses celestial bodies, such as the sun, moon, and stars, to enhance the speakers' dialogue and contribute to Romeo and Juliet's relationship. In their love towards one another, Romeo and Juliet tend to <u>speak of symbols such as stars and the moon to evoke their love and passion for each other,</u> despite the difficult situations that they are forced to endure. Because the <u>sun, moon, and stars are seen as symbols of prosperity, strength, and happiness,</u> they are continually applied to the two lovers. These symbols help explain <u>the role of beauty in Romeo and Juliet's love as well as the effects of fate predetermining the outcome of the play.</u> However, while comparisons of Juliet to celestial bodies elevate Romeo's love towards Juliet and show his romantic personality, <u>Romeo's ability to make Juliet's beauty equivalent to the stars and heaven prompts readers to consider whether beauty and attraction are the primary basis of Romeo and Juliet's love.</u> Yet even though the two lovers are forced to endure many hardships and difficult times, their love for one another never terminates, even at their death. <u>The celestial bodies help explain the role of beauty in Romeo and Juliet's love, the effects of fate predetermining the outcome of the play and the necessity to overcome their families' wishes for true love.</u>

1. Gather Information

Carter has already examined the evidence from the play as an aid to develop this essay.

2. Ask Questions

Carter's group has already asked questions that helped him define the purpose of these symbols.

3. Qualify

This question—whether Romeo's love is based primarily on beauty or not—lends interesting nuance to the discussion.

4. Make Connections

While the concept of fate is not directly linked to Carter's main thesis, it is an important motif in the play that Carter's class discussed and that he can use in his paper.

5. Organize and Discuss

Carter gives clear indications of how he will present the discussion at the end of this paragraph.

Student Example 2: Engineering and Design

The Task

Our class challenge this week has revolved around the difficulties Kenyan women have with hand washing stations in isolated areas. Come up with a possible solution to this problem. Develop your ideas through research, group collaboration, and trial and error. Then, build a hand washing station of your own that addresses the problems of the Kenyan women.

As part of a cross curricular design project, middle school science teacher Donna Budynas challenged students with this task in order to help build their engineering, design, and innovation skills. To make the challenge work, students needed to generate ideas and then spend several days developing those ideas and making them realistic.

Kaitlin and Riley began the process of designing a hand washing station with guided thinking on a worksheet Ms. Budynas provided them:

The Engineering Design Process Worksheet

Directions: Use this worksheet to ensure you complete every step in the Design Process. Use the spaces provided to show your work. If you need more room, you may attach additional pieces of paper. You must have me check and sign each completed step before you begin the next one.

Name Group 1_____**Class** _____ **Date** _____

STEP	WRITE YOUR RESPONSES IN THESE BLOCKS.
1. ASK What is the problem?	Kenyan women must walk many miles to get water. They use a Tippy Tap hand washing station to wash their hands. Washing your hands is important because when you eat you could get germs and bacteria in your body. These germs can cause you to get very sick. In Kenya, soap isn't readily available. We have two problems to solve. First, the Tippy Tap needs to be short enough so small kids that are about 3.5 Ft tall can reach them. Also, the soap is being stolen. In the middle of the night, people come and cut the rope to get the soap.
2. ASK What are the requirements?	There has to be soap and water in a jug. It has to be small enough for a small child.
3. ASK What are the constraints?	The budget is fifteen dollars or less. We have to think about what they have in Kenya. Our budget was 15 dollars because the average amount that a person makes in Kenya is a dollar a day. They have water, string, jugs (bottles), sticks, pocketknives, and gravel. They don't have piping, metal, a lot of money, and proper tools.

 Available for download from **www.resources.corwin.com/burkeacademicmoves**

As they worked, Kaitlin and Riley researched online and discussed a number of possibilities with one another and with Ms. Budynas. Kaitlin expressed concern about the theft of soap at stations—how could they attach a bar of soap securely enough to keep it from being stolen? As their ideas developed, Kaitlin came up with a possible solution—liquid soap. This would be far more difficult to steal, she reasoned, so she researched and found a process for turning bar soap into liquid by shaving and boiling it. After a trial of this process overseen by Ms. Budynas, the girls included a permanently fixed liquid soap dispenser on their final project.

Throughout the week, students worked to develop their ideas through a number of steps, including brainstorming, testing, and discussing problems. Finally, the girls arrived at a plan (see photo on right).

And eventually, their plan became reality.

At the end of the project, Kaitlin reflected on all of the places during the process where she had encountered obstacles:

Kaitlin and Riley's Plan on Paper

If we put two full jugs on one stick it would break. We found that the sticks were too close together and that is a problem because the bottom jug gets stuck. We had to get taller sticks because the part for the adult was too short and the child one was too short. We had to use clay to make the sticks stand up because sediment is not strong enough. We had to dig more narrow holes because when they were wider the sticks wobbled. Another problem was that when you let go of the tension for the soap for too long, too much soap came out. It was good enough but there were a few minor things we had to fix.

Kaitlin and Riley's final hand washing station. The jugs can be operated by pressing on a stick with one's foot. The liquid soap dispenser can be seen in the upper left corner of the photo.

The continued development of ideas—resulting in not a single solution but a series of emerging solutions to minor problems—became a key lesson of the activity. Ms. Budynas summed up what she saw during the week with her students this way:

> The girls were really surprised at how the ideas they had in the classroom didn't work exactly the same in the real world. With each hurdle, they talked about the original problem, the design, and then tried something new. The final design was a compilation of ideas from all three girls and several prototypes that had been designed and redesigned over a 2 day period.

Work Cited

Johnson, S. (RiverheadBooks). (2010, September 17). Where good ideas come from [Video file]. Retrieved from https://www.youtube.com/watch?v=NugRZGDbPFU

Scaffolding Development With Webb's DOK

WHAT CARTER DID

Level One (Recall)

- *Sample Task:* Recall all references you can to a single image from the play.

- *What Carter Did:* Listed all of the references to words such as *stars* or *Sun* he could recall from the play.

Level Two (Skills)

- *Sample Task:* With a group, discuss the references you found to make sense of them individually within the context of the scene where they appear.

- *What Carter Did:* Discussed individual quotations and references with his group to determine whether or not they would be useful.

Level Three (Strategic Thinking)

- *Sample Task:* With your group, compose a single paragraph that relates the image thread you have discussed to overall themes and meanings of the play.

- *What Carter Did:* Carter worked with his group to develop an analytical paragraph that tied imagery to themes of the play.

Level Four (Extended Thinking)

- *Sample Task:* Using all of the material you have collected, write an essay analyzing the use of a symbol in the play.

- *What Carter Did:* As part of writing this particular essay, Carter went back to his notes from class discussions that took place over several weeks. He worked with numerous pieces of information—his notes, online sources, evidence from the text, and the results of group work—to create his final paper, which itself went through a series of revisions and conferencing with his teacher.

Rubric for the Development of Ideas or Projects

SCORE	THESIS AND IDEA DEVELOPMENT	ORGANIZATION	STYLE, VOICE, AND CLARITY	CONVENTIONS AND MECHANICS
5 Outstanding	There is ample evidence that the idea has been thoroughly developed through research, questioning, and making connections	Clear and consistent organization presents the development of the idea in a compelling and logical manner	The response is clear and original and employs appropriate stylistic elements for effect in an exceptional manner	Syntax, grammar, and conventions are correct and add to the effectiveness of the response
4 Exceeds Expectations	There is clear evidence that the idea has been developed through research, questioning, and making connections	The organization is clear and makes the development of the idea apparent	The response is clear and employs appropriate stylistic elements for effect	Few or no errors are present in usage or syntax
3 Meets Expectations	There is some evidence that the idea has been adequately developed through research, questioning, and making connections	The organization is adequate to represent the development of the idea	The response is mostly clear and adequately employs stylistic elements	Minor errors in usage or syntax may be present, but without repetition or undermining overall effectiveness
2 Approaching Expectations	Evidence that the idea has been developed through research, questioning, and making connections is unclear or lacking in some areas	Some flaws in organization or lack of clarity makes the development of the idea unclear or hard to follow	The response may be unclear or misuses stylistic elements in ways that interfere with voice and meaning	Patterns of errors in usage or syntax undermine the effectiveness of the response
1 Well Below Expectations	Evidence of development of the idea is missing or unclear	The organization lacks focus and clarity; development is unclear	The response is vague or lacks clarity; stylistic choices may confuse rather than enhance meaning	Significant errors in usage or syntax obscure the meaning and effectiveness of the response

Planning Page: Develop

Develop: improve the quality or substance of; extend or elaborate upon an idea in order to give it greater form; add more complexity or strength to an idea, position, or process

Learning Goal
What will your students develop? What learning outcomes or assessments do you wish to see?

Before	During	After
How will you prepare students to develop ideas about texts, issues, situations, or works?	What activities will you use to model, scaffold, and engage students in development?	How will you measure the effectiveness of your lesson?

Notes From This Chapter
What ideas or activities from this chapter do you wish to remember as you teach students to develop?

7

Evaluate

establish value, amount, importance, or effectiveness

assess • figure out • gauge

Evaluate: determine the value, amount, importance, or effectiveness of something in order to understand if it matters or means something

CORE CONNECTIONS

- Integrate and **evaluate** content presented in diverse formats and media, including visually and quantitatively, as well as in words (R7)

- Delineate and **evaluate** the argument and specific claims in a text, assessing whether the reasoning is valid and the evidence is relevant and sufficient; identify false statements and fallacious reasoning (RI8.9–10, W9b.9–10)

- Integrate and **evaluate** information presented in diverse media and formats, including visually, quantitatively, and orally (SL2)

The Main Idea

In **Bloom's taxonomy,** revised (2001), the skill of *evaluating* was demoted slightly from the highest level of cognitive tasks to the second highest, below *creating*. Some illustrations of Bloom's place the two side by side. Either way, there is little doubt that when the word *evaluate* appears in a set of academic instructions, students are being called upon to bring together a number of other skills—the ability to analyze, to determine, to argue, and to support, for instance.

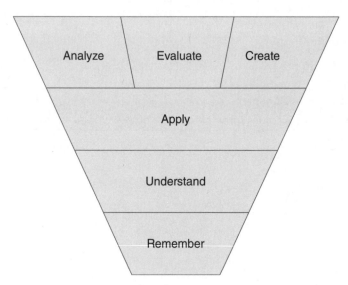

Source: Bloom (1956/2001).

Underlying Skills:

- **Make comparisons.** Evaluation requires knowledge of other works of similar type as a basis for comparison, as well as an understanding of the elements of those works that might serve as strengths or weaknesses.

- **Apply evidence.** Evaluation without *evidence* is merely personal opinion (though personal opinion backed with evidence can serve as one form of evaluation).

- **Consider both strengths and weaknesses.** Some students seem predisposed to see only the "good" or "bad" in a work or issue (or what they "like" or "don't like"). As with other sophisticated tasks, evaluation requires a tolerance for ambiguity and a willingness to accept that reasonable opinions might disagree.

CORE CONNECTIONS

Continued

- **Evaluate** a speaker's point of view, reasoning, and use of evidence and rhetoric (SL3)

- **Evaluate** the validity and reliability of multiple claims that appear in scientific and technical texts or media reports, verifying the data when possible (NGSS, HS-PS4-4, grades 9–12)

Before: Preparing Students to Evaluate

Students evaluate all of the time: They like one movie and not another, they prefer one superhero over another superhero, and they choose one book instead of another book. Each of these choices involves evaluation, but that evaluation may not be convincing to others ("I chose this book because the text is bigger and it has fewer pages than others" may be an acceptable reason for selecting personal reading, but it wouldn't stand up to a discussion of relative literary merits). Part of evaluation is collecting evidence rather than merely voicing opinion.

Before you teach students to evaluate, therefore, make sure you've taught them to ask important questions about evidence that sometimes trip adolescents up.

Is the evidence reliable and relevant? Before drawing a conclusion based on information, students should ask questions about credibility, authorship, how data were collected, or whether a quotation is taken in context. *Example:* • Yes: A student assesses a website's credibility, sees it is a US government website, and cites it. • No: A student looks at the number of subjects in a data set and notices there were only nine. He decides to use different data.	**Does the task leave room for personal connections?** Sometimes, an assignment asks students to make text-to-self connections. Students need to recognize when this is or is not the case (you may prefer to distinguish between *examples* and *evidence*). *Example:* • Yes: A student is asked to evaluate how a work of art makes her feel (see student example one in this chapter). • No: An essay assignment requires students to use only quoted material and to avoid first person pronouns.

Am I looking for the best answer instead of the correct answer?

Sometimes a task has a right answer; sometimes it asks students to evaluate evidence to make a reasonable judgment about which outcome is better.

Example:

• Yes: Math students are asked to choose between two processes that both produce correct answers (see student example two).
• No: Math students are asked to choose between two processes to determine which will produce a correct answer.

Before you teach students to evaluate a text, issue, situation, or work, try these four things.

- **Model:** Evaluation is a broad enough skill that you may need to use several activities to ensure your students have the skills they need. Be sure to model several types of work as you teach evaluation, including websites (emphasize credibility), speeches (emphasize rhetorical techniques), and data (emphasize reliability), as well as discipline-specific texts, such as articles or poems.

- **Define Expectations:** Teachers whose students write—in any discipline—need to outline specific expectations for evaluation tasks. Are students allowed to use first person? Do they need to cite? If so, how? What types of evidence are needed? Without such clear expectations, evaluation tasks are likely to slide toward opinion pieces.

- **Build Content Knowledge:** Evaluation requires a clear understanding of specific types of evidence. Students can judge which poem they *like*, for instance, but academic evaluation requires them to recognize and interpret literary devices, uses of language, and subtext. Evaluating data means understanding axis labels and values. Be sure to provide students with the appropriate tools for any evaluation task.

- **Practice Mental Moves:** Give students a sample task or a short work to evaluate. In small groups or pairs, have them practice the mental moves in the sidebar by discussing the questions. Post these questions and moves on the wall and keep circling back to them as students practice their evaluation skills so that students internalize them.

Obstacles to the Moves

When teaching students to evaluate, watch out for these areas of difficulty:

- **Weak Connections.** Evaluating requires students to hold an idea or work up to others of its kind; if students are unfamiliar with material of this kind, they need exposure to similar ideas or works.

- **Personal Bias.** No matter how often we discuss the difference between opinion and evidence, students may fall back on their own biases when evaluating material.

Mental Moves

Evaluate

1. Determine Criteria

What are the elements I am being asked to evaluate? Is personal preference involved? Comparison? Outcome?

2. Identify Strengths and Weaknesses

Which pieces of this item are effective, and which are not?

3. Consider Improvements or Alternatives

What could be done to make this item better?

4. Gather Evidence

Which details prove my assessment of the item?

5. Draw Conclusions

In the end, how do I judge this item according to the criteria of this task?

During: **Practicing Evaluation**

Choose a text to evaluate with your students—a written passage, a data set, or a visual text, for instance. Then, in pairs or as a class, use the following activities as a starting place for discussion about how we evaluate and how evaluation differs from opinion.

Note: if you have access to a Smart Board, tablet, or other projection device, this activity will benefit from modeling on screen as you walk students through the steps. Jim often pulls texts or images up on his iPad and annotates with or for his classes, for instance.

- Write three statements about the text on the board—two based on evidence and one on opinion. Ask the class to distinguish between the two. Then, ask them to specify the evidence used in the two evidence-based statements.

  → *Example 1: These data show: (1) Lemonade profits increase when it is hot outside, (2) sales on most days start at about one dollar, (3) the sellers should have charged more for each cup of lemonade.*

  → *Example 2: This poem, "The Road Not Taken" (Frost, 1916), is written in first person. The poem describes a choice between two roads. The poem is actually about choices we make in our lives.*

- Work together to form an evidence-based statement about the text by asking students to find an example of *relevant* evidence. Then, have pairs of students work together to create their own statements and post them for discussion.

  → *Example 1: We can tell that lemonade profits increased in June because the line goes from $2/day to $4/day during that month.*

  → *Example 2: Because the speaker describes both roads as "about the same," the choice he makes is not actually to take the road less traveled, no matter what he claims.*

- Have students generate questions that require further research or might spark discussion.

  → *Example 1: What might have happened if the sellers charged more per cup? Do we have enough evidence to make an educated guess?*

  → *Example 2: Is it possible the speaker is lying to himself, or to us, in the final stanza? Is there evidence in the poem that suggests this?*

- Suppose someone asked you whether or not this item is "good." What criteria might you use to evaluate it?

  → *Example 1: We'd consider how useful the data are for helping to improve the lemonade stands sales.*

→ *Example 2: We'd consider whether the poem makes us think of an important question in a new and provocative way. We'd also compare the language, imagery, and literary techniques to other great poems we have studied.*

ELL Focus: Do This One Thing to Help

ELL students may not have the same body of knowledge from which to draw when evaluating works, but they do bring a body of knowledge to the classroom with them. Harness their knowledge to help them deepen comparisons and evaluations. Allow them to write about—and share in class—works or texts in their native language that have similar themes, style, or approaches or about how works tend to differ. These discussions will help structure the basis for comparison students need to make effective evaluations.

Discussion, Presentation, Technology, and Multimedia

- **Discuss.** Start a whole-class discussion by allowing students to voice opinions, and then move them toward evaluation:

  → Post a statement or question that is arguable.

    ○ *Example 1: "Men do not need paternity leave from work."*

    ○ *Example 2: "In Shakespeare's play, Julius Caesar is a tragic hero."*

  → Allow students to voice their opinions in a whole-class discussion.

  → Have students research, look at the text, or otherwise find evidence to support their positions. Return to whole-class discussion with evidence in hand.

    ○ *Example 1: Students search online for statistics, studies, and laws about the pros and cons of paternity and maternity leave.*

    ○ *Example 2: Students find quotes from the play* Julius Caesar *to support or refute the idea that Caesar is a tragic hero.*

  → After the second discussion, have students write down evidence-based conclusions as notes or planning for future assignments.

- **Present.** When students speak formally or informally, "evidence" of a personal nature can be of enormous value. Stories, anecdotes, and examples are often just as useful, if not more useful, in persuading or engaging an audience. Discuss the appropriate uses of such examples, along with audience awareness, with your students before they give presentations, write speeches, or create personal reflections.

- **Surf.** The ability to evaluate the quality of websites is a crucial element of digital literacy and research. Pick a topic and ask students to find any web page related to that topic. Then, ask them to look for evidence of *authorship, date, objectivity, citations, validity of the information, presentation,* and *clarity.* Afterward, discuss how students can apply such criteria to their research online outside of class. Again, this is a good place to project, annotate, and discuss together using a projector or other device.

YouTube Moment: To practice evaluation and also expose students to an interesting global phenomenon, search YouTube for *The Power of Kiva* (2012), and you'll find a video describing the work of Kiva, an online website that allows users to donate small amounts to provide microloans to individuals in developing countries. Then, allow students to browse the stories on the Kiva website at www.kiva.org. Tell students they have an imaginary $100 to donate to one project on the site. How will they choose a microloan? What criteria will they employ to evaluate the stories on the site? As an extension, have students research the location and issue of a particular Kiva story and report back to the class on what they find.

After: Producing Evaluative Work

Student Example 1: Letter to an Author

John Green's (2012) powerhouse novel *The Fault in Our Stars* was all the rage when Samantha reached eighth grade. She read the book at the recommendation of a friend but was drawn into the story by the strength of its characterization, plot, and dialogue. When Samantha's teacher made an assignment to write a letter to any author, Samantha knew that she would be writing to Mr. Green. And, she knew, she planned to *send* the letter.

Samantha's audience, in this case, was the author of the work itself. With her teacher, she had discussed parts of the book she enjoyed as well as parts she thought could be better, but her awareness of audience and task meant that her letter would focus mainly on strengths. She also decided to make her letter personal—to praise the aspects of the book that offered connections to her own life rather than focusing on academic language or analysis, for instance. Thus, Samantha's evidence relied more on her personal experience than quotations from the novel, as was appropriate to this particular assignment.

When Samantha dropped her letter into a mailbox (with a real, old-fashioned stamp on it), she knew she understood the book—and its value to her—better than she had when she first finished reading. While she had not found individual quotations and written a five-paragraph essay, she had *evaluated* the book and defended her evaluation along lines other than purely scholarly.

> **The Task**
>
> *Write a persuasive letter to an author, living or dead, of a work you admire. Do not summarize the plot or merely flatter the work—instead, identify the strengths of the work and why they matter to you. How did the work affect you? Be specific in your letter.*

Samantha's Letter

Dear Mr. Green,

Some say that love can be measured by distance. After reading your book, The Fault in Our Stars, I found that it is really a test of heart and effort. Hazel and Augustus constantly show their love for one another, and although they are only teens, they love one another like an adult couple would. <u>Your book not only holds several secrets that only careful readers will discover, but it gives me hope and teaches me a very important lesson: how to love someone.</u> Those secrets are all of the keys that must be collected in order to open the door of true love—not a relationship, not a what-stage-are-we fling, but real, irreplaceable love.

Hazel Grace and Augustus always stay together, in sickness and in health. I'm only a 13-year-old girl who has never had an illness as severe as theirs, so I have not experienced the heartfelt love that Hazel and Augustus shared . . . but I have witnessed it. My parents are my biggest role models, and it took reading your book to realize that they were showcasing the most important lesson that they could ever teach my siblings and me. They have unconditionally loved one another for the past 17 years, and every year has been better than the one before. These days, it takes a lot for two individuals to fall in love and stay in love, as the divorce rate is near 50%. I have always worried that my parents may divorce, leave, or split up on one of their "unhealthy" days, but after reading your book, I have been given a great sense of security. You demolished my fear by creating and connecting two emotionally and physically strong characters who have a passion for loving one another. <u>I saw that my parents are those two characters, somehow as solid as foundation stones.</u> Without needing to prove their strength, they are forever joined and living in the storybook of life.

<u>My mom, like Hazel and Augustus, was diagnosed with cancer: skin cancer.</u> She was rushed to the hospital and was tested by unknown people she was forced to trust. Skin cancer meant melanoma, and melanoma meant death. The beeps of machines with names so long and complicated still ring in my ears, as I sat in uncomfortable office chairs waiting to see when my family would just fall apart. I couldn't help but race to this finish line without contemplating any other outcome. All of the characters in your story at some point or another show love. My dad proved to fill that exact pattern: he never left my

---

1. Determine Criteria

For this purpose, Samantha wanted to discuss theme and personal impact rather than, for instance, literary techniques.

2. Identify Strengths and Weaknesses

Samantha sees the ability to create links to her own life as one of the book's greatest strengths.

mom's side and constantly showed his pure adoration towards her by keeping her updated with the rest of the family and by bringing flowers and cards to her on tough days. All of the cards seemed to never matter; it was the way my mom would light up when she saw my dad after only a few rotations of the smallest hand on a clock. It was the times that she would wake up and smile and be happy around him, even when the darkest clouds were over her head.

It brought goose bumps to my arms and made the hairs on the back of my neck stand up when I would notice these details, when I would see two people so innocently yet truly in love.

My dad never left my mom's side, and like most things, the tables eventually turned. After being rushed to the hospital, a recurring event in my house, my dad was diagnosed with shingles in his left eye causing blurry vision to the point of legal blindness, along with an amount of pain that no scale can detect. My mom's main focus became healing my dad. I had never seen someone go through so much for another person. She continuously waited with him through the 3-year process, and leaving never once came to her mind. Arrangements for my siblings and me were made immediately so that she could spend every waking hour by my dad's side. I found that in an adult relationship, this commitment is rare and valuable. In the future, when my spouse is unhealthy, I will know exactly what to do and how to handle the situation. Unlike Isaac's girlfriend who left when times got tough, my mom stayed then and will always stay because love is a promise, just as you describe on every page of the story. It is not, as some seemed to demonstrate, like an exhaled breath in winter, strongly visible at first but then dissipating over time until it simply disappears.

There are middle-school and high-school relationships blossoming all around me, and I have actually experienced one. I've learned that those relationships can be fun and bittersweet, but when you find the one, you'll know, and you will never forget him. The naive relationships lead to a certain heartbreak that time can and will heal, but if you are lucky enough to have someone who will do anything to be considered your everything, that is a true rarity. That special person will make the world seem like it is yours. They will never forsake you or purposely mislead you. They will give you those supportive compliments you need, they will understand your feelings, and most of all, they will see through any flawed imperfections and will accept you as you are.

4. Gather Evidence

While this letter is more about her own life than a summary of the novel, Samantha still refers to moments from the book.

5. Draw Conclusions

Samantha's penultimate paragraph draws conclusions throughout.

3. Consider Improvements

The nature of this assignment means that Sam will not explicitly discuss alternate ways in which the book could have been written. However, it is clear that she has read other books that are less effective, by her estimation, than Green's novel.

Before reading The Fault in Our Stars, I was unaware that the adoration surrounded me, but after finishing the last page, you have strengthened my understanding of love and the effect it has on individuals. <u>Your book acted more like a friend to me than a combination of chapters, and I thank you.</u> I'm beyond blessed to have read your book and to have been able to witness true love in action, as my parents share their little infinity and while I await mine beginning soon.

Sincerely,

Samantha

Student Example 2: Evaluating a Math Process

Step One: Working and Comparing

Damon liked puzzles, so when his eighth grade math teacher gave him this simplified Sudoku, he wasn't flustered. Instead, he went to work and nearly solved the puzzle within the four-minute time frame he was allowed. He could see the process clearly, and when his teacher asked him to write it down, Damon quickly listed these steps:

1. *First I checked all of the ones, then the twos, etc.*
2. *I tried to see if a 1 or 2, etc., had to go in a certain column. Like there has to be a 1 in the bottom box of column 6 because it can't go in column four.*
3. *Then I tried checking rows across the same way.*
4. *Then I checked the shaded and unshaded areas.*

As he was writing, Damon felt good about his process. He actually couldn't imagine any other way to complete this problem. He was surprised, therefore, when one of his peers, Jamie, read his process:

> *I started writing down all of the numbers that could go in each box, and I tried to figure out if there was one box where only one number could go. For instance, the very first box could have a 1, 3, or 5 but nothing else.*

And then another student at Damon's table, Cameron, wrote this:

> *I went row by row and tried to see if any number could only go in one box.*

And finally, the fourth student at Damon's table, Ben, wrote this:

> *I guessed at the first box then tried to see if it would work. As soon as it didn't, I went back and guessed a different number and tried that.*

Step Two: Evaluating

Damon's teacher reminded the class that they needed to *evaluate* the processes and decide which one they liked best. Here is a bit of the conversation from Damon's group:

Ben: Now that I've listened to everyone, I don't think I should have guessed. But I don't quite understand how to do it.

Cameron: Did you ever get it right?

Ben: Nope.

Damon: I like my solution. It makes sense to go number by number.

Cameron: It makes sense to go row by row just as much.

The Task

Look at the box below. To complete the puzzle, you must enter numbers so that each row includes the numbers 1–6, each column includes the numbers 1–6, and each shaded or unshaded area includes the numbers 1–6. Once you have worked on the puzzle for four minutes, write down your process in words. Then compare your process to that used by others at your table and evaluate which process worked best.

	2				
6	4		1		
2	3				
				2	6
		2		3	5
				4	

 Available for download from **www.resources.corwin.com/burkeacademicmoves**

Jamie:	I think my way works really well, but it was a pain writing those numbers in.
Damon:	How close did you get to solving it?
Jamie:	I was still writing numbers when we had to stop.
Ben:	Damon got closest to solving it. Do you think that means his was the best?
Cameron:	Maybe you could mix my method and Damon's method?
Damon:	Sure. I think you do mine first, then yours. Those are the steps.

Sudokus, of course, rely more on critical thinking skills than computation. But Damon's teacher had another point in mind: The need for students to evaluate methods of problem solving. Most of her students had learned multiple ways of doing long multiplication, for example (what she termed the "old-fashioned" way and "new" way). She wanted them to think about when to use each method.

The next day, the teacher posed a different question: *How many of you had to backtrack in order to solve the puzzle?* The class went on to have a good discussion about "backtracking" in math problems and the value of checking and rechecking answers, especially to complicated math calculations, regularly. Finally, the teacher rounded off the class by tying the exercise explicitly to calculations with these questions: *What is the proportion of filled squares to unfilled squares in the original puzzle? How might you change this proportion to make the puzzle harder? Easier? Is that the only factor that contributes to how hard or easy the puzzle is?* Damon, incidentally, found himself working Sudokus from the newspaper all year on his own.

For your convenience, we've included the solution to this puzzle below.

5	2	1	4	6	3
6	4	3	1	5	2
2	3	6	5	1	4
1	5	4	3	2	6
4	1	2	6	3	5
3	6	5	2	4	1

 Available for download from **www.resources.corwin.com/burkeacademicmoves**

Works Cited

Bloom, B. S. (2001). *Taxonomy of educational objectives: Handbook I: The cognitive domain.* New York, NY: David McKay. (Original work published 1956)

Frost, R. (1916). The road not taken. In *Mountain interval* (p. 9). New York, NY: Henry Holt.

Green, J. (2012). *The fault in our stars.* New York, NY: Dutton.

Kiva. (Producer). (2012, November 29). *The power of Kiva* [Video file]. Retrieved from https://www.youtube.com/watch?v=TLQX_5kQHyo

Scaffolding Evaluation With Webb's DOK

HOW SAMANTHA WORKED

Level One (Recall)

- *Sample Task:* Identify elements of the novel that you might like to talk about in a letter to the author.

- *What Samantha Did:* Thought about specific scenes from Green's novel that she might use in her letter and described them in class to a partner.

Level Two (Skills)

- *Sample Task:* Discuss the major themes of the book and how these relate to your own life, drawing on specific scenes or elements of the book.

- *What Samantha Did:* Talked in a small group of students in class about why she loved the book, eventually settling on the idea the book teaches readers how to love.

Level Three (Strategic Thinking)

- *Sample Task:* Compose a letter to an author that addresses the effect of the book on the reader, including an appropriate message, clear and correct writing, and persuasive elements.

- *What Samantha Did:* Wrote a letter several paragraphs long that addresses the expectations of the assignment and was also meaningful to her.

Level Four (Extended Thinking)

- *Sample Task:* Over time, make connections to the book by conducting research about the topic and making thematic connections to later and prior reading selections.

- *What Samantha Did:* Went on to read more novels by John Green on her own, gradually building an understanding of the author's voice, style, and content that she was able to apply to discussions of how authors think and work.

Rubric for Evaluation Tasks

SCORE	CRITERIA AND OVERALL EVALUATION	USE OF EVIDENCE	ORGANIZATION	STYLE, VOICE, AND CLARITY	CONVENTIONS AND MECHANICS
5 Outstanding	The criteria are presented clearly, are valid for the evaluation, and are fully addressed in a compelling manner throughout the response	Ample and appropriately selected details effectively support the assessment throughout the response	Clear and consistent organization with well-executed transitions excellently supports the evaluation, including an excellent introduction and conclusion	The response is clear and original and employs appropriate stylistic elements for effect in an exceptional manner	Syntax, grammar, and conventions are correct and add to the effectiveness of the response
4 Exceeds Expectations	The criteria are clear and valid for the evaluation and are fully addressed throughout the response	Appropriately selected details support the assessment throughout the response	The organization is clear and supports the evaluation; the introduction and conclusion are well executed	The response is clear and employs appropriate stylistic elements for effect	Few or no errors are present in usage or syntax
3 Meets Expectations	The criteria are mostly clear and valid for the evaluation and are adequately addressed throughout the response	Details adequately support the assessment but may demonstrate some inconsistencies in execution or application	The organization, including introduction and conclusion, are adequate to support the evaluation	The response is mostly clear and adequately employs stylistic elements	Minor errors in usage or syntax may be present, but without repetition or undermining overall effectiveness
2 Approaching Expectations	The criteria may be vague or insufficient for the evaluation or may not be adequately addressed throughout the response	There is insufficient evidence to support the assessment, or details are not always adequate to support points	Some flaws in organization or lack of clarity and transitions make the evaluation hard to follow	The response may be unclear or misuses stylistic elements in ways that interfere with voice and meaning	Patterns of errors in usage or syntax undermine the effectiveness of the response
1 Well Below Expectations	The criteria are unclear or missing and are not adequately addressed throughout the response	Evidence and details are missing or insufficient to support the assessment	The organization lacks focus and clarity; transitions may be unclear	The response is vague or lacks clarity; stylistic choices may confuse rather than enhance meaning	Significant errors in usage or syntax obscure the meaning and effectiveness of the response

Planning Page: Evaluate

Evaluate: determine the value, amount, importance, or effectiveness of something in order to understand if it matters or means something

Learning Goal
What will your students evaluate? What learning outcomes or assessments do you wish to see?

Before	**During**	**After**
How will you prepare students to evaluate texts, issues, situations, or works?	What activities will you use to model, scaffold, and engage students in evaluation?	How will you measure the effectiveness of your lesson?

Notes From This Chapter
What ideas or activities from this chapter do you wish to remember as you teach students to evaluate?

Explain

provide reasons for what happened or one's actions

clarify • demonstrate • discuss

Explain: provide reasons for what happened or for one's actions in order to clarify, justify, or define those events, actions, causes, effects, results, or processes

CORE CONNECTIONS

- **Explain** how an author develops the point of view of the narrator or speaker in a text (RL6.6)

- Analyze a complex set of ideas or sequence of events and **explain** how specific individuals, ideas, or events interact and develop over the course of the text (RI3.11–12)

- Analyze the main ideas and supporting details presented in diverse media and formats (e.g., visually, quantitatively, orally) and **explain** how the ideas **clarify** a topic, text, or issue under study (SL2.7)

The Main Idea

Explanation is an exercise in backward thinking. Unlike hypothesizing or prediction, which look to an unknown future for multiple possibilities, explanation involves the observation of an issue, topic, or process already in place and seeks out its causes. When explaining, students must question: *How did this come to be? Why does it work? Where did it begin?* Explanation is a key skill good teachers possess, so helping students to explain effectively is, in essence, helping them learn to teach others.

Underlying Skills:

- **Order logically.** A certain amount of retelling is involved in explanation. The ability to reorder key events or steps is necessary for effective explanation.

- **Understand component parts.** In order to explain an end result, students must bring to bear knowledge of how and why similar texts, issues, or processes function. Activating this prior knowledge should thus be part of any assignment or activity.

- **Support an idea.** *Evidence* in the realm of explanation may range from identifying textual support to recognizing guiding principles.

Before: Preparing Students to Explain

The value of explanation as a learning tool is important for students to recognize. Consider, for example, an experiment in which Michael, a middle school student, participated. Michael's teacher set up two upright tubes with a connecting tube between them. One tube contained ice at the bottom, and the other, a lit candle. In his prediction, Michael stated that he thought "the air will travel through the connecting tube back and forth, but the air won't rise."

After conducting the experiment in class, Michael's teacher made three assignments, each of which is described below.

Memorization	Description
Michael memorized the definitions of terms such as *convection current* and *density*. These terms appeared on a quiz later in the week.	In his science notebook, Michael described the experiment: "The air traveled in a circle. It went down in the cold tube and up in the hot tube."

Explanation

The next day, Michael explained to a partner what had occurred. He then wrote an explanation in his notebook: "The warm air sinks because of the ice, goes through the tube, and then the candle hotness pushes it up by creating a convection current. This is the same as a sea breeze and land breeze, where the land air is warmer and it makes a circle."

CORE CONNECTIONS

Continued

- Construct a scientific **explanation** based on valid and reliable evidence obtained from sources (including the students' own experiments) and the assumption that theories and laws that describe the natural world operate today as they did in the past and will continue to do so in the future (NGSS, MS-LS1-5; MS-LS1-6)

Explanation embeds knowledge far more deeply than mere memorization or repetition can do. It also gives students immediate feedback about their own learning—if they can't explain it, they may not really know it—and offers a different vehicle for processing information. As you discuss with students how to approach instructions to explain, don't overlook the value of explanation as a study tool.

Before you teach students to explain a text, issue, situation, or work, try these four things:

- **Model:** For younger students in particular, explanations are unlikely to be long or precise. Model your expectations for explanations in an *I do, You do, We do* manner by giving students an example of an

Mental Moves

Explain

1. Capture the Big Picture

What happened? What was the outcome? What is your topic or purpose? Who is your audience and what do they need or want to know?

2. Reorder Events or Steps

Where did the process or event begin? What steps did it go through?

3. Look for Key Causes

What events stand out as important shifts?

4. Gather Evidence

Which are the most important details?

5. Summarize or Draw Conclusions

What did I learn from this examination?

explanation of your own, then allowing them to try it in writing or with a partner, and then discussing as a class.

- **Define Expectations:** Consider being very specific about what a good explanation should include. Complete sentences or bullet points? A full paragraph or one sentence? Numbered steps? Without providing unnecessary straitjackets, help challenge students to explain thoroughly and completely with such guidelines.

- **Build Content Knowledge:** All explanations rely on information specific to the discipline—otherwise they are unfounded opinions. Remind students to use specific *evidence* or *observations* in explanations and arm them with the terminology and process understanding they need.

- **Practice Mental Moves:** In small groups or pairs, have students practice, with a short text, experiment, or process, answering the questions described in the Mental Moves feature in the sidebar. Post the mental moves on the wall and keep circling back to them so that students internalize them and use them again.

Obstacles to the Moves

When teaching students to develop, watch out for these areas of difficulty:

- **Vagueness.** Explanations require specificity and an appropriate level of elaboration to be useful to readers or listeners; students may skip crucial steps or generalize processes that need more precision.

- **Poor Organization.** A clear explanation allows the reader to follow easily and does not skip or misorder steps or events.

During: Practicing Explanation

As we noted earlier, studying by explaining is an invaluable tool for leading students to reflect on their own understanding. In class, have students identify particular skills or problems they can explain to a classmate; then put students in pairs or small groups to do just that.

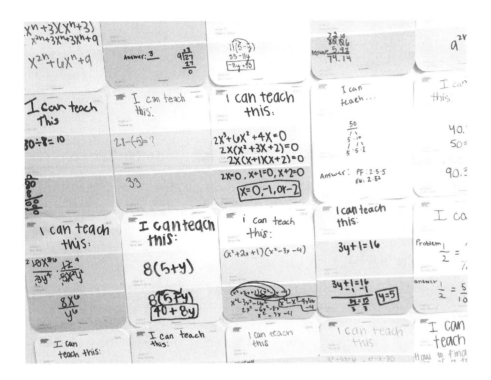

For a nice twist on this activity, consider the example of eighth grade student Gabriel, who struggled in math. Gabriel's teacher brought in dozens of paint swatches donated by a local paint store and allowed each student to choose one color. Gabriel's teacher knew that many of her students felt little **self-efficacy**—the sense that they *could* do the work. She wanted to build confidence and reinforce knowledge at the same time, so she had each student write on a swatch, "I can teach this." Then she posted the swatches on a bulletin board. Before the next quiz, she allowed students to study in class by referring to the board and then asking peers in the class for help with particular problems.

But Gabriel's teacher didn't stop there. She pulled Gabriel and a few other students aside and helped them with their samples, ensuring that they knew how to do at least one problem solidly enough to explain the process to others—and, where possible, she made sure it was a problem with which others in the class struggled. In Gabriel's case, the problem had to do with the area of a triangle. Gabriel taught a number of other students the skill and was also more motivated to ask his peers for help and to prepare for the quiz.

ELL Focus: Do This One Thing to Help

The opportunity to explain orally may offer both relief and pressure for ELL students. To help your ELL students, prepare explicit scripts or question lists to which they can refer. For instance, imagine an ELL student is being asked to teach the process of solving a problem, as Gabriel did above. Having words already prepared in a script may make the process easier.

1. *List the key steps for solving this problem.*
2. *What English words do you need to know to explain this?*
3. *What might go wrong in solving this problem?*
4. *Why is it important to be able to solve this problem?*

Discussion, Presentation, Technology, and Multimedia

- **Present.** Oral presentation is an excellent medium for explanation. Have students practice both their speaking skills and their ability to organize an effective explanation by picking a common process and walking a class through it or by giving the background of a current event in social studies, for instance.

- **Surf.** Probably the most common source of explanations students see online is Wikipedia. Have students examine a few pages on this site (or similar informational sites) and then discuss reliability, format, and how useful Wikipedia explanations are in an everyday or academic setting.

- **Discuss.** Discuss the importance of audience and assessing prior knowledge with students. Use web resources to demonstrate this by looking at complicated and simple explanations of the same event or phenomenon. Be sure to turn this discussion back on students and how they themselves learn.

YouTube Moment: One of the most popular young adult novelists in the world, John Green, has produced a series of videos you can find on YouTube by searching for "John Green Crash Course." In these short productions, Green explains historical movements or other educational issues. Look for an introductory video called "How and Why We Read" (2012), for instance. Students will enjoy hearing a favorite author teach this material, and you can discuss how Green approaches the skill of explanation in his videos.

After: Producing Explanations

Student Example 1: The Personal Essay

In ninth grade, Ali's English teacher assigned her the above prompt—now covered in the CCSS under the umbrella of *informational text*, but commonly referred to as a personal essay. Such essays are often seen in college applications, and Ali's teacher shared a number of actual college essays from students at the school as models. The challenge, she noted, lay in quickly explaining yourself to a stranger—an unknown audience—in a manner that seemed authentic and purposeful. Ali's teacher also shared similar pieces from professional publications such as *The New Yorker* to discuss audience and purpose further.

> ### The Task
>
> *How did you get to be the person you are today? What key moments, events, relationships, or people made you into a unique individual? In a personal essay, explain how you became (or are becoming) a unique individual.*

Ali's Personal Essay

Unlike most teenage girls, the highlight of my summer consists of spending numerous hours in a car with my mom, my dad, and my dog driving cross-country just to visit family. Every summer, my family jams the car full of "necessities" including my guitar, the port-a-potty, and plenty of egg salad while my father constantly asks me "Got everything?" Ultimately, our goal is to journey nearly half way across the US from Memphis to Palm Springs within a week, but pretty soon I pretty much forget the destination and am lost in the epic journey.

To be honest, spending up to twelve hours a day in a car with two college professors can drive some people mad. Luckily, I've developed some tolerance for their habits of taking the wrong turns and their inflexible schedule. But past the background music of Frank Sinatra or The Cure, I hear how my parents really talk and see how they really feel. I guess some kids don't get to see their parents often or really know who they are, but from my experiences I definitely can tell someone all about my parents and their opinions. My parents are pretty different from me, so taking spending so much time with them allows me to accept their little quirks, and once we get home, I definitely am pretty accepting of other people's quirks too.

The most important thing that these yearly trips have provided me with is independence and exposure. I've seen many things the average girl would call strange. I've seen that not all people

> ### 1. Capture the Big Picture
>
> Ali begins her essay by establishing a key theme: she's different from other teenage girls.

> ### 2. Reorder Events
>
> Ali chooses a key moment at which to begin her essay.

> ### 3. Look for Key Causes
>
> In paragraph two, Ali homes in on the heart of her topic: what makes her different.

look and live like me. I've learned how to fend for myself and to be "aware," as my mother would say. I credit these vacations with the source of my fashion sense, music taste, and food preferences. <u>I remember seeing a girl in LA one summer wearing a long skirt and short hair, when in my hometown the fad was to wear short skirts and long hair.</u> I still can't find a reason to why I wanted to dress like that girl, but I did. One of the most unforgettable memories I have of these trips was hearing one of my favorite songs in the Stratosphere hotel—"Young Folks" by Peter Bjorn and John. I had no idea what the song was called or who was the artist, but it consisted of bongos and whistling, and I felt this unbearable need to listen to it again. I've never heard music like that, and being exposed to something as simple as new music has made me want to know more about the world outside of my home and school. <u>Seeing these things in my travels has made me brave enough to be what is considered "different" back home.</u>

4. Gather Evidence

Ali has selected key details to make her point—evidence of her self-evaluation.

5. Draw Conclusions

The essay rounds off with a summative statement about Ali's personality.

Student Example 2: Writing About Math

The Task

Look at the picture of the Rubik's Cube. How many small cubes does the object contain in all? How many small cubes can you <u>not</u> see in this picture? Explain your answers.

On its surface, the Rubik's Cube problem posed here is a simple geometry problem, but it throws some middle school students for a loop, since they need to consider each small cube as a three-dimensional object regardless of how many of its sides they can see (some students want to count corner blocks three times, for instance). Given only a mathematical answer—such as $27 \times 2 = 54$, for instance—a math teacher might guess about a student's misconceptions without being completely certain about the accuracy of that guess.

Two middle school students, Zoe and Caleb, each completed this task in their math classes. Here are their responses:

Zoe's Response

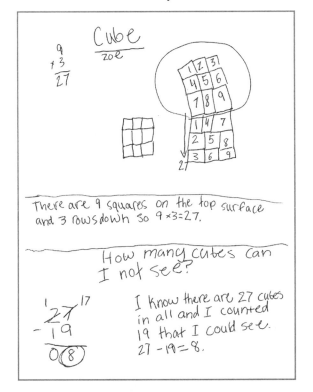

Caleb's Response

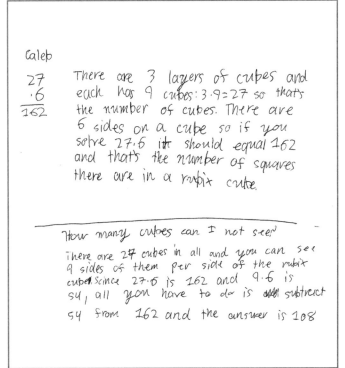

The power of explanation is clear. Both students got the number of cubes correct, but their teacher called both students aside to check for further understanding. Zoe, she felt fairly certain, understood the concept; while Zoe's first explanation indicated that she *probably* comprehended the relationship between volume and multiplication, the second explanation—related to the number of cubes Zoe couldn't see—solidified the teacher's perception of Zoe's understanding. She asked Zoe to explain her drawing and praised her for trying both a visual and a mathematical approach.

Caleb's explanations offered crucial information to the teacher. Had Caleb's math been all of his response, the teacher would have assumed he misunderstood the problem. However, Caleb's explanation shows that he actually understood the initial problem completely. He then went on, however, to figure the number of sides of the cube incorrectly. Based on that misunderstanding, Caleb solved the second part of the problem—the number of cubes he couldn't see—incorrectly as well. The written explanation allowed the teacher to work with the material Caleb figured correctly and build understanding of the remainder of the problem in a conference.

Work Cited

Green, J. (2012, November 15). How and why we read: Crash Course [Video file; Crash Course series]. Retrieved from https://www.youtube.com/watch?v=MSYw502dJNY

Scaffolding Explanation With Webb's DOK
HOW ZOE AND CALEB WORKED

Level One (Recall)

- *Sample Task:* Identify the number of sides of a cube and the number of squares on each side of a Rubik's Cube.

- *What Zoe and Caleb Did:* Completed this step of the problem in their heads, but did draw upon knowledge of cubes learned earlier in school.

Level Two (Skills)

- *Sample Task:* Estimate an answer based on the quick use of logic, not mathematical calculation.

- *What Zoe and Caleb Did:* They may have completed this step in their heads, coming up with a quick range into which likely answers might fall. This is a typical mental step for math students.

Level Three (Strategic Thinking)

- *Sample Task:* Explain how you might use certain calculations to determine the exact number of small cubes in a Rubik's Cube.

- *What Zoe and Caleb Did:* Used different processes to determine the number of sides, rows, or squares, applying prior knowledge of geometry and algebraic thinking to their answers and then writing down this process, trying to recapture the steps they used.

Level Four (Extended Thinking)

- *Sample Task:* Create and solve your own math problems using the rules of geometric figures you have learned throughout this year. In each problem, have users solve for both the parts of the object they can see and the parts they cannot. *Explain* the problem clearly to the user.

- *What Zoe and Caleb Might Have Done:* Zoe and Caleb had also studied rules of volume and area for a number of shapes. They could have applied these formulae, revisiting material from earlier in the course, to their own problems and shared them with classmates, writing explanations for what was expected as well as possible solutions.

Rubric for Explanations

SCORE	OVERALL EXPLANATION	USE OF DETAILS AND EVIDENCE	ORGANIZATION	STYLE, VOICE, AND CLARITY	CONVENTIONS AND MECHANICS
5 Outstanding	The explanation is compelling and complete and demonstrates a clear awareness of purpose, audience, and task	Ample and appropriately selected details effectively support the explanation throughout the response	Clear and consistent organization with well-executed transitions excellently supports a logical explanation that skips no steps	The response is clear and original and employs appropriate stylistic elements for effect in an exceptional manner	Syntax, grammar, and conventions are correct and add to the effectiveness of the response
4 Exceeds Expectations	The explanation is complete and demonstrates an awareness of purpose, audience, and task	Appropriately selected details support the explanation throughout the response	The organization is clear and supports the explanation in a satisfactory manner	The response is clear and employs appropriate stylistic elements for effect	Few or no errors are present in usage or syntax
3 Meets Expectations	The explanation is adequate and demonstrates some awareness of purpose, audience, and task	Details adequately support the explanation but may demonstrate some inconsistencies in execution or application	The organization supports the explanation but may lack transitions or miss steps	The response is mostly clear and adequately employs stylistic elements	Minor errors in usage or syntax may be present, but without repetition or undermining overall effectiveness
2 Approaching Expectations	The explanation is somewhat unclear and may demonstrate a lack of awareness of purpose, audience, or task	There is insufficient evidence to support the explanation well	Some flaws in organization or lack of transitions or clarity of steps makes the explanation difficult to follow	The response may be unclear or misuses stylistic elements in ways that interfere with voice and meaning	Patterns of errors in usage or syntax undermine the effectiveness of the response
1 Well Below Expectations	The explanation is vague or insufficient to the task	Evidence and details are missing or insufficient to support the explanation	The organization lacks focus and clarity; transitions may be unclear	The response is vague or lacks clarity; stylistic choices may confuse rather than enhance meaning	Significant errors in usage or syntax obscure the meaning and effectiveness of the response

Planning Page: Explain

Explain: provide reasons for what happened or for one's actions in order to clarify, justify, or define those events, actions, causes, effects, or processes

Learning Goal
What will your students explain? What learning outcomes or assessments do you wish to see?

Before	During	After
How will you prepare students to explain texts, issues, situations, or works?	What activities will you use to model, scaffold, and engage students in explanation?	How will you measure the effectiveness of your lesson?

Notes From This Chapter
What ideas or activities from this chapter do you wish to remember as you teach students to explain?

9

Imagine

create a picture in one's mind; speculate or predict

Imagine: create a picture in one's mind; speculate or predict what might happen under certain conditions; envision a range of possible outcomes, obstacles, or opportunities

CORE CONNECTIONS

- Write narratives to develop real or **imagined** experiences or events using effective technique, well-chosen details, and well-structured event sequences (W3)

- Develop claim(s) and counterclaims fairly, supplying data and evidence for each while pointing out the strengths and limitations of both claim(s) and counterclaims in a discipline-appropriate form and in a manner that **anticipates** the audience's knowledge level and concerns (WHST1b.9–10)

The Main Idea

It's easy to see how the word *imagine* relates to narrative writing. Students must learn to draw upon their own experiences to compose narratives, but they must also learn to stretch their thinking and creativity. Too often, however, imagination is presented as something students either have or do not, rather than as an academic skill that can be practiced and learned.

Imagining is anticipatory; it requires us to start in the present and consider the future. The word itself suggests visualizing or forming an *image* of a possible future. Similarly, the roots of the word *predict* and *hypothesize* suggest *speaking* or *arguing* in advance of a possible outcome. In each case, there's a methodical process at work. We start with one idea and then picture, describe, or contend with some difference in that idea.

Underlying Skills:

- **Brainstorm.** Imagination requires a willingness to entertain the unusual and to stretch. It also requires that we *actively* look for inspiration and ideas.

- **Visualize.** Most of us imagine through the visual; we must be willing to take the time to envision possibilities and then move into the realm of concrete ideas.

- **Accept possible failures.** Imagination may involve wild ideas and even failure; students need to be encouraged to take risks and to think broadly and creatively.

- Ask questions that can be investigated within the scope of the classroom, outdoor environment, and museums and other public facilities with available resources and, when appropriate, frame a **hypothesis** based on observations and scientific principles (NGSS, MS-PS2-3)

Before: Preparing Students to Imagine

Nothing about an assignment is so daunting as the blank page. Using imagination, whether a student is writing a poem or envisioning an engineering design, feels like jumping off a cliff. It's easy to give up, to turn back after the first failure, because failures hurt.

But imagining, designing, hypothesizing, and seeing predictions through to the end are parts of a process. It's easy to come up with an idea—seeing that idea through requires a certainty that process leads to product. As you make assignments that will lead students through this process, consider how you frame goals and purpose.

Imagine an ending.	**Imagine a beginning.**
Start with a given issue or problem and predict consequences, outcomes, or possible solutions.	Start with an end situation or goal and consider how it might come to pass.
Examples: Describe a plan that will entice more young people to vote.	*Examples: An inexperienced woman in her twenties wins a mayoral race against an experienced politician in her sixties. Imagine what her campaign strategy might have been.*
Write a sonnet in the style of Shakespeare in which you discuss the passage of time and mortality.	*Examine the pictured design for a new chair. What problem was it intended to solve? What steps might the designer have taken in creating it?*

As you design tasks for students, consider using both approaches over time and discussing how the process of addressing such assignments is the same and different.

Before you teach students to imagine, hypothesize, or predict, try these four things:

- **Model:** Too often, teachers know the outcomes of all that happens in a class: How a novel ends or how an experiment will turn out, for instance. Look for places to discover and predict along with students and show them how you visualize possible outcomes and hypothesize about results.

- **Define Expectations:** Imagination tasks should often be assessed based more on process than product. You don't always know how a skit, experiment, or picture will turn out, but you can gauge a student's ability to follow steps in a process and to plan and reflect. Be clear with students about what will or will not be assessed and where the value lies in completing nonassessed parts of the task.

- **Build Content Knowledge:** Predicting in any discipline requires, in part, a familiarity with other works that allows a basis for comparison. Help students understand the elements of a work or situation that allow educated guesses to come about in particular subject areas.

- **Practice Mental Moves:** Give students a brief example of the kind of problem you will give them in their later assignment and have them discuss it in small groups or pairs, focusing on the mental moves and questions in the sidebar. Post these moves on the wall and keep circling back to them throughout the unit so that students internalize them.

Obstacles to the Moves

When teaching students to imagine, watch out for these areas of difficulty:

- **Fear of "Getting It Wrong."** Imagination requires students to try ideas out and, often, to generate wild ideas; students who are used to looking for the "right" answer and fear taking risks may struggle with imaginative tasks.

- **Hasty Generalizations.** Predicting the outcome of a novel or creating a scientific hypothesis requires examining evidence, making comparisons, and applying prior knowledge. Students must take the time to apply both creative and critical thinking to imaginative tasks.

Mental Moves

Imagine

1. Consider Purpose

What is the problem, issue, or goal of my thinking?

2. Visualize

How could this problem or issue be different?

3. Generate Multiple Ideas

How many avenues toward a solution can I envision?

4. Design and Redesign

What works? What doesn't?

5. Commit

Which of my ideas am I willing to see through to its very end?

During: Practicing Imagining

Generally speaking, students must be led to generate ideas. Coming up with multiple avenues to address a problem or idea is hard work, and many students will avoid the process if given an option, falling back on expressions such as "I can't think of anything" or "I don't know what to do." To avoid such acceptance of failure, use two tools that lure students into the expression of ideas: drawing and **looping**. Drawing, of course, gives a concrete dimension to idea generation. *Looping* in idea generation involves revisiting ideas again and again, homing in on the pieces that one wishes to explore further (be careful not to confuse this with the term *looping* as it is used to discuss the practice of teachers working with students over multiple years). Consider these examples:

- **Narrative Writing.** A student draws the floor plan of a house or apartment in which she lived for an extended period of time, including the location of objects, furniture, and even people. She then writes a description of the house as one walks through it. Reading over the description, she circles three items that could lead to further stories. Then she writes one of those stories.

- **Social Studies.** A teacher wishes students to imagine the differences between trails west during the American era of westward expansion. Using research and his textbook, a boy in her class draws a picture for each of three trails that includes a distinct feature and then explains his pictures to a classmate. He then goes on to research more about the specific features in each picture to gather evidence for a class discussion.

- **Science.** A life science teacher introducing the concept of classification of organisms has each student draw a crazy creature— one with multiple legs, horns, wings, and so on. She photocopies the pictures and gives a set of copies to pairs of students; she then asks them to organize the pictures in any way and present their organization to the class. The class then looks at multiple ways to classify the creatures and researches some ways such classification is accomplished in the real world. When the class has learned about the actual classification system, they return to their drawings to discuss where they might fit in this system were the creatures real.

Discussion, Presentation, Multimedia, and Technology

- **Discuss.** Having students *predict* is a staple of most literature-based classrooms. Questions might include "What do you think will happen to this character in the next several chapters?" or "Can you think of three possible ways this story could end?" Similarly, art teachers might discuss the moment captured in a painting by asking students to *imagine* or *predict* what might happen next, thus homing in on why an artist chose this moment to portray. Consider *prediction* as a discussion tool in any discipline, perhaps using a **decision tree** to guide students in their thinking (a decision tree looks almost like a sports tournament bracket, with multiple potential outcomes for each new step in a student's thinking). Ask students to anticipate what consequence might follow the delivery of a historical speech, a scientific invention, or the application of a mathematical idea to a real-world process (e.g., *"Using your understanding of circumference, predict which horses on a merry-go-round would have to travel fastest, those on the inside or those on the outside."*).

- **Surf.** The ability to search images online changes the nature of many imagination-based tasks. Students can easily get help in visualizing, whether they look up pictures of Afghanistan before reading *The Kite Runner* (Hosseini, 2003) or look for sample designs for an egg cage to protect an egg dropped from twenty feet for a science challenge. Including this step as a part of the process of speculating and anticipating is not cheating, but an opportunity to discuss the nature of ideas, how we build off the ideas of others and add to them, and how we attribute information and ideas—think of it as building a visual vocabulary for unfamiliar concepts. Conduct such searches in class to model this process and the thinking behind it for students.

- **Present.** As technology allows students to adapt old forms to new media, we can look for those opportunities to imagine what, for example, an essay might look like in more digital formats by letting them experiment with presentation software like PowerPoint or Keynote, or even more nonlinear options like Prezi where students can embed everything from audio and video to art and photographs. In such "digital essays," students are still doing the same thinking as they might in an essay but learn to imagine other possibilities as writers who face the problem of how best to convey their ideas about a subject. The word *essay* means "to make an attempt" to explain something, but nothing about the word demands a response in paragraphs or only in words. Doing a search for "photo essays" quickly reveals a whole new range of opportunities for the imaginative student who wants to use a cell phone, for example, to capture and convey the ideas in a digital essay.

YouTube Moment: Search for "Ideo Shopping Cart" and you'll find a video from ABC's *Nightline* (Neri, 2009) that focuses on design company IDEO and their efforts to reimagine the everyday shopping cart. Have students take notes as they watch this video and then share their observations about how IDEO employees approach tasks without limiting themselves to conventional thinking.

After: Producing Imaginative Works

Student Example 1: Planning a Science Project

The Task

Beginning with a real-world problem, create a science fair project to enter in the county science fair. Your project must solve the problem. Document your steps for presentation.

When Elizabeth began her science fair project in sixth grade, she may have had the idea from previous labs that creating a hypothesis was a somewhat boring, dusty process—guessing at what will happen in a lab when the answer has been predetermined already. Certainly, she did not expect her project idea to require a great deal of imagination—she planned to build a small robot to turn out a light, a task that seemed ambitious but straightforward. Certainly, she needed imagination to construct the robot, but it seemed more a matter of putting the right pieces together than creating something new.

By the time Elizabeth's project moved on to win first place in her county's science fair competition, she had learned more, not just about science but also about the process of *imagining, hypothesizing, predicting,* and *speculating.*

Step One: Imagining Purpose

Elizabeth knew she wanted to build a robot. But her teacher had added an interesting twist: Every science fair project had to solve a real-world problem. Elizabeth's first step in imagining, therefore, involved imagining *purpose*:

> Since I was very small, I have always loved to know how things worked. When I was in first grade, a Lego robotics class became available at my school. Being the Lego lover I am, I signed up without hesitation. In the class, we used Lego motors and Legos to build robot helicopters, cars, boats, and even robotic Lego people. So I had already created a working robot that moved toward a light source. However, I wasn't quite sure of its purpose. Then I thought of my grandmother who was elderly and had difficulties turning out lights. That was when I decided to make the robot's purpose to turn out the lights for those who cannot.

With a purpose in mind, Elizabeth also had to re-envision the technical aspects of her robot to make sure it fit that purpose:

> After much researching and constant redesigning, I had created a working robot that moved toward a light source. I built my robot using a breadboard with an on-off switch connected to CDS cell light sensors (light sensors that turn light into voltage, making the robot move towards lights). The light sensors were monitored by MOSFETs and resistors. These were connected to two vibration motors, one on either side of the breadboard, which turned the

energy from the CDS cell light sensors into energy to activate the
vibration motors. The vibrations caused two toothbrush heads,
glued under the motors, to vibrate and move forward; finally, I had
a working robot.

Elizabeth began with a Lego robot, but by the time she had connected practice and purpose, the device had changed. It took multiple trials (and many trips to Radio Shack with her father) to figure out which parts she needed— and even this was not enough to make the idea work. She was able to order, for instance, her "breadboard with an on-off switch" and the light sensors, but the idea of connecting toothbrush heads to her robot came directly from the need provided by her goal of helping the elderly turn out lights. Real-world thinking thus combined with her practical knowledge to help Elizabeth focus her imagination.

Step Two: Design and Redesign

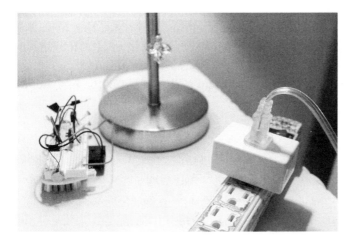

Elizabeth had already researched and redesigned her robot, but then she ran into a bigger problem: The robot moved toward a light, but it wouldn't turn the light off. The project already seemed like an accomplishment: After all, hadn't she built a working robot? But purpose changed the outcome, first in building the robot and then in coaxing it to do its work. Elizabeth's teacher played cheerleader and coach throughout without ever doing the heavy lifting for her:

I would run all of my theories by my earth science teacher. She
never gave me the answers to my problems; she would just look at
me and say, "I don't know; what do you think?" until I figured them
out myself. I redesigned all of my ideas six or more times, and she
helped me keep going even when I was about to give up.

Elizabeth thought she had reached the easy part of the project—she had the robot, she just needed it to turn out a light:

> I thought the robot would be strong enough to push or pull a lever, but after several attempts at building a lever connected to a lamp, I discovered I was wrong. I also went through a similar experience with several touch sensors and switches. After a long period of brainstorming, I came up with a Lego "pusher" (a Lego piece that moves forward when a gear is turned). This was placed at the top of a lamp with the pusher in front of the switch. I engineered a gear train reaching up to the pusher and planned for my robot to move a spinning gear into place, causing the gear train to spin the gear connected to the pusher, activating the pusher, and turning out the lights. The gears, however, were not strong enough; this idea failed.

Students are rarely rewarded for failure in school. Educators speak of risk taking, but the reality is that risks, especially those that don't pay off, are too often met with poor grades or recrimination. Yet failure is the spark for imagination; without failure, no one re-envisions, creates a new hypothesis, or bothers to anticipate a new outcome. Elizabeth was frustrated that her robot would not turn out the light no matter what she did to it, so after a long string of failed attempts, her teacher asked her to imagine a different way of achieving the goal. Soon, Elizabeth had an answer. She had built the robot for the task; now she needed to build *the lamp*.

> The idea that eventually worked was a specially designed lamp for the robot. I took a large, plastic cup, turned it over, and cut a hole in the bottom. I inserted an LED light through the hole and used batteries and wires to make a simple circuit through the lamp, leaving a loose wire at the lamp base. When the robot was turned on, it moved toward the lamp and bumped into the wire, turning off the lights.

The lesson Elizabeth learned, of course, went to the heart of imagination and hypothesis—the real work of imagining is not just about creativity but process too:

> I learned to never give up even though my project provided many obstacles. I desperately wanted to quit during my redesigning process, but my stubbornness won out. I never give up, no matter how much time it takes or how much effort I must exert.

Ultimately, the most valuable result of Elizabeth's science fair project (which at the time of this writing is entered into a national competition, awaiting results) was that it taught her to *imagine* as an academic skill.

As you read Elizabeth's summary of the entire project and process, consider how similar the act of imagining in science can be to the same act in creating a work of art, such as a painting, musical composition, or novel.

Elizabeth's Project Description

I learned to never give up even though my project provided many obstacles. I built a robot, dismantling and redesigning it several times. <u>Elderly and disabled people may experience difficulties with simple tasks such as getting up to turn off lights.</u> To solve this problem, <u>I designed and built a robot that would perform this job for them, simply by turning on the robot and allowing it to do its work.</u> One original idea involved a lever connected to the lamp's on-off switch that the robot would push, turning out the lights. My robot was not strong enough to push the lever. <u>After repeatedly redesigning my lever, I switched course.</u> I attached a touch sensor to the lamp; when the robot touched the sensor, it would activate the sensor, turning out the lights. The robot had too little mass to activate the sensor; it was unsuccessful. I created a Lego "pusher" placed at the lamp's neck. If a gear turned, the pusher would move forward and push the light switch off. I built a gear train reaching up to the pusher; I planned for the robot to push a spinning gear into place. The gears leading up the lamp would spin causing the pusher to do its job. Unfortunately, the Legos were not strong enough to support the heavy gears; they kept snapping. <u>My final decision was to make a special lamp where my robot would run into a wire at the lamp base, knock it loose, disconnect the circuit, and turn out the lights. I desperately wanted to quit during my redesigning process, but my stubbornness won out.</u> I never give up, no matter how much time it takes or how much effort I must exert.

1. Consider Purpose

Elizabeth states an explicit goal with real-world connections.

2. Visualize

Elizabeth *imagined* a robot that could perform the task she wished.

3. Generate Multiple Ideas

Elizabeth knew from the start of her project that she might have to try several designs.

4. Design and Redesign

Elizabeth tried a number of different avenues to make her idea a reality.

5. Commit

Elizabeth could have given up and simply presented a working robot as her project, but she stuck with her idea and saw it through.

Student Example 2: Narrative Writing

The Task

The year is 2050. The city in which you live, Memphis, flooded one year ago, leaving only the tallest buildings above the water line. Imagine this new future and how it might affect the government, social rules, and viewpoints of its citizens. Write a vignette set against this backdrop in which you predict the effects of this future on a single person.

As part of his summer reading assignment, tenth grader Emilio elected to read the dystopian novel *Ship Breaker*, by Paolo Bacigalupi (2010). His classmates read similar selections of young adult (YA) dystopian literature, and upon their return to school in the fall, they began by discussing *why* dystopian fiction had become so popular. As an offshoot of that discussion, they began to classify kinds of dystopian futures and to think about the differences that different settings might lend to them. As his teacher, Jane McAlister, led the discussion, Emilio took notes in the form of a concept map.

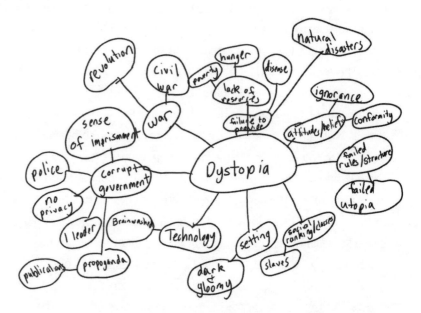

Emilio's notes on a class discussion of dystopias

Mrs. McAlister then decided to carry the assignment a step further. She asked Emilio's class to *imagine* a dystopian future for the city of Memphis—the city in which they lived. Here are the steps she used:

Step One: Individual Visualization

Emilio and each of his classmates were given a blank piece of paper without lines. Mrs. McAlister asked each of them to visualize a possible dystopian future for the city in one of three ways: they could use text, they could draw a picture, or they could draw a map. There had to be consistency and **verisimilitude** in these futures, Mrs. McAlister warned. In other words, while the students could let their imaginations run free, everything they included needed a reason. Why would aliens attack? Why would a government become totalitarian? Where would zombies come from? The students eagerly started drawing.

Step Two: Class Brainstorming

After the students spent a few minutes in individual creativity and had a chance to share at their tables, Mrs. McAlister took ideas from the class and started listing them on the board without being too discriminatory. After just a few minutes, she had a list of possibilities ranging from mutant ninja monkey attacks to more realistic viral outbreaks. She then spent a few minutes discussing the needs of good fiction (again, the word *verisimilitude* came up) and then had each table vote for three possibilities.

With a little negotiation, the class decided on a single desperate future for their city: weeks of rain would cause the Mississippi river to flood the entire region, and a virus spread by the water would destroy much of the city's food supplies, leading to a breakdown of social norms. (The scenario was not so far-fetched; Memphis had just survived some of the worst floods in its history at the time.)

Step Three: Creating a Class Wiki

A **wiki** is a website on which any approved user can create a page and post text or images. Mrs. McAlister made such a page and wrote a scenario on the first page. It included the dystopian future the students had created and a brief description of the city in its postflood stage; by writing the first page, Mrs. McAlister participated and modeled in the writing project. She then approved and created a page for each of the twenty-four students in the class. She discussed the assignment with the students and then gave them time to work.

Here is part of Emilio's entry. Emilio set his vignette in two neighboring tall buildings in the neighborhood where he went to school, Clark Tower and the iBank building.

Emilio's Vignette

BAM! A sharp crack startles me from my slumber. I look around and see the others wide-eyed, as well—I then notice Anthony's silhouette in the doorway, pistol in hand, confirming everyone's worst fears.

"Bankers—come to loot our food and vaccines," he states. "Is . . . is he dead?" I ask tentatively. Anthony nods with a victorious expression.

"That's the third one this month; their food stock must be getting desperately low," an elderly man comments. We all murmur in agreement, each secretly aware that we were only a few months away from the Banker's state of starvation. However, in that time we may all be dead from disease, a full-blown attack from the Bankers, or even the reptile escapees from the Memphis zoo, hungry for flesh— either way, unless help came soon, the flood would consume us all.

"Remember, Clark Towerees: Bankers vie for our demise. They are greedy, as demonstrated by the Banker I just eliminated," Anthony bellows.

I look at the thirty of us remaining. Our professions dictate our ranking, and the doctors are our leaders. A vat in the attic, installed in case the building caught on fire, supplies us with fresh water when Anthony permits it. I look out the window at Memphis; the sun is just peaking over the toxic water, casting a brilliant light across the destroyed city. Tops of buildings are visible, as well as scads of billboards; the perpetual smell of rotting humans and decay is sickening. Anthony clears his throat to initiate "Thought Time," thus interrupting my pensiveness. Reluctantly I chant the principles of a Clark Toweree with the others:

"Bankers are evil, greedy, and vile.
Clarks are superior in every way.
Hate the Bankers. Hate the neighbors.
Together, Clarks will prevail."

Anthony and his cronies monitor us, and strike those who don't chant along. When we finish, our daily ration of a pack of Lay's potato chips and a small cup of water is distributed. We all stare enviously at the doctors, who sit atop desks gobbling three bags each, a gallon of water at each of their sides. They explain that as our leaders, they must sustain themselves to protect us from the Bankers—this justification doesn't satisfy my growling stomach.

Step Four: Reading the Wiki

One of the best aspects of the class wiki emerged in the revision stage. Mrs. McAlister told the students that she planned to share their writing with some younger classes in the school, but that first they needed to make sure it was error free, appropriate, and complete. She set students in groups of four to read and edit one another's pages. The students worked hard to correct any errors, knowing that others would read the pages, but they also went a step further: As they read their classmates' entries, some of the students went back and revised their own entries to take other students' ideas into account. They began to imagine scenarios in which their own characters interacted with the characters in other students' vignettes, or in which the same events transpired within multiple vignettes. Most of the students read far more than the four pages they were assigned to edit; they read them all. By the time Mrs. McAlister actually shared the wiki with others, students had already shown it to their friends, parents, or other teachers.

Works Cited

Bacigalupi, P. (2010). *Ship breaker*. New York, NY: Little, Brown.

Hosseini, K. (2003). *The kite runner*. New York, NY: Riverhead Books.

Neri, A. (ABC Nightline, Producer). (2009, December 2). ABC Nightline—IDEO Shopping Cart [Video file]. Retrieved from https://www.youtube.com/watch?v=M66ZU2PCIcM

Scaffolding Imagination With Webb's DOK
HOW ELIZABETH WORKED

Level One (Recall)

- *Sample Task:* List the steps of a science experiment.

- *What Elizabeth Did:* Gathered materials, made a schedule, and worked with her teacher to prepare for the study.

Level Two (Skills)

- *Sample Task:* Generate a hypothesis and research question that will guide you in your project.

- *What Elizabeth Did:* Formed the hypothesis that "if a robot was constructed with a photo axis, which turns light into energy, it would move toward a lamp and then be able to turn off the lights." This, along with her stated purpose (to help elderly or disabled people turn off lights), guided her work.

Level Three (Strategic Thinking)

- *Sample Task:* Draw a conclusion from your observations of a science experiment and consider further experiments that would help you understand the phenomenon.

- *What Elizabeth Did:* Designed and redesigned her robot as part of the project, testing it and observing its performance. Ultimately, she added a second layer to her experiment by designing a lamp as well. She reflected on each of these steps in writing.

Level Four (Extended Thinking)

- *Sample Task:* Design and conduct a science fair project that requires investigation, reinvestigation, research, and presentation over an extended time period.

- *What Elizabeth Did:* Refined her model in light of feedback from others and observations; presented her project, explaining as she did not only how it worked but also how she solved the different problems she encountered along the way.

Rubric for Imaginative Tasks

SCORE	BRAINSTORMING, VISUALIZATION, AND PREDICTION	CREATIVITY	ORGANIZATION	STYLE, VOICE, AND CLARITY	CONVENTIONS AND MECHANICS
5 Outstanding	The process of imaginative thinking is thoroughly evident from student materials, including the generation and evaluation of multiple ideas	The response is creative, original, and compelling; it demonstrates a unique approach to the problem or task	The organization is appropriate to the imaginative task and showcases creative elements throughout the response	The response is clear and original and employs appropriate stylistic elements for effect in an exceptional manner	Syntax, grammar, and conventions are correct and add to the effectiveness of the response
4 Exceeds Expectations	The process of imaginative thinking is evident from student materials, including the generation and evaluation of multiple ideas	The response is creative; it demonstrates an interesting approach to the problem or task	The organization is appropriate to the imaginative task and includes creative elements throughout the response	The response is clear and employs appropriate stylistic elements for effect	Few or no errors are present in usage or syntax
3 Meets Expectations	The process of imaginative thinking is adequate; multiple ideas may have been considered	The response shows some creativity; it demonstrates an adequate approach to the problem or task	The organization is adequate for the imaginative task	The response is mostly clear and adequately employs stylistic elements	Minor errors in usage or syntax may be present, but without repetition or undermining overall effectiveness
2 Approaching Expectations	The process of imaginative thinking is inconsistent or shallowly applied; ideas need more depth and development	The response is lacking in evidence of creative effort, or the approach does not augment the problem or task	The organization is unclear or does not allow creative elements to be understood	The response may be unclear or misuses stylistic elements in ways that interfere with voice and meaning	Patterns of errors in usage or syntax undermine the effectiveness of the response
1 Well Below Expectations	The process of imaginative thinking is unclear or absent	The response lacks evidence of creative effort	The organization lacks focus and clarity and interferes with comprehension	The response is vague or lacks clarity; stylistic choices may confuse rather than enhance meaning	Significant errors in usage or syntax obscure the meaning and effectiveness of the response

Available for download from **www.resources.corwin.com/burkeacademicmoves**

Planning Page: Imagine

Imagine: create a picture of in one's mind; speculate or predict what might happen under certain conditions; envision a range of possible outcomes, obstacles, or opportunities

Learning Goal
What will your students imagine? What learning outcomes or assessments do you wish to see?

Before	During	After
How will you prepare students to imagine, predict, or hypothesize?	What activities will you use to model, scaffold, and engage students in imaginative tasks?	How will you measure the effectiveness of your lesson?

Notes From This Chapter
What ideas or activities from this chapter do you wish to remember as you teach students to imagine, predict, or hypothesize?

10

Integrate

make whole by combining the different parts into one

combine • incorporate • synthesize

Integrate: make whole by combining the different parts into one; join or make something part of a larger unit; synthesize many disparate parts into one form

CORE CONNECTIONS

- **Integrate** and evaluate content presented in diverse formats and media, including visually and quantitatively, as well as in words (R7)

- Gather relevant information from multiple print and digital sources, assess the credibility and accuracy of each source, and **integrate** the information while avoiding plagiarism (W8)

- **Integrate** and **evaluate** information presented in diverse media and formats, including visually, quantitatively, and orally (SL2)

The Main Idea

In most books of study skills, **synthesis** is reserved for the final chapters. Because they see it as a higher-order cognitive skill, teachers may talk about its importance but shy away from actually teaching it as a reproducible skill. Yet the ability to integrate material—whether it comprises two or three quotations from a single poem or twenty sources in a research paper—is one students should be learning all along, at every grade level.

Underlying Skills:

- **See the big picture.** What is the overall theme, concept, or situation to which the material relates? The ability to zoom out (and then zoom back in) is crucial to the integration of academic pieces.

- **Organize.** The more pieces one is trying to incorporate, the more crucial solid organizational strategies become. Does the material fall into two categories, three, or more?

- **Create.** Many tasks that fall into Bloom's synthesis level are actually creative tasks, such as writing a sonnet, creating a dramatic scene, or proposing an experiment. Integration of academic material always requires the ability to make pieces of knowledge more than the sum of their parts—a research paper is more than a collection of quotations from sources; it is a new argument with original ideas.

Before: Preparing Students to Integrate

Whether they realize it or not, students are asked to synthesize ideas constantly (if they are not, they are probably not learning much). It may help to break down the levels at which students are asked to integrate ideas, skills, or knowledge on a regular basis:

CORE CONNECTIONS

Continued

- **Integrate** qualitative scientific and technical information in written text with that contained in media and visual displays to clarify claims and findings (NGSS, MS-PS4-3)

Within a Topic

Sample Tasks:

- Make sense of a text by building new knowledge as one reads
- Combine findings from two sets of data on one topic
- Conduct research on a single, specific topic
- Write an essay that applies quotations from throughout a text to a single thesis
- Find material on the Internet to apply to a classroom presentation

Within a Class

Sample Tasks:

- Connect themes of multiple readings
- Create a project that draws on skills learned throughout the year
- Write an essay based on multiple documents encountered throughout a unit
- Respond to a discussion board on an ongoing basis to collect ideas and communicate as a class

Across Classes

Sample Tasks:

- Discuss how a historical era relates to a development in science
- Use math processes to complete a lab experiment in a science class
- Write a paragraph with correct grammar and style in any discipline
- Create a portfolio of your work from throughout the year in multiple subjects and reflect on your learning

From small tasks to large ones, each time students incorporate material into a bigger idea they are practicing the skill that, in many ways, ties all other academic skills together. Being explicit about this step of academic progress is a valuable way to help students gain confidence about their ability to collect and connect in your classroom.

Mental Moves

Integrate

1. Consider Your Artifacts

What does each work I wish to integrate tell me?

2. Construct a Thesis

What is the purpose of integrating these works? What is the bigger picture?

3. Gather Evidence

Which details of each work will help make my point?

4. Organize

In what order do I present my evidence?

5. Draw Conclusions

What have I learned from this combination of artifacts?

Before you teach students to integrate texts, issues, or data, try these four things:

- **Model:** Create a synthesis task to complete as a class—a short research project, reading, or creative activity. Have students use sticky notes of different colors to reflect different types of findings; then, collect these on the board and discuss the big ideas they call to mind. Emphasize that integrating the notes requires more than just collecting information but also thinking about the big picture.

- **Define Expectations:** It helps students to know the number of sources they are expected to use, along with what types of sources, for research projects (if you do not wish to suggest a specific number, suggest a range). Similarly, other integration tasks that require students to collect their own data or material need specific expectations and rubrics.

- **Build Content Knowledge:** Help students by focusing their attention on elements of sources or data they may otherwise overlook in their integration of material. When comparing texts, for instance, students will often gravitate toward content and away from rhetoric or style. When integrating data, make sure students look at specific principles and processes as appropriate.

- **Practice Mental Moves:** When working on your synthesis task as a class, have students practice the mental moves in the sidebar by asking themselves these questions in pairs or groups. Post these questions and moves on the wall and keep circling back to them as students practice their integration skills so that they internalize them.

Obstacles to the Moves

When teaching students to integrate, watch out for these areas of difficulty:

- **Poor Organization.** In many synthesis projects, organization is important not only in producing the final product but also in collecting, tracking, and arranging material as a process; help students plan to organize along the way during a project, not only at the end.

- **Answering the Question.** Synthesis tasks such as completing a document-based question or some research papers require students to approach the task in specific ways; failure to recognize the demands of the questions can result in failure to complete the task properly.

During: **Practicing Integrating Assignments**

- Teach students to integrate by making pieces of the task visible. Try color coding sources or outlines to show students how integration might work. Imagine, for instance, that students *compare* an article about Albert Einstein to one about Isaac Newton. In each article, students might highlight scientific discoveries in blue, statements about historical context in yellow, and aspects of their personal lives in green and then connect their findings by comparing colors and ideas. (See the sticky note activity related to modeling earlier in this chapter for a twist on this idea.)

- For younger students, the ability to synthesize and integrate begins with adding new knowledge to prior knowledge as they read or study. Try a simple "At first I thought/Then I learned/Now I understand" chart for students to trace their understanding of a topic or text.

- For more mature students, integration can become a complex process that requires careful note keeping and management of sources or ideas. Discuss the logistics of assignments with students, including how to keep track of web sources and web searches, how to take notes in preparation for research, or how to document a science project using photographs, notes, and journaling. See the ideas for incorporating technology that follow this section for more specific ideas.

ELL Focus: Do This One Thing to Help

- Simpler synthesis tasks, such as reading a work that continually adds new knowledge to prior knowledge, require clear understanding of the material before the student moves on to the next section or idea. Have ELL students stop often to check their understanding. You may wish to suggest a particular online source such as a summary of a text that students can use in combination with reading original material.

- Complex synthesis tasks, such as constructing a longer research paper, may take ELL students more time because of the layers of language involved. Use graphic organizers to help make expectations clear. After an ELL student collects sources for a research paper, for instance, help make an outline that includes boxes where quotations from each source could be inserted to help create a whole.

Discussion, Presentation, Technology, and Multimedia

- **Discuss.** The very purpose of discussion is to incorporate multiple points of view and ideas into student thinking. Use **jigsaw activities** with larger classes to help students incorporate views and ideas by following this example, based on a class of twenty-four students:

→ Randomly assign students to eight groups of three to discuss an idea or problem. *Example: What are the ten most important problems candidates need to address in the upcoming presidential election?*

→ Have each group combine with another (four groups of six) and repeat the same task. *Example: Combine your two lists into one list of ten problems. Write your list on poster-sized paper.*

→ Again, instruct each group to combine with another (two groups of twelve) and repeat the task. One student acts as facilitator and attempts to find common ground between the lists. *Example: Look for similarities between the lists and write those on a new sheet of paper or on the board. Then, discuss differences and try to come to a consensus on which items are most important. If discussion breaks down, vote on your answers.*

→ Facilitate a whole class discussion in which students look for similarities between the two new lists, creating a list of ten or fewer outcomes, which you can use to prompt further research, discussion, or personal reflection. *Example: Now that we have agreed on eight major problems candidates should discuss, each of you will choose one and conduct research on the pros and cons of one solution to that problem.*

- **Discuss.** Increase synthesis activity in your classroom by using online discussion boards that require students to post a thought and respond to others' thoughts and then collect and incorporate ideas into a reflective piece. For example, have students post a response every day at the end of class regarding their learning about a new concept. After a few days, have them respond to others' posts each day at the start of class. When enough students have posted, have them read back through the posts and discuss overall reflections on the nature of learning they glean from the posts of the entire class.

- **Organize.** There are many excellent online tools available that will help students keep track of source material and stay organized as they collect and combine research to integrate into a final project. Introduce sites such as noodletools.com or easybib.com that not only create citations but also help to bookmark, save, and retrieve sources.

- **Connect.** Twitter, Instagram, Vine, and other social media tools are a natural place for adolescents to synthesize and connect material of diverse types. Create a class account you can monitor on a social networking site or have students use such tools in their group work and presentations; be sure to discuss how we use social media and the pathways to integration it offers.

- **Present.** Have students keep digital portfolios of their work, preferably on a free website or wiki (consider weebly.com, wix.com, or wikispaces.com as possible tools for this activity). In the portfolio, students should display artifacts of their learning over time, including documents, photographs, or videos, and also write short reflections on those artifacts and how they connect to their learning over time. Where possible, have students share these portfolios with each other, their parents, or even their teachers at the start of the next year.

YouTube Moment: Mashups (popular works such as songs combined into one new work) and parodies require integration of a sophisticated sort, even though students may think of such works as simple fun. Search for "Maccabeats Les Miserables" to find a video (Drive-In Productions, 2013) of an a capella college group that cleverly combines popular songs and Jewish holidays, in this case, the Passover story and the musical based on Hugo's famous novel. Discuss how such clever combinations of material require the mental moves required for integration.

After: Producing Integrated Assignments

Student Example 1: Informational Writing (The Research Paper)

The Task

Choose one of the historical documents we have studied in class this semester; all of these documents reflect important historical moments of the past fifty to sixty years. In addition to analyzing the document itself, you will conduct research about the historical event and conduct an oral interview of someone who was alive at the time of the event. Then, you will integrate *all of your findings into a single paper about the event.*

When Claire's English and World History teachers teamed up to assign a single research project, she was overwhelmed. The project included literary analysis, historical research, and even an oral interview, all focused on a single historical text. With a sense of foreboding, Claire chose John F. Kennedy's (JFK's) address during the Cuban Missile Crisis primarily because her mother said it would make a good topic.

Claire dutifully did her research and studied the speech, but it wasn't until she conducted the oral interview with a military veteran who lived through the crisis that her interest was truly sparked. *Then,* she returned to her historical documents and textual analysis with more interest. The historical event was important to the veteran, who appreciated the opportunity to share his own experience and thinking with an adolescent; thus, it became more important to Claire.

But how to mesh all of the material together?

Fortunately, Claire's teachers helped her develop an outline and a plan for integrating the diverse sources: her own analysis, her research sources, and the oral interview. She wrote a thesis in English class and then revisited it in history, but it wasn't complete until after the oral interview. Then, Claire realized she could organize around the pieces of the interview, taking the major points shared by the veteran and backing them up with research and her analysis of the speech as a piece of rhetoric.

Claire's final product was quite long, so we have included only a piece of it here, including the original citations and bibliography just as Claire turned them in with the paper. However, this piece is enough to see the mental moves in action and to examine Claire's approach to the integration of multiple sources in her own work.

Keep in mind that the same process Claire uses here to compose a fairly traditional research paper could be used to make a multimedia presentation, a website, or a video. Integration is as necessary in the digital world as it is in the world of print.

Claire's Excerpt

In Kennedy's address to the nation, a historical analysis of the events in the situation, and an oral interview with a member of the Marine Corps during the Cuban Missile Crisis, the theme of the president's stability persisted.

Before addressing the Soviets and Cubans, Kennedy makes a promise to his people: "Our unswerving objective, therefore, must be to prevent the use of these missiles against this or any other country and to secure their withdrawal or elimination from the Western Hemisphere" (Kennedy). This promise is sincere, yet formal and comprehendible, and prompted the American people to trust in him as both the president and as an ordinary citizen of the United States. Yet for over a week, Kennedy and his Executive Committee of the National Security Council (ExComm), a committee dedicated to helping Kennedy overcome the crisis, had debated about which option to choose. If the air raid were to be used against them, the invasion could result in many deaths, and an action against Berlin could lead to nuclear war. Although Kennedy wanted to appear steadfast and strong, "...he was also very concerned that the crisis would escalate out of control" (Munton and Welch, 2007). After considering many options and undergoing almost two weeks of debate, it became obvious that the strongest peaceful option was to initiate a naval blockade surrounding Cuba. "All ships attempting to enter Cuba were to be stopped and searched for missiles and related military material" (Phelps and Lehman, 2005). Kennedy's main hope was that "...the blockade most likely would not trigger immediate war" (Hanes, Hanes, and Baker, 2004). The same authors suggest that the strength that Kennedy demonstrated in choosing his method of action continued when he learned that "the Soviets were using the missiles to test his will." In order to pass this test of strength and willpower, Kennedy resolved to broadcast a national speech to explain the crisis to Americans, Soviets and Cubans.

As a father, husband, and son, Mr. Hayden could relate to the fearful American people, but as a member of the air force he had a greater understanding of the conflict. During Kennedy's address regarding the Cuban Missile Crisis, Mr. Hayden was "sitting there with [his] two small children," and he remembers thinking, "they might not grow up, but there is no place to go." Even though Mr. Hayden experienced the

1. Consider Artifacts

Claire identifies the primary source, her oral interview, and her research.

2. Construct a Thesis

This is merely an excerpt of Claire's multipage paper, but it nevertheless presents a clear goal: to give evidence of Kennedy's strength during the crisis.

3. Gather Evidence

Claire quotes from all three of her sources: the interview, the speech, and research material.

4. Organize

Claire has chosen to present historical material first and then color it with snippets of her interview.

war in the marine corps, he remembers feeling "more tense having come back from the war to the civilian life with [his] wife and children sitting there than [he] ever was in any confrontation that [he] ever had anywhere in the world as a US marine because it was just a different situation." Fortunately for America, the Russians made a major mistake: they recognized that Kennedy was young and "had only been in office for two years," so they "thought that they could bully him, but the counsel that he got from the secretary of defense and also from his military commanders was pretty solid and that was an extreme benefit to Kennedy and the entire United States during the crisis." Throughout the entire speech, Kennedy "consistently identifies himself as the one who [is] handling the situation" (Long and Swett, 2012).

5. Draw Conclusions

Claire sums up the point of this section with another quote from her research.

Claire's Sources

Hanes, Richard C., Sharon M. Hanes, and Lawrence W. Baker, eds. *Cold War Reference Library.* Vol. 2nd of Cold War: Almanac. Cuban Missile Crisis 9. Detroit: UXL, 2004. Accessed February 14, 2012. http://ic.galegroup.com/ic/uhic/ReferenceDetailsPage/ReferenceDetailsWindow?displayGroupName=Reference&disable Highlighting=true&prodId=UHIC&action=e&windowstate=normal &catId=&documentId=GALE%7CCX3410800033&mode=view&user GroupName=tel_k_hutchison&jsid=d274fdd8611fb461cb573abb4e108256.

Kennedy, John F. "Cuban Missile Crisis Address to the Nation." 22 Oct. 1962. *American Rhetoric.* Web. 24 Jan. 2012. <http://www .americanrhetoric.com/speeches/jfkcubanmissilecrisis.html>.

Long, Jamie Thomas, and Sean Swett. "John F. Kennedy and the Cuban Missile Crisis: An Analysis of crisis communication within our nation." *Jamie Thomas Long.* Wordpress, n.d. Web. 23 Jan. 2012. <http:// jamiethomaslong.wordpress.com/writing-2/john-f-kennedy-and-the-cuban-missile-crisis-an-analysis-of-crisis-communication-within-our-nation-written-by-jamie-long-and-sean-swett/>.

Munton, Don, and David A. Welch. *The Cuban Missile Crisis: A Concise History.* 2nd ed. 2007. Reprint, New York: Oxford University Press, 2012.

Nathan, James A. *Anatomy of the Cuban Missile Crisis.* Westport, CT: Greenwood Press, 2001.

Phelps, Shirelle, and Jeffrey Lehman. "Cuban Missile Crisis." In *West's Encyclopedia of American Law*. Gale U.S. History In Context, 2005.

Accessed February 14, 2012. Last modified 2005. http://ic.galegroup .com/ic/uhic/ReferenceDetailsPage/ReferenceDetailsWindow?display GroupName=Reference&disableHighlighting=true&prodId=UHIC&ac tion=e&windowstate=normal&catId=&documentId=GALE%7C CX3437701241&mode=view&userGroupName=tel_k_hutchison& jsid=273f2e3ff2c01b0e67eca28a070c2970.

Student Example 2: Informational Writing (The DBQ)

The task included here is a spin-off from actual AP test tasks often referred to as DBQs. The name makes it clear that students are expected to individually *interpret* and then integrate multiple documents. On an AP exam of this sort, documents would be provided to students, who would then have forty-five minutes in which to construct a response. We should note that the actual AP prompts do not generally include the word *integrate*, but the skill clearly lies at the heart of this task.

This task places more autonomy in the hands of the student. It's the task that Max's teacher assigned his class in March, as the class of sophomores neared the first AP exam most of them would take.

Max set to work to find documents. He enjoyed reading *The Grapes of Wrath* in his English class, even though many of his peers had disliked the book, so after discussion with his teacher, he decided to focus on the Great Depression for his DBQ. He knew immediately that he wanted to include a photograph by Dorothea Lange; his English teacher had shared these during their study of the 1939 Steinbeck novel, and Max was fascinated by the stark images of travelers during this time. He quickly found a nonfiction piece by Steinbeck, a speech from President Herbert Hoover, a political cartoon featuring FDR, and a chart showing the unemployment rate in the United States throughout the 1930s. In his search, he came across an *actual* DBQ from the 2003 AP exam, which he showed his teacher; she had been planning to use it as a review exercise for the class, so she asked him to avoid using those documents in his own DBQ.

Once Max had collected ten artifacts, he then scoured the documents to come up with his own prompt.

"I knew I couldn't just ask about the cause of the depression or something basic," Max wrote in his final reflection on the project. "And I didn't want to steal from the previous AP question. So I came up with my own twist. The prompt was, *Analyze how the life of the common person changed as a result of government policies and interventions during the Great Depression.*"

Max presented his DBQ to the class; then, he went home to write an essay in response to his own assignment. Over the course of the year, Max had learned what was expected by the College Board of such an essay, including

- A strong, clear thesis
- Use of a majority of the documents
- An understanding of the basic meaning of the documents
- Organization of the documents into groups

The Task

Throughout your tenth grade year, you have been asked to answer document-based questions (DBQs), such as those you will see on the upcoming Advanced Placement (AP) test. Now, it's your turn. Construct a specific essay prompt related to 20th century American History and find six to ten documents that relate to the prompt, including at least one speech, one visual document, and one chart or graph. Then, write an essay in which you integrate *the documents into one analysis of the issues raised by the historical period and an answer to your own essay prompt.*

As he worked, Max kept in mind that he was expected not only to use the documents as evidence, but also to *integrate* them into his argument. Here is one paragraph of his final response:

> As the archetype of "the common man" began to spread during the Great Depression, it became common for depictions to show out-of-luck workers as tired, long-suffering victims. But in fact, many people had the rug pulled out from under them. Document 5, the graph of unemployment during the 1930s, demonstrates that unemployment reached a high of 25% in 1933, up from just 10% three years earlier. One quarter of the American people were out of work, and more than half of those lost jobs they'd had just a few years before and had no prospects for work. Document 6, a photograph of a man in the depression by Dorothea Lange, shows a man waiting for work. This is a perfect image of the resolute "common man" waiting patiently, not angrily, for the government to fix his problems, but not with much hope. Likewise, in document 7, Roosevelt criticizes those who have "too little contact with the true America" and do not understand the common man's plight. By contrast, the president stereotypes the rich as "gentlemen in well-warmed and well-stocked clubs." This image is all-important to understanding how the government began to form policies that would address the nation's problems.

Max's teacher was fond of warning students against creating a "laundry list" of documents—a simple summary of what each document communicated. Instead, she instructed students to connect the documents to themes and place them in categories. Max worked hard to do just that. He brought together his prior knowledge, his understanding of a variety of sources, and his ability to think about overarching questions and themes to combine the material into a more unified whole.

Works Cited

Drive-In Productions. (Producer). (2013, March 19). The Maccabeats—Les Misérables, A Passover story [Video file; MaccabeatsVideos]. Retrieved from https://www.youtube.com/watch?v=qmthKpnTHYQ

Steinbeck, J. (1939). *The grapes of wrath*. New York, NY: Viking Press.

Scaffolding Integration With Webb's DOK

HOW CLAIRE WORKED

Level One (Recall)

- *Sample Task:* Identify the key events and dates of the Cuban Missile Crisis.

- *What Claire Did:* Before even beginning initial research, she familiarized herself with the basic dates and moments of the event she was to study.

Level Two (Skills)

- *Sample Task:* Annotate and interpret JFK's speech in response to the crisis, including initial research to understand the context of the speech.

- *What Claire Did:* Studied and interpreted the speech, preparing to use it as evidence and to construct arguments about it, and read for background understanding of the time period before beginning her research in earnest.

Level Three (Strategic Thinking)

- *Sample Task:* Conduct an oral interview with an eyewitness to a historical event, using your own knowledge of the event as well as prepared questions to prompt discussion.

- *What Claire Did:* Interviewed a veteran who served during the Cuban Missile Crisis after preparing thorough research and careful question construction.

Level Four (Extended Thinking)

- *Sample Task:* Gather your notes, research, understanding of a primary text, and interview transcript and use them to create a coherent research paper with a clear argument.

- *What Claire Did:* Over several weeks, she analyzed and culled sources to combine key details and ideas into a larger whole, returning to sources as needed and organizing findings; she then synthesized all of the material into one final paper.

Rubric for Integration and Synthesis

SCORE	THESIS AND OVERALL SYNTHESIS OF MATERIAL	USE OF EVIDENCE	ORGANIZATION	STYLE, VOICE, AND CLARITY	CONVENTIONS AND MECHANICS
5 Outstanding	A well-developed thesis introduces material that has been synthesized in a sophisticated and meaningful manner	Ample and appropriately selected details are effectively combined to enhance meaning	Clear and consistent organization with well-executed transitions excellently supports the integration of material and leads to well-developed overall conclusions	The response is clear and original, and employs appropriate stylistic elements for effect in an exceptional manner	Syntax, grammar, and conventions are correct and add to the effectiveness of the response
4 Exceeds Expectations	The thesis is clear and introduces material that has been synthesized in ways that contribute to meaning	Appropriately selected details are combined to enhance meaning	The organization is clear and supports the integration of material throughout the response	The response is clear and employs appropriate stylistic elements for effect	Few or no errors are present in usage or syntax
3 Meets Expectations	The thesis is clear and introduces material that has been adequately synthesized for the task	Details adequately support main points but may lack integration	The organization is adequate but may not allow material to be integrated as smoothly as possible	The response is mostly clear and adequately employs stylistic elements	Minor errors in usage or syntax may be present, but without repetition or undermining overall effectiveness
2 Approaching Expectations	The thesis is vague or unclear; material is not smoothly or meaningfully integrated	Details are not integrated and may not support key points or overall meaning	Some flaws in organization or lack of clarity and transitions interfere with the successful integration of material	The response may be unclear or misuses stylistic elements in ways that interfere with voice and meaning	Patterns of errors in usage or syntax undermine the effectiveness of the response
1 Well Below Expectations	The thesis is vague or absent and the integration of material is unclear or lacks meaning	Details are missing or insufficient to support the task	The organization lacks focus and clarity; transitions may be unclear; material is not integrated successfully	The response is vague or lacks clarity; stylistic choices may confuse rather than enhance meaning	Significant errors in usage or syntax obscure the meaning and effectiveness of the response

Planning Page: Integrate

Integrate: make whole by combining the different parts into one; join or make something part of a larger unit; synthesize many disparate parts into one form

Learning Goal
How will your students integrate material? What learning outcomes or assessments do you wish to see?

Before	During	After
How will you prepare students to integrate texts, issues, situations, or works?	What activities will you use to model, scaffold, and engage students in integration and synthesis?	How will you measure the effectiveness of your lesson?

Notes From This Chapter
What ideas or activities from this chapter do you wish to remember as you teach students to integrate?

11

Interpret

draw from a text or data set some meaning or significance

deduce • infer • translate

Interpret: draw from a text, data set, information, or artwork some meaning or significance; make inferences or draw conclusions about what an act, text, or event means

CORE CONNECTIONS

- **Interpret** words and phrases as they are used in a text (R4)

- **Interpret** information presented in diverse media and formats (e.g., visually, quantitatively, orally) and *explain* how it contributes to a topic, text, or issue under study (SL2)

- Read closely to determine what the text says explicitly and to make logical **inferences** from it (R1)

- Analyze and **interpret** data to provide evidence for phenomena (NGSS, MS-LS2-1)

The Main Idea

When the instruction to *interpret* appears in an assignment or prompt, it tends to be followed by a specific object: a poem or story, a work of art, or a graph or data set, for instance. It could also carry more specific instructions, such as to interpret the actions of a character or the effects of a particular speech on a historical event. All instructions to interpret, however, share in common the need for students to reach beyond the literal and to make leaps—often of intuition—to construct meaning.

Underlying Skills:

- **Draw inferences.** Students must be able to draw *connotations*, understand *subtext*, and *read between the lines*.

- **Think metaphorically.** Metaphorical thinking goes beyond inferring—it involves attaching meaning to symbols or *archetypes*, understanding *allegory*, and recognizing *allusions* and their importance.

- **Think causally.** Interpretation of history, science or math data, or current events, for instance, requires that students connect causes and effects. This thinking can also include separating correlations and coincidences from causes.

Before: Preparing Students to Interpret

Interpretation is often seen—and, frankly, too often taught—as merely a subjective enterprise. One problem with an approach that accepts statements such as "I just don't like it" or "I think it can mean whatever I want it to mean" is that it doesn't teach students the value of using evidence, context, and prior knowledge to construct a valid line of communication and reasoning between author and audience. More importantly, however, the message that interpretation is subjective, while often meant to draw in young students to talk about works of art or literature, actually scares them off as time goes by, and it leads older students to feel that they "don't get it" or "can't understand" art or poetry.

There is, of course, room for multiple interpretations of all works, but that truth does not eliminate the value of evidence-driven reconstructions of meaning. Students are often ready to judge music, movies, or television shows as entertainment, but it takes training to move that judgment process into an academic skill (with his classes, Jim talks about "reading rhetorically" as opposed to reading merely for pleasure). Consider the distinction:

The Entertainment Audience	The Academic Audience
Asks these questions:	Asks these questions:
• *How did it make me feel?* • *Was it better or worse than similar works I've experienced?* • *Was it worth what I paid for it?* • *Was it fun?* • *Did it conform to my expectations?*	• *What was the author trying to communicate?* • *What techniques did the author use to create a message?* • *How did the work challenge assumptions, genres, or ideas?* • *How did the work attempt to transform its audience?*

We place an arrow between these two boxes to show that, of course, there is room to be both intellectually engaged and entertained at the same time. Ideally, students can learn to balance both sets of questions at once. (Try using the questions to discuss a popular young adult novel or song lyrics with your class—but if you do so, make sure to check your own prejudices at the door and accept that for adolescents, the answers on the right may be different from yours.)

Before you teach students to interpret a text, issue, situation, or work, try these four things:

- **Model:** Show your students how you work through an interpretation of a work or set of data by talking out loud as you approach the task. What are the steps you use? Actually lead them through your own mental process, using phrases such as "First, I . . ." or "After I've figured that part out, I usually . . ." If you want to challenge yourself, use a work or data with which you're largely unfamiliar—the process will be more authentic and teach students more about how you think through tricky issues.

- **Define Expectations:** Interpretation often involves multiple levels of understanding. Recognizing a trend in the data, for instance, is not the same as providing reasons for that trend, just as recognizing that a poem contains a metaphor is not the same as explaining the metaphor. Be clear about the levels of understanding on which you will evaluate students.

- **Build Content Knowledge:** Techniques and methods—how dialogue is written, how data were collected, or the purpose of a technical document, for instance—can be key in interpreting and evaluating material. Be sure students are armed with the vocabulary and discipline-specific understanding they need before they begin an interpretive task.

- **Practice Mental Moves:** Give students a sample task and have them work in pairs, using the questions in the sidebar to practice the mental moves. Post these questions and moves on the wall and keep circling back to them as students practice their interpretive skills.

Obstacles to the Moves

When teaching students to interpret, watch out for these areas of difficulty:

- **Vague Associations.** The importance of zooming out and zooming in—sometimes repeatedly—is that students connect impressions to evidence; skipping the second of these steps may lead students back toward the idea that "it can mean whatever I want it to mean" and allow for generalizations unsupported by details.

- **Lack of Sequencing.** An interpretation of a poem, for instance, needs to proceed stanza by stanza (or section by section); students sometimes want to start with the end of a piece when interpreting and may miss important elements.

Mental Moves

Interpret

1. Zoom Out

Gauge your overall reaction: What emotions or thoughts does this work elicit?

2. Zoom In

Look closely: Which elements of the work serve as the best evidence of its meaning?

3. Consider the Source

What might the creator of this work be trying to convey? Who was the audience?

4. Consider Ambiguities

What possible coexisting or conflicting messages might the work convey?

5. Summarize Meaning

Using the evidence, explain the meaning or purpose of the work in your own words.

During: **Practicing Interpretation**

- Today's adolescents will probably spend as much of their lives interpreting visual media as printed text or data—even if they go on to study fields that focus on printed text and data. Visual literacy, moreover, provides an accessible entry point for students to interpret. Try starting by looking at how some prominent writers have interpreted works of visual art. Here are a few examples you might discuss:

  → Bruegel, *Landscape With the Fall of Icarus* (painting)
    - Auden, "Musee Des Beaux Arts" (poem)
    - Williams, "Landscape With the Fall of Icarus" (poem)
  → Picasso, *The Old Guitarist* (painting)
    - Stevens, *The Man With the Blue Guitar* (poem)
  → Elmer, *Mourning Picture* (painting)
    - Rich, "Mourning Picture" (poem)

- Students are sometimes tempted to accuse teachers of "reaching" for interpretations, refusing to trust that artists or writers "really meant" for deeper meanings to be conveyed through a work. It helps if students can see the artistic process modeled so that they get a sense of the time and thought many writers or artists put into their work. As an example, introduce Norman Rockwell's paintings, including his *Four Freedoms* series (1943) and *Breaking Ties* (1954), which relied on a process of gathering ideas, photographing real people from his town in black and white, painting studies, and making a final version, all of which model the intentional and lengthy nature of the creative act.

- The mental moves for interpretation apply to data as well as to works of art, literature, or music. As with other genres, the interpretation of graphs, charts, or data sets requires both objective knowledge and subjective intuition and insight. Model this work for students multiple times; working with data does not come easily to all. Try taping a grid to your floor and have students stand on different data points; then, discuss their physical relationship to other students in the room and why it matters.

ELL Focus: Do This One Thing to Help

If you feel that language learners in your class may struggle with an interpretative task, provide guiding questions. Consider the level of intuition and nuance involved in the task—the same student may struggle more with a Shakespearian sonnet than with a painting because of the language demands. Pose questions such as "What emotion is the author trying to convey, and how do you know?" or, more specifically, "What aspects of the Sun and the subject of the poem does Shakespeare compare?"

Discussion, Presentation, Technology, and Multimedia

- **Present.** Use the idea of zooming in and zooming out to have students structure short presentations in which they interpret a work of art, a poem, or a data table. Have them create presentation slides that show the text and literally zoom in or out to highlight key details or the whole piece as they interpret it. As part of the assignment, you can specify a certain number of details to include (three or four details would provide a good start).

- **View.** As you teach students to draw inferences from texts, consider starting with video clips from popular movies or television shows. Choose a scene that includes multiple characters and show it once, and then again, with students looking carefully at nonverbal cues and communication the second time. What can you *infer* from facial expressions and body language? Then, transfer their understanding to verbal inferences by reading a passage together and looking for specific words and phrases that allow the reader to infer information.

- **Discuss.** It's important that students learn to interpret political and editorial cartoons, both those that reflect current issues and historical examples. This skill often appears on tests students encounter late in high school. Practice by sharing examples with your classes, and have students discuss possible meanings in pairs, in groups, or as a whole class. Then, have students create their own editorial cartoons (they may use stick figures) and share them in class.

- **View.** The United States Holocaust Memorial includes a lesson on its website to accompany its exhibit, Some Were Neighbors. In the lesson, students are presented with photographs and asked to interpret the images; then they are given full information about the context *after* making an initial interpretation. You can access this lesson online here: http://somewereneighbors.ushmm.org/education/lesson/deconstructing-the-familiar.

YouTube Moment: You may know Khan Academy for its famous online videos that teach math concepts to students, but you may not be aware that Salman Khan also produced videos for Khan Academy in which he discusses interpretations of great works of art with experts in the field. Search for "Khan Academy Mona Lisa" (2012) to find a discussion of da Vinci's painting. As your students watch, instruct them to look and listen for the mental moves for interpretation and the accompanying questions in the discussion.

After: Producing Interpretations

Student Example 1: Interpreting Graphic Novels

<table>
<tr>
<td>

The Task

The works of literature we read in this unit required the reader to visualize. Choose one of these four works and write a single page in which you interpret the visual elements of the work and how they helped the author communicate theme and meaning. Be sure to refer to specific details as evidence of your interpretation.

</td>
</tr>
</table>

Justin's eleventh grade teacher included a two-week unit in which groups of students read one of four works, including the graphic novels *Maus* (Spiegelman, 1987) and *Persepolis* (Satrapi, 2000) and two young adult novels that use visuals as integral pieces of the story, *The Adventures of Hugo Cabret* (Selznick, 2007) and *The Book Thief* (Zusak, 2006). As part of his summative assessment, Justin's teacher included the task presented in the box to the left.

After his teacher gave book talks on each of the four books, Justin chose to read *Persepolis*, the black and white graphic novel about growing up in Iran by Marjane Satrapi. An artist, Justin had never been a particularly avid reader, but Satrapi's combination of simple shapes and unflinching descriptions of her own childhood fascinated Justin, and he read the work within two days.

Here is the piece Justin turned in to his teacher.

Justin's Sample

Marjane Satrapi's memoir, *Persepolis*, serves as a very powerful story in its graphic novel form. Satrapi describes her problems in life in Iran from the ages of six to fourteen through only black and white comics, <u>which makes this stark memoir much more powerful and invigorating.</u> But why black and white only?

1. Zoom Out

Justin begins with a characterization of the work as a whole.

<u>On page five in *Persepolis*, the top frame shows two groups of women shouting at each other. On the left, the veiled women are dressed in black, whereas on the right, the veil-less women are dressed in white.</u> This image shows how opposite things were for Satrapi in this time period. <u>The black indicates compliance to the war, while the white indicates freedom and rebellion.</u> One source, Patricia Storace (2005), suggests that the alternation between black frames to white frames indicates much uncertainty during this time period in Iran. Life is so sporadic that no one knows what is coming next.

2. Zoom In

Justin describes specific scenes to construct his point.

3. Consider the Source

Justin shows an awareness of the author and context of the work.

4. Consider Ambiguities

Justin is willing to entertain multiple possible meanings.

<u>But another idea as to why Satrapi used the black and white color scheme is that it seems very childlike.</u> She wrote this memoir in 2000, so she had the option to go back and try to relive this time period as a child. This is possibly why she

decided to use black and white because it gives her a way to re-experience her childhood. In early frames, Satrapi shows herself in white (as a child) and her parents in black. Her white wardrobe reaffirms this childish spirit because she wants to help. <u>Satrapi seems to [use] only black and white as a way to prove that a child can do a lot.</u>

5. Summarize

Justin rounds out his discussion by summing up the reasons for Satrapi's use of black and white.

Either way, the use of black and white is ironic because something of the magnitude of a war is never as simple as black and white. Satrapi is truly a genius for using black and white in order to passionately describe to the reader what life was like for her in Iran—less colorful and more true.

Work Cited

Storace, P. *A double life in black and white* (2005, April 7). Retrieved January 30, 2008, from http://www.donkeys-party.com/pdfs/satrapi_and_moaveni.pdf

Student Example 2: Interpreting Data

David had studied 20th century China in his tenth grade World Studies class for several weeks when his teacher presented this on-demand assignment to him. The class had practiced tasks similar to this one throughout the year; in fact, though David had rarely been asked to interpret data of this sort in the early years of his education, he found that the skill was more common in high school, particularly in science and social studies classes.

David felt good about such assignments, but he knew some of his classmates dreaded them. Even the first part of the assignment—simply describing the data—threw some of his peers for a loop, not to mention the difficult task of constructing reasons that explained the data.

As part of his response, David wrote the following interpretation of the graph:

> The line on the graph goes steeply up after 1980, indicating that the Chinese economy grew more rapidly, and is pretty much flat before 1980, showing that before that time the Chinese economy didn't rise much. The main reason that the economy changed so much is that there was a change in leadership in China. This change

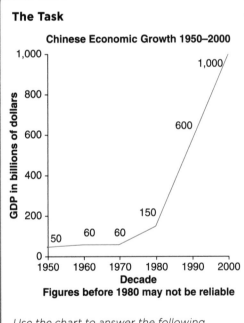

The Task

Chinese Economic Growth 1950–2000

Use the chart to answer the following questions:

a. Describe the different trends in the Chinese economy before and after 1980.

b. Applying your knowledge of China, interpret the data provided on the graph. What are two reasons that explain the trends the graph displays?

c. Explain why, according to the note, "figures before 1980 may not be reliable."

was mainly the change from Mao to Deng Xiaoping as leader. Mao believed more in communism, while Deng Xiaoping believed that a market economy and communist rule could coexist. This is why Deng said, "It doesn't matter if the cat is black or white, so long as it catches mice." Deng allowed for more privatization in which companies could own businesses rather than the government running them. He also allowed limited foreign investment. Mao, on the other hand, tried an economic reform called the Great Leap Forward, but the graph proves that most of China saw almost no improvement economically during Mao's time. In fact, the graph shows a total growth under Mao of around $100 billion compared to growth after Mao of around $850 billion. The figures before 1980 are less reliable because under Mao, China was more tightly controlled, more closed off, and may even have fabricated numbers, whereas once the market opened up, the rest of the world could track the economy better.

While David's response is not expansive, he accomplishes what many students have trouble with—tying explicit descriptions of data to reasons and causes. As with any interpretation, David looks at the raw material presented to him and overlays his background knowledge of the topic to come to a new understanding.

Works Cited

Auden, W. H. (1940). "Musee Des Beaux Arts" [poem]. In *Another time*. London, UK: Faber & Faber.

Bruegel, P. (1558). *Landscape with the Fall of Icarus* [Oil and canvas, painting]. Brussels, Belgium: Musees royaux des Beaux-Arts de Belgique.

Elmer, E. R. (1890). *Mourning picture* [painting]. Northampton, MA: Smith College Museum of Art.

Khan, S., & Harris, B. (2012, December 14). Celebrity & Art: Leonardo's "Mona Lisa" [Video file; Smarthistory, Art History at Khan Academy]. Retrieved from https://www.youtube.com/watch?v=3kQ_p2EZX4Q

Picasso, P. (1903). *The old guitarist* [Oil painting]. Chicago, IL: Art Institute of Chicago.

Rich, A. (1965). Mourning picture [poem].

Rockwell, N. (1943). *Four Freedoms Series: Freedom of speech, freedom of worship, freedom from want, and freedom from fear* [painting]. Stockbridge, MA: Norman Rockwell Museum.

Rockwell, N. (1954, September 25). *Breaking home ties* [painting]. *Saturday Evening Post*, on cover. Indianapolis, IN: Curtis.

Satrapi, M. (2000). *Persepolis*. New York, NY: Pantheon, Knopf Doubleday.

Selznick, B. (2007). *The adventures of Hugo Cabaret*. New York, NY: Scholastic.

Some Were Neighbors. (2014). Deconstructing the familiar: Photo activity. Retrieved from http://somewereneighbors.ushmm.org/education/lesson/deconstructing-the-familiar

Spiegelman, A. (1987). *Maus*. New York, NY: Pantheon, Knopf Doubleday.

Stevens, W. (1939). *The man with the blue guitar* [poem]. In *The man with the blue guitar*. New York, NY: Knopf.

Williams, C. W. (1939–1962). Landscape with the fall of Icarus [poem]. In *Collected Poems: 1939–1962* (Vol. 2). New York, NY: New Directions.

Zusak, M. (2006). *The book thief*. New York, NY: Knopf.

Scaffolding Interpretation With Webb's DOK

HOW DAVID WORKED

Level One (Recall)

- *Sample Task:* List the elements of data being presented in this graph.

- *What David Did:* Quickly identified the pieces of information he would grapple with: figures in billions of dollars, 20th century decades, and China.

Level Two (Skills)

- *Sample Task:* Describe the trends revealed by the graph.

- *What David Did:* Applied his understanding of how graphs work to make simple observations that set the stage for deep analysis. He noticed the sharp spike in gross domestic product (GDP) around 1980 and looked at the steady, slow rise before that date, for instance.

Level Three (Strategic Thinking)

- *Sample Task:* Analyze the data, applying your knowledge to offer explanations for trends.

- *What David Did:* In his essay, he drew on his understanding of Chinese history to explain the major shift that is reflected in the data in 1980.

Level Four (Extended Thinking)

- *Sample Task:* Investigate one decade on the graph in more detail, researching that period to discover what economic reforms China put in place and why they were or were not successful; prepare a presentation that teaches the rest of the class about the topic.

- *What David Might Have Done:* Researched and learned more about the Great Leap Forward, which he touches on only briefly in the essay, and compiled that research into a presentation.

Rubric for Interpretation

SCORE	THESIS AND OVERALL INTERPRETATION	USE OF EVIDENCE	ORGANIZATION	STYLE, VOICE, AND CLARITY	CONVENTIONS AND MECHANICS
5 Outstanding	A well-developed thesis introduces a sophisticated interpretation that includes interesting insights and inferences	Ample and appropriately selected details effectively support the interpretation throughout the response	Clear and consistent organization with well-executed transitions excellently supports the interpretation, including an excellent introduction and conclusion	The response is clear and original and employs appropriate stylistic elements for effect in an exceptional manner	Syntax, grammar, and conventions are correct and add to the effectiveness of the response
4 Exceeds Expectations	The thesis is clear and introduces an interpretation that includes some correct inferences	Appropriately selected details support the interpretation throughout the response	The organization is clear and supports interpretation; the introduction and conclusion are well executed	The response is clear and employs appropriate stylistic elements for effect	Few or no errors are present in usage or syntax
3 Meets Expectations	The thesis is clear; interpretation may be straightforward; inferences may be inconsistent	Details adequately support the interpretation but may demonstrate some inconsistencies in execution or application	The organization, including introduction and conclusion, are adequate to support the interpretation	The response is mostly clear and adequately employs stylistic elements	Minor errors in usage or syntax may be present, but without repetition or undermining overall effectiveness
2 Approaching Expectations	The thesis is vague or unclear; the work may be incorrectly interpreted, or inferences may be inaccurate	There is insufficient evidence to support the interpretation, or details are not always adequate to support analytical points	Some flaws in organization or lack of clarity and transitions make the interpretation hard to follow	The response may be unclear or misuses stylistic elements in ways that interfere with voice and meaning	Patterns of errors in usage or syntax undermine the effectiveness of the response
1 Well Below Expectations	The thesis is vague or absent and interpretation is inaccurate	Evidence and details are missing or insufficient to support the interpretation	The organization lacks focus and clarity; transitions may be unclear	The response is vague or lacks clarity; stylistic choices may confuse rather than enhance meaning	Significant errors in usage or syntax obscure the meaning and effectiveness of the response

Planning Page: Interpret

Interpret: draw from a text, data set, information, or artwork some meaning or significance; make inferences or draw conclusions about what an act, text, or event means

Learning Goal
What will your students interpret? What learning outcomes or assessments do you wish to see?

Before	During	After
How will you prepare students to interpret texts, issues, situations, or works?	What activities will you use to model, scaffold, and engage students in interpretation?	How will you measure the effectiveness of your lesson?

Notes From This Chapter
What ideas or activities from this chapter do you wish to remember as you teach students to interpret?

Organize

arrange or put in order

arrange • classify • form

Organize: arrange or put in order according to some guiding principle; impose coherence, order, structure, or function according to type, traits, or other quality

CORE CONNECTIONS

- Introduce claim(s) and **organize** the reasons and evidence clearly (W1a)

- Introduce a topic; **organize** ideas, concepts, and information (W2a)

- Engage and orient the reader by establishing a context and introducing a narrator and/or characters; **organize** an event sequence that unfolds naturally and logically (W3a)

- Analyze the structure an author uses to **organize** a text, including how the major sections contribute to the whole and to the development of the ideas (RI5)

The Main Idea

It's no accident that the word *organize* appears in the first specific detail of each standard related to the three genres of writing in the Common Core standards: narrative, information, and argument. Yet it's also an essential skill and process in the social sciences, sciences, and mathematics, all of which ask students to identify or generate ways to order the details, data, or other elements being studied, and to do so with some objective in mind.

Underlying Skills:

- **Identify key elements.** Students need to understand the major divisions or aspects of works in order to determine what possible organizational schemes they might consider. A novel, for instance, might lend itself to organization based on characters or themes, while a data set might produce organizational approaches based on cause and effect or order of importance.

- **Display information appropriately.** Students should learn to emphasize the organizational structures most important to their purposes. Presenting a historical trend, for example, such as immigration to the United States, might lead to creating a table that illustrates how the trends change by group, region, era, or reasons for immigrating rather than a traditional paragraph.

- **Use transitions or signal words.** Transitions make clear the nature of a student's organizational approach and further emphasize whatever relationships are at the center of a presentation or paper.

CORE CONNECTIONS

Continued

- Construct a scientific explanation based on evidence from rock strata for how the geologic time scale is used to organize Earth's 4.6-billion-year-old history (NGSS, MS-ESS1-4)

Before: Preparing Students to Organize

Students often gravitate toward the most obvious of the available organizational structures, but there are, in fact, quite a few they can often choose among. Introduce or extend their knowledge of organizational approaches by helping them think about the purpose of various tasks. (For a more detailed discussion of the organizational "moves" listed in the boxes below, see Appendix II: Academic Writing Moves.)

Diving Deep

Students examine and analyze a single text, a current event, a historical period, or a scientific discovery, for instance.

Possible organizational strategies:

Cause and effect

Classification

Illustration

Pros and cons

Problem and solution

Making Connections

Students work to connect two or more texts, issues, or events, or to explain how two items are or are not related.

Possible organizational strategies:

Analogy

Comparison and contrast

Pros and cons

Agree and disagree

Acknowledge alternatives

Putting in Order

Students must define or relate a plot, event, discovery, or process for science or math.

Possible organizational strategies:

Chronology

Definition

List

Narration

Process

As students move into upper grades, they need to become more adept at determining purpose and strategy for themselves, and they may even begin to layer strategies on top of one another, comparing and contrasting in chronological order, for instance, or including definition and illustration within a discussion of pros and cons.

Before you teach students to develop a text, issue, situation, or work, try these four things:

- **Model:** Display a set of details or data on a large screen and go through to show them the different ways you could arrange them depending on your purpose. Talk about the advantages and disadvantages of each approach, and explain why you would choose the one you did.

- **Define Expectations:** Make clear to students that the organizational scheme should be suitable for your purpose and work throughout. Some, for example, will choose to organize their ideas in a paper by using an extended metaphor, but this strategy often weakens over time as the comparison becomes less obvious.

- **Build Content Knowledge:** Provide students a rich and increasingly diverse array of words and phrases they can use to signal their organizational moves when writing. One way to do this is to have them study models from actual experts in your discipline to show how they use language to emphasize or clarify the organizational approach.

- **Practice Mental Moves:** Give students a sample organizational task and have them work in pairs or groups, using the questions in the sidebar to practice the mental moves required for organization. Post these questions and moves on the wall and keep circling back to them as students hone their organizational skills.

Obstacles to the Moves

When teaching students to organize, watch out for these areas of difficulty:

- **Abrupt Transitions.** Even mature students often need reminders to include basic signals that they are making a shift in thinking or argument.

- **Non-Parallel Structure.** Often, students will lose track of their own organizational strategy in a longer essay or presentation, resulting in a paragraph or point that does not fit the pattern already established in the piece.

Mental Moves

Organize

1. Identify the Task

What are the core details, items, or ideas the task asks for? How would I classify these? How are they similar or different?

2. Determine What Matters

Colors? Functions? Plot points? Themes? Types? Values? How do the assignment and the work itself suggest organization?

3. List Possible Strategies

What are the options for organizing my work? Order of importance? Chronological? Problem-solution?

4. Test It Out

When I outline and write my introduction, does the strategy I've chosen support the point I want to make? Does it work for all?

5. Apply to All Content

What is the format through which I should communicate? Should I use a table? Graph? Bullet points? Paragraph?

During: Practicing Organization

Students tend to understand the linear nature of narrative text (even when it includes flashbacks, for instance) somewhat naturally; they grow up with stories. Informational text can be more difficult. When students encounter a math textbook, a procedural manual, or a historical article with charts and maps, for instance, they may face difficulty. Even more so, composing such material may prove quite difficult. Argument, though it may use some of the same strategies as narrative and informational texts, comes with its own set of components that are arranged according to long-established principles of rhetoric and composition and may similarly prove less natural for students to replicate.

Visuals such as those below can make a difference. As you introduce methods of organizing ideas, consider posting anchor charts with simple graphic displays in your room that help students *see* how organization works (see Appendix VII for full-page versions).

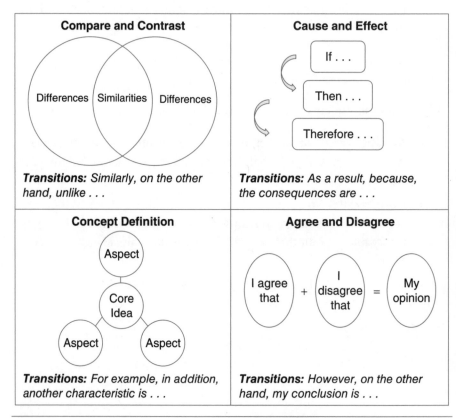

 Available for download from **www.resources.corwin.com/burkeacademicmoves**

ELL Focus: Do This One Thing to Help

Anything you can do to help English learners visualize the concept you are teaching is useful. This means either demonstrating with visuals how to apply the different organizational strategies discussed during this unit (by drawing them or otherwise displaying them through objects you can actually manipulate or by diagrams) or having these students go through their own writing, for example, with a highlighter to indicate all the words that signal their organizational approach. This also helps you to see where they have none and allows you to be more efficient in your examples of transitions they could use.

Discussion, Presentation, Technology, and Multimedia

- **Discuss.** Practice organizational strategies in whole-class discussions:
  - → To practice comparison and contrast, make one side of the room responsible for making comparisons and one for making contrasts.
  - → To practice cause and effect or chronological organization, try handing out historical events, parts of a passage, or steps in a process and having students line up according to what they think the order might be.
  - → To practice pros and cons, stage a series of formal debates.
  - → To practice classification, give each student an aspect of a text, issue, or event; then, have them work to classify themselves into groups and explain the classifications.

- **Present.** Presentations can be organized using the same formulas and processes as papers, but students won't necessarily think of this naturally. Instead, they may retreat to the familiar territory of narrative chronologies, especially in speeches that are reflective. Encourage students to outline their presentations and consider a variety of strategies. Could a personal address be framed as a series of pros and cons? Could a PowerPoint on a scientific idea be organized as cause and effect?

- **View.** Videos—even short videos—often use interesting organizational techniques. Try comparing a brief news clip, a short animated story, and a music video and then discussing how the filmmakers used organizational strategies in each case to communicate a message.

- **Surf.** Websites have unique methods of organization, including menus and hyperlinks. Teach these elements to students (especially younger students) as part of an emphasis on digital literacy and informational text.

YouTube Moment: Search for "Pixar Storyboarding Mini Doc" (Garcia, 2013) to find a short video discussing the process of storyboarding at Pixar, including a demonstration of a storyboard scene and actual animated scene from the movie *A Bug's Life.* Discuss the concept of storyboarding, in which screenwriters draw a series of images as an initial representation of a story, with students. Why does charting a story—or, for that matter, a paper, presentation, or other work—in a visual manner help with organization? How can the power of visual organization help with the works students produce?

After: Producing Organized Student Work

Student Example 1: The Analytical Essay

> **The Task**
>
> *Some critics have argued that Hamlet becomes the very injustice he seeks to redress. In a well-organized essay, defend or refute this idea. Turn in both your outline and essay by the end of class today.*

Because her classes took place in blocks of eighty-five minutes, Gaby was often faced with the task of planning and writing an entire essay within a single class period, especially as she got older and began to take more AP classes. By her senior year, the ability to plan and write an essay in a limited amount of time was expected of her. True, her teachers treated such essays as drafts only, but they expected polished drafts, at least.

Moreover, Gaby's English teacher no longer had much patience for simple five-paragraph essays that used three aspects of a single issue to construct wordy paragraphs. The essays Gaby wrote in class were expected to be concise, have a clear point, and make that point in a logical manner using evidence from the text.

Gaby's response to *Hamlet* came in this way in the fall of her senior year.

Step One: Outlining

When Gaby received the prompt to write about Hamlet and his quest for justice, she wasn't entirely sure what she believed, but she knew she had to take a stand on the issue one way or the other. She hurriedly threw together her outline, thinking as she planned. We have presented Gaby's rough outline exactly as she wrote it. Note, however, that she used a simple but effective organizational strategy: She made a point about the play, offered a possible counterpoint, and then drew a conclusion.

Gaby's Outline

Hamlet:

1. Wants to kill uncle, which is rational, but 2. Goes overboard, therefore, 3. Becomes the injustice he's attacking.

Outline:

- Hamlet takes the "eye for an eye approach."
- Hammie thinks that if he kills his uncle, his father's death will be avenged.
  - → YET there must be a distinction between avenging a death and justice. Justice is not doing in return what has been done.
  - → That decision in itself is unjust. For Hamlet to be just, he should have let him be.
  - → Justice would have found a way for itself to be served. Hamlet needn't become the instrument of justice.
- Then [he] decides he must make his uncle SUFFER.
- My boy Ham has the chance to kill his uncle while he is attempting to pray but does NOT because he wants Claudius to suffer hellfire.
  - → THIS is where Hamlet becomes the embodiment of the very injustice he seeks to redress.
  - → The fact that he not only wants to avenge his father's death but that he wants to make his uncle suffer for his actions is where Hammie becomes increasingly unjust.
  - → In his eye for an eye stage, Ham just wanted to punish Claudius for his actions, but when Hamlet seeks to make Claudius SUFFER for his actions, Hamlet becomes the injustice.

In actual fact, as Gaby grew older, she wrote many essays of this sort without an outline, especially when AP teachers began to reduce the time she was allotted to compose an essay to forty minutes or less. Here, however, Gaby struggled with how to organize her thoughts—the outline became her road map for organization in the essay itself.

Step Two: Writing

With her outline in place, Gaby started writing. Notice that the bullet points in Gaby's outline do not translate directly into full paragraphs, as a fully prepared, numbered outline might be expected to do. Rather, the notes represent Gaby's initial thinking and help her take the next organizational step. As she wrote, Gaby used transitional phrases at the opening of each paragraph to make her train of thought clear.

Gaby's Essay

Hamlet: He Is What He Repeatedly Does

1. Identify the Task

Gaby takes a clear stand (even if she is unsure of her view).

2. Determine What Matters

Because *Hamlet* is a chronological narrative, Gaby organizes chronologically in order to follow the character's development.

3. List Possible Strategies

While her essay is chronologically organized, Gaby has drawn on her experience as a writer and superimposed a point and counterpoint strategy.

At the onset of young Hamlet's quest for retribution in William Shakespeare's Hamlet, he seeks only to equiponderate the unjust death of his father, King Hamlet; however, he eventually decides to cause the murderer to suffer endlessly in hell, thereby, becoming the very injustice he seeks to make right.

At the beginning of his reparative journey, Hamlet walks a justifiable path. He wishes only to kill his uncle, Claudius, to balance out the unwarranted murder of King Hamlet by Claudius's hand; in his own words, Hamlet wishes to "be cruel, not unnatural" (III.ii.428) in his pursuit of justice. At the start, his father, in the form of a ghost, appears and bids that Hamlet "revenge his foul and most unnatural murder" (I.v.31). In a sense, at the beginning of his quest for justice, Hamlet is only following his father's final request, and he honestly believes that he "was born to set it right!" (I.v.211), only because he has a duty to do right by his father.

However, Hamlet does go so far as to make his revenge "th[e] commandment [by which he] all alone shall live" (I.v.109), and at this very point, Hamlet begins sliding down the slippery slope on which he tumbles into becoming the very injustice himself. He badly wants to avenge his father's death and to set right what his uncle has done wrong, but when his obsession with justice transforms into an outright desire to punish his uncle for his father's death, Hamlet becomes the instrument, even the embodiment, of the very injustice he attempts to redress. Hamlet resolves to kill Claudius while he kneels and attempts to confess his many sins, but Hamlet then decides that killing his uncle after he had repented for his transgressions would be too light of a punishment; Hamlet feels "a more horrid hent" (III.iii.94) is appropriate for his uncle and his crime.

To this effect, Hamlet proclaims, "... And I am then revenged / To take him in the purging of his soul, / When he is fit and seasoned for his passage? / No." (III.iii.89–93). This utterance marks the turning point for Hamlet. This decision serves as his *hamartia*; this decision is his fatal one. Hamlet openly wishes for his uncle to suffer in the worst way possible, saying his wishes to kill his uncle "about some act / That has no relish of salvation in' t— / Then trip him, that his heels may kick at heaven, / And that his soul may be as damned and black / As hell, whereto it goes" (III.iii.96–100). Thus, Hamlet's resolution to damn his uncle to eternal burning and suffering is the same resolution that Claudius makes in killing the elder King Hamlet; thus, by this decision, Hamlet has indeed become the very injustice he seeks to redress. He has abandoned the just path on which he set out and has adopted a path of ruthlessness and of a will to punish. Hamlet has moved from wanting to justly take an eye for an eye to unjustly wanting to take an entire body for an eye, and this decision determines his tragic downfall, for he cannot live as he seeks to dole out injustice instead of justice.

As some critics argue, Hamlet becomes the very injustice he seeks to redress, and in that transformation is his misstep that leads to his eventual and tragic downfall. Yet Hamlet did not set out on a path of injustice; rather, he sets out to right a wrong. But, when his desire to right the wrong transforms into a desire to not only right the wrong but to also punish the wrongdoer indefinitely, Hamlet seals his fate. At that decision to make an act of equalization become an act of endless punishment, Hamlet metamorphs into the very injustice he attempted to remedy.

4. Test It Out

Gaby's outline provided a road map for her to reach this argument about the play. Her first test was the outline; her second is the essay itself.

5. Apply to All Content

By the time she has reached her conclusion, Gaby has proven that her organizational strategy works.

Student Example 2: Science Writing

As a middle school science student, Quinn had not been asked to do a great deal of scientific research, much less write a paper based on that research. Her original notes for her paper comparing tap water in the city of Memphis, Tennessee, to a brand of bottled water were more or less a list of information she found in no particular order:

- FIJI water meets all federal health standards
- FIJI is bottled water from the source of Viti Levu (Fiji Islands)
- 2nd largest bottled water brand in the U.S.A.
- Source is a natural aquifer located in Yaqara river valley
- Water is continually replenished by rainfall
- Also purified by trade winds blown across the Pacific Ocean to the Fiji Islands
- This is a product of one of the last virgin ecosystems on the planet
- This water is very rare
- Natural pressure pushes FIJI water out of the aquifer deep below the earth's surface
- Then squeezed into iconic square bottles
- Afterwards shipped off to humans
- Memphis aquifer produces some of the highest quality water in the nation
- Aquifer is located 350 ft. below the surface of downtown Memphis
- Its thickness is 800 ft.
- Water is delivered to the surface from the use of wells
- Memphis is one of the only cities that relies on underground water

When it came time to turn these notes into a full paper, Quinn realized that her notes contained valuable information but did not help her organize that material. She talked to her teacher about organization, and together they arrived at a *comparison and contrast* format. In planning for her paper, Quinn wrote, "I will examine the differences between the Memphis aquifers and the source of Fiji water, as well as lead in drinking water. The first two paragraphs will compare water purity and location. The third paragraph will compare lead in the water."

Using this comparison and contrast strategy, Quinn was able to translate the content in her bullet points to a clearly organized paper. Here is part of her final product:

Our Memphis aquifer produces some of the highest quality water in the nation. The aquifer is located 350 ft below the streets of downtown Memphis. The aquifer is 800 ft wide ([University of] Memphis.edu, 2003). The source of Memphis water comes from an underground source called the Memphis Sand Aquifer. The remaining water comes from a deeper source called the Fort Pillow Sand Aquifer. These are little particles of a bigger water foundation called the Mississippi Embayment. No other water source has been used since 1885. The water is pumped from the aquifers through a large pumping station. At the station, the iron is removed, and small levels of chlorine and fluoride are added to the water. They add chlorine because it kills bacteria in the pipes when the water travels to the houses of Memphis. The fluoride helps tooth decay. However, lead is commonly found in drinking water. Memphis homes built before 1986 likely have lead plumbing, and even when an ad says "lead free plumbing," it most likely has 8% lead in it.

Fiji water is the second most popular brand in the United States. Each bottle of Fiji water produced meets all health standards. The source of the water is in Viti Levu, which is in the Fiji Islands. The true source is in a small natural aquifer in the Yaqara river valley. The actual water is continuously refilled by rainfall. The water is also purified by trade winds swept across the Pacific Ocean to the Fiji Islands. The water is very rare, for it is a result of one of the last virgin ecosystems on the globe. Natural pressure pushes the water out of the aquifer deep below the earth's crust. Then, it is squeezed into square bottles which are shipped to the United States and beyond.

In comparison, even if Memphis drinking water is pure, the city is old. This means that there are probably many lead plumbing fixtures that release the lead into the drinking water. The Fiji water will probably be purer and have better water quality than Memphis tap water because it goes straight from the source to the bottle.

Ultimately, Quinn decided this comparison was interesting enough that she based her science fair project around it; her organization of the paper helped her see that she could easily conduct an actual comparison of the lead content in the tap and bottled water.

Works Cited

Garcia, D. (2013, March 20). Pixar storyboarding mini doc [Video file]. Retrieved from https://www.youtube.com/watch?v=7LKPVAIcDXY

University of Memphis. (2003, August 12). Memphis water clearly among the best [News release]. Retrieved from http://www.memphis.edu/newsarchive/aug03/gwi.html

Scaffolding Organization With Webb's DOK

HOW GABY WORKED

Level One (Recall)

- *Sample Task:* Identify three scenes in the play in which Hamlet kills or nearly kills another character.

- *What Gaby Did:* Mentally cataloged these scenes, including scenes she ultimately used in her essay.

Level Two (Skills)

- *Sample Task:* Outline an argument that Hamlet's actions might be considered just or unjust, including evidence for your thesis.

- *What Gaby Did:* Collected her rough thoughts in writing, focusing on a scene in which Hamlet almost kills Claudius but stops himself and makes a decision about the justice or injustice the scene conveys.

Level Three (Strategic Thinking)

- *Sample Task:* Write a well-organized essay in which you argue that Hamlet becomes or does not become the injustice he seeks to end.

- *What Gaby Did:* Constructed a solid essay with a clear thesis and evidence (in a short amount of time), employing a point and counterpoint organizational strategy.

Level Four (Extended Thinking)

- *Sample Task:* Consider the nature of injustice in Shakespearian plays and, using two or more plays as sources of evidence, write an essay in which you draw conclusions about Shakespeare's sense of justice.

- *What Gaby Might Have Done:* Used her reading of multiple Shakespeare plays from eighth to twelfth grades, including not just *Hamlet* but also *Julius Caesar, A Midsummer Night's Dream, Romeo and Juliet,* and others to construct a thoughtful argument about Shakespeare's portrayals of justice.

Rubric for Organization

SCORE	ORGANIZATION	IDEAS AND CONTENT	USE OF EVIDENCE	STYLE, VOICE, AND CLARITY	CONVENTIONS AND MECHANICS
5 **Outstanding**	Clear and consistent organization with well-executed transitions excellently supports the argument, including an excellent introduction and conclusion and appropriate organizational strategy	Focus is evident; topic is exceptionally well developed and suited to the audience and purpose	Ample and appropriately selected details effectively support the argument throughout the response	The response is clear and original and employs appropriate stylistic elements for effect in an exceptional manner	Syntax, grammar, and conventions are correct and add to the effectiveness of the response
4 **Exceeds Expectations**	The organization is clear and supports the argument; the introduction and conclusion are well executed, and the organizational strategy is appropriate	Focus is evident; topic is well developed and suited to the audience and purpose	Appropriately selected details support the argument throughout the response	The response is clear and employs appropriate stylistic elements for effect	Few or no errors are present in usage or syntax
3 **Meets Expectations**	The organization, including introduction and conclusion, is adequate to support the argument	Focus is evident but possibly inconsistent; topic is somewhat developed and suited to the audience and purpose	Details adequately support the argument but may demonstrate some inconsistencies in execution or application	The response is mostly clear and adequately employs stylistic elements	Minor errors in usage or syntax may be present, but without repetition or undermining overall effectiveness
2 **Approaching Expectations**	Some flaws in organization or lack of clarity and transitions make the argument hard to follow	Focus is inconsistent or the topic is underdeveloped or not suited to the audience and purpose	There is insufficient evidence to support the argument, or details are not always adequate to support points	The response may be unclear or misuses stylistic elements in ways that interfere with voice and meaning	Patterns of errors in usage or syntax undermine the effectiveness of the response
1 **Well Below Expectations**	The organization lacks focus and clarity; transitions may be unclear	Response lacks focus and the topic is underdeveloped or unsuited to the task	Evidence and details are missing or insufficient to support the argument	The response is vague or lacks clarity; stylistic choices may confuse rather than enhance meaning	Significant errors in usage or syntax obscure the meaning and effectiveness of the response

Planning Page: Organize

Organize: arrange or put in order according to some guiding principle; impose coherence, order, structure, or function according to type, traits, or other quality

Learning Goal
What will your students organize? What learning outcomes or assessments do you wish to see?

Before	During	After
How will you prepare students to organize ideas about texts, issues, situations, or works?	What activities will you use to model, scaffold, and engage students in organization?	How will you measure the effectiveness of your lesson?

Notes From This Chapter
What ideas or activities from this chapter do you wish to remember as you teach students to organize?

Summarize

retell the essential details of what happened

outline • paraphrase • report

Summarize: retell the essential details of what happened, what someone did or said, in order to better understand and remember it; outline key details in accessible language

CORE CONNECTIONS

- Determine central ideas or themes of a text and analyze their development; **summarize** the key supporting details and ideas (R2)

- Respond thoughtfully to diverse perspectives, **summarize** points of agreement and disagreement, and, when warranted, qualify or justify their own views and understanding and make new connections in light of the evidence and reasoning presented (SL1d.9–10)

- Quote or **paraphrase** the data and conclusions of others while avoiding plagiarism (W8.6–8)

The Main Idea

The ability to retell a sequence of events objectively is a key skill in every discipline. Students must be able to observe and report in science, to condense complicated situations to bullet points in history, to relate a plot succinctly in language arts, and to repeat the steps of a lengthy solution in math. When dealing with text, students must also, importantly, possess the skill of summarizing without plagiarizing. And, perhaps most important of all, students need to know when *not* to summarize and, thus, must recognize summary as distinct from *analysis*.

Underlying Skills:

- **Comprehend texts, steps, or events.** In order to summarize, students must possess comprehension skills (e.g., the ability to condense an article to key points) and the ability to follow events within a discipline (e.g., understand how a science experiment works).

- **Outline and organize.** Restating key points or concepts in a logical manner is not intuitive for every student, nor is looking for an author's organization through headings or topic statements; these are learned skills.

- **Avoid plagiarism.** The line between summary and *plagiarism* can seem blurry to students; students must understand how to attribute when necessary and when *attribution* is unnecessary.

CORE
CONNECTIONS

Continued

- Gather, read, and synthesize information from multiple appropriate sources and assess the credibility, accuracy, and possible bias of each publication and methods used, and describe how they are supported or not supported by evidence (NGSS, MS-LS1–8)

Before: Preparing Students to Summarize

The following three categories are essential for students to understand if they are ever to summarize effectively. The distinction between them might arise in any number of academic contexts, but it is most likely to come up when students are conducting and synthesizing research, especially for written research papers. Don't overlook, however, the necessity of understanding the distinction between summary, paraphrasing, and plagiarism for oral presentations, online projects, or discussion.

In order to demonstrate these categories of using material, we'll give examples based on the final paragraph of Gaby's essay about *Hamlet* from the last chapter.

> As some critics argue, Hamlet becomes the very injustice he seeks to redress, and in that transformation is his misstep that leads to his eventual and tragic downfall. Yet Hamlet did not set out on a path of injustice; rather, he sets out to right a wrong. But, when his desire to right the wrong transforms into a desire to not only right the wrong but to also punish the wrongdoer indefinitely, Hamlet seals his fate. At that decision to make an act of equalization become an act of endless punishment, Hamlet metamorphs into the very injustice he attempted to remedy.

Plagiarize	**Paraphrase**	**Summarize**
What it is: The student lifts material from an original source word for word without citation.	*What it is:* The student expresses the words of an author in his or her own words.	*What it is:* The student retells the main points of a text.
Example: The author states that Hamlet's desire to punish leads to his eventual and tragic downfall.	*Example:* The author suggests that Hamlet begins to act unjustly when he allows himself to seek punishment rather than merely the correction of a mistaken act. (citation required)	*Example:* The author states that Hamlet does act unjustly and that this injustice leads to his tragic demise. She then cautions that Hamlet did not intentionally act unjustly, but that his desire to punish leads him down this path. She ends by reiterating the connection between his desire for punishment and his descent into unjust action. (possible citation required)
Corrected: The author states that Hamlet's desire to punish "leads to his eventual and tragic downfall" (citation required)	*Use it:* When you need to convey the main idea of a passage in a short space. Also paraphrase when you need to clearly and simply relate core ideas of a complex text.	*Use it:* When you convey the scope of an entire text (or a large portion of it) in a short space.
Use quotation and citation: When you wish to use a key term, a phrase, or a longer passage in the author's original words.		

Teachers may use the above terms *summarize* and **paraphrase** interchangeably, so it's worth warning students to pay attention to context and their own needs. Knowing how to handle information from other sources is a core academic skill and becomes more crucial as students grow older.

Before you teach students to summarize a text, issue, situation, or work, try these four things:

- **Model:** Demonstrate summary for students by showing them a product in the format you wish to see—a paragraph, bulleted list, or PowerPoint, for instance. In your model, highlight main points, transition words, or other elements you wish students to imitate.

- **Define Expectations:** Clarity is especially important when students summarize as part of relating research findings. Most students *want* to summarize, paraphrase, and cite without plagiarizing, but it can be very confusing to them regarding which information calls for which approach. Be prepared to give students simple guidelines for this process and help them when they are confused.

- **Build Content Knowledge:** In order to isolate the main points in a text or work, students must understand the point of the work and its context within a discipline. Be sure to have students practice challenging texts, but not without guidance or assistance as necessary.

- **Practice Mental Moves:** Give students a short practice text and have them work in pairs to summarize the selection. Have them use the questions in the sidebar as a guide and to practice the mental moves required for this kind of work. Post these questions and moves on the wall and keep circling back to them as students hone their summary skills.

Obstacles to the Moves

When teaching students to summarize, watch out for these areas of difficulty:

- **Too Much Detail.** A basic error made by too many students in their argumentative essays or presentations is summarizing the plot rather than analyzing; teach students to summarize quickly and effectively in order to move on to their own ideas.

- **Abrupt Transitions.** Effective summary relies on clear transitions, such as *but, so, then,* and *therefore;* be sure students organize summaries so that they are easy to follow and not just lists of events.

Mental Moves

Summarize

1. Study the Text

How is this material laid out? Are there clues such as headings I should use?

2. Identify the Main Idea

What is the central point of this material?

3. Identify Key Moments

What shifts, elements, or developments will help me organize my summary?

4. Select Details

Which details are important and which can I safely ignore?

5. (Re)Organize

What format—paragraphs, bullet points, using headings—will best communicate a summary of this material?

During: Practicing Summaries

Any teacher has probably encountered the twin sins of summary: Giving too much information and not giving enough. These sins can be particularly painful when students present orally, either boring the class into submission or leaving them confused.

- When summarizing fiction, most students tend toward the former practice: They're confused about which details to leave out. For such summaries, try having students outline in threes: Three major parts of a story (the beginning, middle, and end); three important developments within each of those parts; three details for each development. You might do this first as a class with sticky notes—one per student so that everyone contributes—and make pyramids on the board to show students the hierarchy of importance.

- With nonfiction texts, students may tend toward the opposite practice—summing up entire works with a single sentence. A good place to start with such text is by teaching the elements of nonfiction, such as the headings, table of contents, captions, subheads, and index of a work. Students don't learn these elements unless we teach them explicitly (we suggest anchor charts with the elements on the wall of your classroom to remind students). Then, try the same sticky note activity described earlier for a nonfiction text.

ELL Focus: Do This One Thing to Help

For ELL students (or other struggling readers), consider offering a summary guide. Here's an example:

The main idea of this passage is _____.

One idea or detail that supports this idea is _____.

A second idea or detail that supports this is _____.

These details support the main idea because they _____.

Discussion, Presentation, Technology, and Multimedia

- **Discuss.** Use discussion stems to prompt students to include summary as they discuss texts or issues. For example, write these models on the board before beginning a class discussion:

  → What I think the author is saying is _____, and I agree/disagree with this because _____.

  → Overall, this work makes the point that _____. We need to consider this because _____.

  → The first half of this work suggests that _____, but the second half suggests that _____.

- **Present.** Use PowerPoint to help students summarize by having them create one slide per major point. Limit the word count of each slide to twenty words.

- **Create.** Have students use software to create diagrams, tables, or software to create succinct, concise summaries of material. Consider flowcharts, webbing strategies, and the SmartArt feature of Microsoft Word or PowerPoint (under the Insert menu) to prompt thinking about how a visual summary can represent ideas.

YouTube Moment: Show students summary videos from the Royal Society for the Encouragement of the Arts at www.thersa.org. After watching these videos, let students try a thirty-second version on your board or use software that captures writing on a screen.

After: Producing Summaries

Student Example 1: Summarizing Main Ideas in a Text

The Task

Choose one of the poems in our poetry packet and paraphrase it. Your paraphrase should restate the poet's message in your own words, though you may quote if you wish. Be sure to summarize the poem's message as well as its component parts.

When David Templeton's high school sophomores began a unit on modern poetry, he found that they often wanted to skip straight to the "meaning" of a poem, as if each poem he taught equated to no more than its central meaning. Along the way, however, he discovered that his students were missing key details and often misinterpreting poems. He wanted them to read carefully and separate the literal from the figurative, so he turned to the practice of paraphrasing poems before discussing them in class.

Perhaps ironically, one boy in the class, Cody, chose to paraphrase the poem "Introduction to Poetry" by Billy Collins, a poem about how students read poems. Cody's paraphrase provided the springboard for an excellent discussion in class the next day about reading and interpreting poetry.

When we asked Cody how he went about creating his summary, he told us about a strategy he'd learned from Mr. Templeton. "He has us draw lines across the page," Cody said. "Horizontal lines. You find transition words or you group stanzas or just look for punctuation. Then, you take each piece of the poem between the lines and find a few key words to circle. From that, you summarize each part."

Cody's Sample

In the poem, "Introduction to Poetry," the author, Billy Collins (2006), tells his readers that <u>poems are not meant to be analyzed as soon as one reads the poem.</u> Instead, Collins suggests, readers should listen to what the poem says and how it says it instead of trying to force an academic meaning the first time we read the poem. He implies that sometimes it is unnecessary to analyze a poem.

<u>The first stanza of the poem describes his students:</u> "I ask them to take a poem / and hold it up to the light / like a color slide / or press an ear against its hive" (p. 58). Here, Collins describes a poem as a work of art—one to be savored, not deconstructed.

<u>The second section of this poem states,</u> "I say drop a mouse into a poem / and watch him probe his way out, / or walk inside the poem's room / and feel the walls for a light switch" (p. 58). Collins is trying to get across that sometimes the meaning of the poem is ambiguous and takes thoughtful probing of the text.

<u>In the third section, Collins surprises us with a violent description:</u> "But all they want to do / is tie the poem to a chair with rope / and torture a confession out of it. / They begin beating it with a hose / to find out what it really means" (p. 58). Collins describes students who treat a poem with force, not finesse. They assume there is a central meaning, so [they] force it into the poem rather than waiting for understanding.

True meaning will not always be found in the elements of the text in a poem. Descriptions of similes, metaphors, and even "meanings" are representations of what the author says, not what the author actually says. <u>Collins reveals that it is sometimes better just to read than to break down.</u>

2. Identify the Main Idea
Cody begins his summary with a statement of the poem's overall message.

1. Study the Text
Cody knows the poem comes in both stanzas and implied sections.

3. Identify Key Moments
Cody points out the shift in the third section of the poem with this sentence.

4. Select Details
Cody quotes specific lines to back up his summarization.

5. (Re)Organize
Cody has chosen to summarize one section of the poem at a time and ends by again revisiting the poem's overall message.

Student Example 2: Summary in Speech

When seventh grade student Ansley was assigned to represent Cuba in a Model United Nations (MUN) simulation by her social studies teacher, she knew she would have to do a great deal of research—and she did. In the end, Ansley entered the formal MUN debate armed with pages of data, a long written description of the problem she wished the other students to address, and a document to submit to the MUN group for debate.

The next difficulty, however, was that at the end of the debate, Ansley knew she would have only one minute to summarize her entire argument and plan and convince her peers to vote for it. Such formal debate experiences offer excellent opportunities for students to practice summarization skills. Not only did Ansley have to boil her argument down to a few key points, but she had also to consider her audience: How much information was enough to engage them without boring them? There were dangers in being either too terse or too expansive.

In the end, Ansley settled on a single paragraph for her summation during the debate. Here is what she wrote:

> Water pollution is a major problem in Cuba and people there are infected every day. If water purification systems are built within range of citizens, then people will no longer be infected with cholera from contaminated water. Countries near Cuba will no longer be highly threatened by the infection from travelers carrying cholera. Our solution will provide 2 million lifesaving water filtration bottles [that] will support the children in Cuba less than 14 years of age with safe and clean water. It will also provide 100,000 large water filtration systems for Cubans. Fixing this problem could save Cuba from a deadly cholera epidemic. We urge high ranking and yield our time to the chair.

Work Cited

Collins, B. (2006). "Introduction to Poetry" [poem]. In *The apple that astonished Paris*. Fayetteville: University of Arkansas Press.

Scaffolding Summarization With Webb's DOK

HOW CODY WORKED

Level One (Recall)

- *Sample Task:* Write down frequent transition words that might appear in a poem.

- *What Cody Did:* Learned to recognize key terms that, in addition to stanza breaks and punctuation, would help to break down a poem into sections—words such as *but, however, moreover, still, yet, although,* or *thus.*

Level Two (Skills)

- *Sample Task:* Determine the key transition points or breaks in a poem after reading it.

- *What Cody Did:* Broke the Collins poem into a few pieces, each of which could become a paragraph of his summary.

Level Three (Strategic Thinking)

- *Sample Task:* Summarize the poem, capturing the main ideas and restating them in a way that is clear and captures both literal and figurative meaning.

- *What Cody Did:* Wrote his summary, detailing stanza by stanza what the author said and meant.

Level Four (Extended Thinking)

- *Sample Task:* In a letter to next year's students, summarize what you have learned about reading poetry and how you think they should approach it.

- *What Cody Might Have Done:* At the end of an entire unit on poetry, collected his thoughts and written a letter detailing his strategy.

Rubric for Summarizing

SCORE	MAIN IDEAS	SELECTION OF DETAILS	ORGANIZATION	STYLE, VOICE, AND CLARITY	CONVENTIONS AND MECHANICS
5 **Outstanding**	The purpose of the summary is clear, and main ideas are related in a logical, meaningful order with all essential content included	Appropriately selected details effectively support the summary throughout the response	Clear and consistent organization with well-executed transitions excellently supports the summary, including an excellent introduction and conclusion	The response is clear and original and employs appropriate stylistic elements for effect in an exceptional manner	Syntax, grammar, and conventions are correct and add to the effectiveness of the response
4 **Exceeds Expectations**	The purpose of the summary is clear, and main ideas are related in a logical order with essential content included	Some appropriately selected details support the summary	The organization is clear and supports the summary; the introduction and conclusion are well executed	The response is clear and employs appropriate stylistic elements for effect	Few or no errors are present in usage or syntax
3 **Meets Expectations**	The purpose of the summary is clear; main ideas are related in a mostly logical order with most essential content included	Details adequately support the summary but may demonstrate some inconsistencies in execution or application	The organization, including introduction and conclusion, are adequate to support the summary	The response is mostly clear and adequately employs stylistic elements	Minor errors in usage or syntax may be present, but without repetition or undermining overall effectiveness
2 **Approaching Expectations**	The purpose of the summary is somewhat unclear, or main ideas are related in an order that confuses or leaves out important elements	There is insufficient detail to support the analysis, or details are not always adequate to support key points	Some flaws in organization or lack of clarity and transitions make the summary hard to follow	The response may be unclear or misuses stylistic elements in ways that interfere with voice and meaning	Patterns of errors in usage or syntax undermine the effectiveness of the response
1 **Well Below Expectations**	The summary is insufficient to the task; main ideas are missing or presented in confusing or incorrect order	Details are missing or insufficient to support the summary	The organization lacks focus and clarity; transitions may be unclear	The response is vague or lacks clarity; stylistic choices may confuse rather than enhance meaning	Significant errors in usage or syntax obscure the meaning and effectiveness of the response

Planning Page: Summarize

Summarize: retell the essential details of what happened, what someone did or said, in order to better understand and remember it; outline key details in accessible language

Learning Goal
What will your students summarize? What learning outcomes or assessments do you wish to see?

Before	During	After
How will you prepare students to summarize texts, issues, situations, or works?	What activities will you use to model, scaffold, and engage students in summarizing?	How will you measure the effectiveness of your lesson?

Notes From This Chapter
What ideas or activities from this chapter do you wish to remember as you teach students to summarize?

14

Support

offer evidence or data to illustrate your point

cite • justify • maintain

Support: offer evidence, examples, details, or data in order to illustrate or bolster your claim or conclusion; cite those sources of information that justify your position

CORE CONNECTIONS

- **Cite** specific textual evidence when writing or speaking to **support** conclusions drawn from the text (R1)

- Write arguments to **support** claims in an analysis of substantive topics or texts (W1)

- Draw evidence from literary or informational texts to **support** analysis, reflection, and research (W9)

- Construct and present oral and written arguments supported by empirical evidence and scientific reasoning to **support** or refute an explanation or a model for a phenomenon or a solution to a problem (NGSS, MS-PS2-4)

The Main Idea

The importance of support in the physical world will be obvious to students: imagine rows of columns holding up a building, cables on a bridge, a victorious team holding up their star player. But what's expected of them when the word *support* appears in a prompt or assignment can be ambiguous; evidence comes in many forms across content areas. Yet from using detail in descriptive writing to data in science or content elements to critique a website, all types of support involve connecting key pieces of a work, issue, or process to larger concepts and themes.

Underlying Skills:

- **Select details.** Teaching students which evidence to pull from a large text or body of information—including words, data, or images, for instance—is important in every discipline.

- **Structure paragraphs or points.** When students support points in writing or speech, they work at the level of paragraphs and must consider how two or three pieces of information combine to make one substantial point. They must also consider whether to quote or paraphrase and even whether a table or chart might represent the evidence better than prose.

- **Draw inferences.** Utilizing evidence to support an argument requires both explicit and implicit thinking about how information is compiled.

Before: Preparing Students to Support Ideas

When a student sees the word *support* in an assignment or task, he or she needs to sort through several questions very quickly:

- What is the main idea I want to express?
- What type of detail and evidence is appropriate for expressing this idea convincingly?
- What do I need to know about this particular genre or discipline in order to select the most salient evidence and details?

Teachers often expect students to work through these questions mentally *before* the actual task of writing or arguing begins. Consider these examples:

A student must answer a *persuasive* writing prompt.

The student determines that she needs to use *observations* and *personal experience* to support her opinion.

The student *brainstorms* possible pieces of evidence in order to communicate her thinking.

A student is asked to interpret a poem and write an *analysis* of it.

The student determines that she needs *quoted evidence* from the text to support a thesis.

The student *reads the poem closely* and gathers lines that best support a specific interpretation.

In science class, a student makes a series of observations. She is asked to predict future *data* and support her predictions.

The student determines that she needs to use a *mathematical graph* to provide *evidence*.

The student writes an explanation of the *graphing process* that shows her understanding.

Mental Moves

Support

1. Plan

What kind of evidence do I need? Do I plan to quote, paraphrase, or use examples to illustrate?

2. Collect

Where do I find this evidence? How do I keep track of evidence as I gather it?

3. Organize

What's a good way to present my evidence?

4. Cite

How do I refer to my sources? Can my audience find the original source of my evidence?

5. Discuss

Why is this evidence important? What does it prove?

Before you teach students to draw support from a text, issue, situation, or work, try these four things:

- **Model:** Use mentor texts to show students examples of professional authors—or other students—using support appropriately, including the logistics of how authors quote, paraphrase, cite, and underscore points. Where possible, show students the original source material from which a writer quotes in order to demonstrate how that writer chose limited examples from numerous possibilities.

- **Define Expectations:** Don't assume that students will know how to identify, gather, or create supporting information for a new assignment. Walk students through the process of making notes or creating marginalia, including showing them the kind of information to note or, almost as importantly, not to note.

- **Build Content Knowledge:** When using evidence, students need content-area vocabulary to make the context of their supporting material obvious; words such as *stanza* or *axis* can offer the reader important information about the material students are drawing upon. Additionally, students need to cite appropriately for each discipline and to be aware, as they grow older, of different citation methods that apply to different disciplines and why they matter.

- **Practice Mental Moves:** Give students a short practice text and thesis and have them work in pairs to locate supporting evidence for the thesis they have been provided. Then, have them co-construct a short essay incorporating this support. Have them use the questions in the sidebar as a guide and to practice the Mental Moves required for this kind of work. Post these questions and moves on the wall and keep circling back to them as students hone their skills.

Obstacles to the Moves

When teaching students to support, watch out for these areas of difficulty:

- **Disorganized Research.** In every discipline, students need systems to keep track of evidence they find; otherwise, they may be tempted to use genuine material that they are not able to attribute correctly.

- **Lack of Relevance.** Sometimes, students have trouble choosing the most appropriate evidence to make a point; practice this skill by discussing a sample text or data set with students and asking them to find appropriate details to back up a main idea.

During: Practicing Support

No matter what subject you teach, a **graphic organizer** can help students make the leap from *collecting* evidence and *applying* that evidence to support a point. You'll see an example of such an organizer in the first student example in this section.

Extremely simple graphic organizers can be surprisingly useful to students who may face an on-demand prompt that requires support, such as prompts for American College Testing (the ACT). As a rule of thumb, coming up with three supporting details or ideas is a good goal for students analyzing a passage, paragraph, or argument. Even a quick concept map can be a great jump-start device for a student in a pinch, as this eighth-grade example demonstrates:

Should all schools require students to wear uniforms?

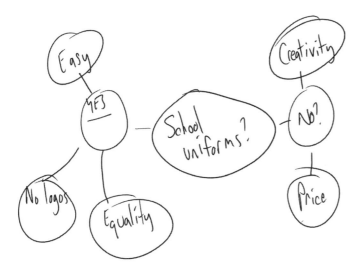

ELL Focus: Do This One Thing to Help

Some academic cultures do not approach quotation and citation in the same way American education expects. Quietly conference with your non-native speakers to be sure they understand how to quote and cite material, especially if you require a specific citation format such as Modern Language Association (MLA). You may find that such a conversation helps to avoid uncomfortable misunderstanding about support and even plagiarism.

Discussion, Presentation, Technology, and Multimedia

- **Discuss.** Before you conduct a class discussion on a text or topic, have each student write three supporting facts, quotations, or ideas on three different sticky notes.

  → As students participate in the discussion, have them hand you any sticky notes they use to make a point (this is also a good way to make sure everyone participates).

  → Put the sticky notes on your board or wall.

  → Halt the discussion from time to time or take time at the end to organize the sticky notes—what categories or overarching ideas can you think of that would include several of the notes?

- **Present.** Assign short presentations on a topic in which students use PowerPoint or other presentation software to answer a specific question.

  Example: What were three important causes of the Great Depression?

  → Limit the use of slides to only specific supporting evidence—a quotation, photo, graph, data set, or problem solution, for instance.

  → Students should explain the supporting material to the class orally.

- **Surf.** Provide students with the vocabulary and tools they need to draw evidence from a web page, video, or other sources. For example, what elements should students consider in evaluating a website? Suggestions might include evidence of authorship, citations (or links), design, URL, bias, or date. Make an anchor chart with these tools and display the chart in your classroom.

YouTube Moment: Almost any Technology, Entertainment, Design (TED) talk you find online will offer students a chance to examine and discuss the concept of support; these interesting addresses on a variety of subjects feature experts who bring varying types of evidence to bear on their topics. We recommend searching for "Amy Cuddy TED Talk" to find one of the most popular of these videos on the subject of body language. Ask students to watch the kinds of support Cuddy uses, and how she employs it, throughout her talk (her examples range from simple images to scientific research). What is most effective and why? How important is support to her persuasiveness?

After: Producing Support

Student Example 1: The Analytical Essay

As a ninth grade student, Landon had been asked only once or twice to conduct an analysis of a text in essay format using specific quotations. "I wrote one essay about a poem in eighth grade where the teacher provided the prompt and the lines to use," he told us. "So that was easy. We all used the exact same quotes. But the idea that I could just decide which lines to use to make a point about a poem was really confusing to me."

Here, Landon's teacher outlines the process of first studying and then writing about William Blake's (1866) poem "The Chimney Sweeper."

The Task

Read the poem "The Chimney Sweeper," by William Blake, closely. Then, write an essay in which you analyze how the speaker's experience is conveyed through such elements as tone, structure, and imagery.

Landon's Teacher's Comments

I wanted the students in my class to analyze an accessible but challenging poem. I didn't want to hand them "themes" and "meanings" but to have them uncover the meaning for themselves. So we took a slightly different approach.

First, I had the entire class brainstorm elements of a poem that might be useful in supporting an analysis of the poem's meaning. This was a refresher; we'd covered these terms and so had their previous teachers. I made a big list on the board for reference of terms such as *simile or personification.*

1. Plan

Landon's teacher allowed students to recall useful terms, prompting them to look for certain elements with each poem.

Then, I put the students in pairs and had each do a *think-pair-share* where they worked with a particular poem and annotated it with their own thoughts and interpretations. We transferred those ideas to a graphic organizer.

2. Collect

This pairing activity served as a chance for students to gather evidence.

When it was time to write, we talked about how to quote lines and what to do about line breaks, though I stressed that the most important part of the assignment had to do with the quality of the evidence, not how it was formatted—that could be fixed in later drafts. Finally, we talked about drawing bigger conclusions based on the notations students made, and I had each pair discuss their thesis statements at length, both with each other and with me. Then we were ready to write.

3. Organize

The graphic organizer allowed students to add structures to the information they found in the poem.

4. Cite

Though the conversation is brief, Landon's teacher helps students think about how evidence will be incorporated into their essays to support their arguments.

5. Discuss

Landon works on a thesis statement, preparing to use the evidence as support for a larger argument about the poem.

Here is the process in more detail, with the work students in the class actually completed:

Step One: Planning

Landon's teacher asks students in the class to list elements of a poem that might be useful in supporting an analysis of the poem's meaning. She writes the ideas on the board for reference:

tone words	imagery	interesting rhymes	similes
personification	symbols	word choices (diction)	setting
metaphor	allusions	characterization	repeated words
punctuation	meter	juxtaposition	dialogue

Step Two: Collection

Landon reads "The Chimney Sweeper" in class and makes careful notes with a partner on the first two stanzas:

sold/cry = sad

When my mother died I was very young,
And my father sold me while yet my tongue
Could scarcely cry " 'weep! 'weep! 'weep! 'weep!"
So your chimneys I sweep & in soot I sleep.

There's little Tom Dacre, who cried when his head
That curled like a lamb's back, was shaved, so I said,
"Hush, Tom! never mind it, for when your head's bare,
You know that the soot cannot spoil your white hair."

speaker
simile
repetition—like a cry
rhyme for emphesis
black/white

Step Three: Organization

Using a graphic organizer, Landon connects the *evidence* to his overall *analysis* of the poem.

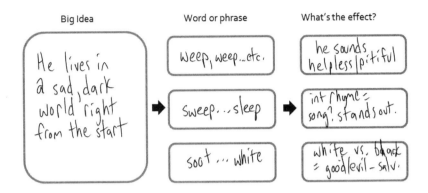

Landon then plans his essay around the evidence he has found:

Body para. one: first two stanzas—little boy is abandoned and his world
is dark

- "my father sold me..."
  - → His tongue "cannot speak," so he is helpless
- "weep, weep," etc.
  - → Repetition shows how helpless he is
- "chimneys I sweep and soot I sleep"
  - → internal rhyme give emphasis to this line and makes it stand
    out
  - → soot = dark and depressing world
- "Hush, Tom..."
  - → Very casual like someone is speaking, narrative style
- "soot/white hair"
  - → Black vs. white connects to the salvation later in the poem

Step Four: Citation

Because Landon is analyzing one poem only, his teacher determines that he
can simply refer to line numbers throughout his essay.

Step Five: Discussion

Landon writes his essay, using the evidence he gathered with his partner to support his argument.

In the first two stanzas, the reader meets a little boy, the speaker, as an abandoned infant and soon realizes how dark the world is for this little boy. In the first stanza, the speaker shows that the world is dark by telling readers that "my father sold me while yet my tongue / could scarcely cry weep weep weep" (2–3). Because the speaker cannot speak or scarcely even cry, he is helpless against being sold away from his parents. His world is dark from the beginning. Blake uses repetition of the word "weep" to show how helpless the speaker as an infant is. When said aloud, "weep" isn't a word that commands much attention; therefore, the speaker has no power to do anything but be sold away. Blake also uses internal rhyme when he writes, "So your chimneys I sweep and in soot I sleep" (4). The true rhyme of sweep and sleep brings attention to the line. This boy's life is sweeping and sleeping and waking up to sweep again then drifting off to sleep afterwards. This quote also shows how dark and gloomy the speaker's world has become. In the second stanza, readers meet Tom Dacre, a timid little chimney sweep. This stanza is very narrative; it tells of how Tom cried when having to get his head shaved and how the speaker comforted him saying, "Hush Tom never mind it, for when your head's bare / you know that the soot cannot spoil your white hair" (7–8). Blake juxtaposes the word *soot* with the white hair knowing that soot is dark black and the white hair is pure white. The juxtaposition symbolizes how darkness and suffering can fill one's life, but a perfect, white salvation can follow it. Overall, the first two stanzas display how gloomy, dark, and melancholy the chimney sweep's world is from the very beginning.

Student Example 2: Science Writing

For sixth grade student Micca, interpreting visual data and drawing conclusions was not a natural leap. But Micca's teacher knew the skill is one demanded by both the Common Core State Standards and Next Generation Science Standards. A series of observations of shadow length at various times of day provided an excellent springboard for deduction and the use of support in expressing those deductions in writing.

Micca's teacher suggested that strong student answers would use one of the following phrases:

- *For instance . . .*
- *For example . . .*
- *The data prove that . . .*
- *On the graph, we can see that . . .*

Micca then used these transitions to construct her answer:

> You could use the graph to figure out the length and location of some of the shadows that were not plotted and traced by seeing which way the lines go. For example, during 10:00–11:30 a.m., we didn't record the shadow's length. But the dots at those times prove that the shadows will get smaller the closer we get to noon, changing from 15 cm down to around 9 cm.

Work Cited

Blake, W. (1866). The chimney sweeper. In *Songs of innocence and experience*. London, UK: Basil Montagu Pickering.

The Task

This week, we recorded and charted the length of shadows. Pick a time for which we did NOT observe shadow length. How could we use a graph to determine shadow length at that time of day? Support your answer with specific evidence from your graph.

Table 1 Shadow Length

Time of Day	9:10	9:25	9:40	11:45	12:00	12:15	12:25	1:20	1:35	1:50	2:05	2:20
Shadow Length	27	25.5	21	10	9	9.5	9	8.5	9	9.5	10	10.5
Time of Day	2:35	2:50	3:05									
Shadow Length	11	11.5	12.5									

Graph 1 Shadow Length Over Time

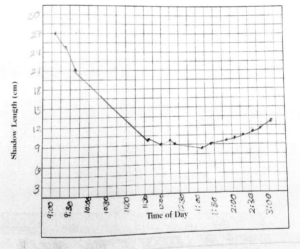

Micca's observations and graph

Scaffolding Support With Webb's DOK
WHAT LANDON DID

Level One (Recall)

- *Sample Task:* List elements common to poems that are useful in analysis tasks.

- *What Landon Did:* With his class, he brainstormed and recalled elements of poetry and listed them on the board.

Level Two (Skills)

- *Sample Task:* Find specific rhetorical and poetic elements within a poem and note their function within the context of the line or section of the poem.

- *What Landon Did:* Discussed the poem with a partner, drawing out specific elements that could be useful for an overall analysis and support.

Level Three (Strategic Thinking)

- *Sample Task:* Structure and write an analysis of the poem using evidence from throughout the poem to support your thesis.

- *What Landon Did:* Wrote an essay in which he analyzed the poem section by section, supporting his thinking by quoting from the text and coming to an overall interpretation of the poem's meaning.

Level Four (Extended Thinking)

- *Sample Task:* Compare the use of rhetorical devices across several poems you have studied to come to a conclusion about the use of those devices as a global literary tool.

- *What Landon Did:* After his class completed their essays, he participated in a class discussion about tools such as *alliteration or metaphor* in a number of the poems (all of which the entire class read) to discuss *how* and *why* poets might employ these devices.

Rubric for Support

SCORE	USE OF EVIDENCE AND DETAIL	IDEAS AND CONTENT	ORGANIZATION	STYLE, VOICE, AND CLARITY	CONVENTIONS AND MECHANICS
5 Outstanding	Ample and appropriately selected details effectively support the main ideas throughout the response; evidence is correctly cited and smoothly incorporated so that it contributes to overall meaning	Focus is evident; topic is exceptionally well developed and suited to the audience and purpose, drawing on support to make an overall point	Clear and consistent organization with well-executed transitions excellently supports the main ideas and allows for connection of details or evidence to main points	The response is clear and original and employs appropriate stylistic elements for effect in an exceptional manner	Syntax, grammar, and conventions are correct and add to the effectiveness of the response
4 Exceeds Expectations	Appropriately selected details support the main ideas throughout the response; evidence is correctly cited and incorporated so that it contributes to overall meaning	Focus is evident; topic is well developed and suited to the audience and purpose, drawing on support to make an overall point	The organization is clear and supports the main ideas with details or evidence connected to main points	The response is clear and employs appropriate stylistic elements for effect	Few or no errors are present in usage or syntax
3 Meets Expectations	Details adequately support the main ideas but may demonstrate some inconsistencies in execution or application; most evidence is correctly cited; details may be incorporated in a straightforward manner	Focus is evident but possibly inconsistent; topic is somewhat developed and suited to the audience and purpose, somewhat drawing on support to make an overall point	The organization is adequate to support the main ideas; details and evidence may be inconsistently connected to main points	The response is mostly clear and adequately employs stylistic elements	Minor errors in usage or syntax may be present, but without repetition or undermining overall effectiveness
2 Approaching Expectations	There is insufficient evidence to support the main ideas, or details are not always adequate to support points; citations may be inconsistent or missing; incorporation of evidence may not flow smoothly	Focus is inconsistent or the topic is underdeveloped or not suited to the audience and purpose; details are not related to the overall point clearly	Some flaws in organization or lack of clarity and transitions make the main ideas hard to follow; details may be disconnected from main points	The response may be unclear or misuses stylistic elements in ways that interfere with voice and meaning	Patterns of errors in usage or syntax undermine the effectiveness of the response
1 Well Below Expectations	Evidence and details are missing or insufficient to support the main ideas; citations are missing or incorrect	Response lacks focus, and the topic is underdeveloped or unsuited to the task with irrelevant or missing details	The organization lacks focus and clarity; transitions may be unclear	The response is vague or lacks clarity; stylistic choices may confuse rather than enhance meaning	Significant errors in usage or syntax obscure the meaning and effectiveness of the response

Available for download from **www.resources.corwin.com/burkeacademicmoves**

Planning Page: Support

Support: offer evidence, examples, details, or data in order to illustrate or bolster your claim or conclusion; cite those sources of information that justify your position

Learning Goal
What ideas or concepts will your students support? What learning outcomes or assessments do you wish to see?

Before	During	After
How will you prepare students to support ideas about texts, issues, situations, or works?	What activities will you use to model, scaffold, and engage students in using support?	How will you measure the effectiveness of your lesson?

Notes From This Chapter
What ideas or activities from this chapter do you wish to remember as you teach students to support ideas?

15

Transform

change in form, function, or nature to reveal or emphasize

alter • change • convert

Transform: change in form, function, or nature in order to reveal or emphasize something; convert data from one form into another; alter something through a process

CORE CONNECTIONS

- Analyze how an author draws on and **transforms** source material in a specific work (e.g., how Shakespeare treats a theme or topic from Ovid or the Bible or how a later author draws on a play by Shakespeare) (R9.9–10)

- Compare and contrast a fictional portrayal of a time, place, or character and a historical account of the same period as a means of understanding how authors of fiction use or **alter** history (RL9.7)

- Apply properties of operations to calculate with numbers in any form;

The Main Idea

At its simplest level, transformation requires understanding a process: How to convert decimals to fractions, for instance. More complicated transformation—such as turning bullet points into a well-crafted paragraph—layers processes on top of one another. Even more complicated is the transformation of *ideas* and *concepts*, which requires using analysis, synthesis, and imagination. All levels of transforming information, however, entail similar steps.

Underlying Skills:

- **Recognize patterns.** Transformation often requires understanding how information works and the process for changing it into another form.

- **Reduce a work to elements.** In order to transform information into another form, students must be able to see the components of that information: A poem, for instance, becomes a collection of themes, uses of language, contexts, form, and images.

- **Think critically.** Students may wish to approach transformation tasks as intellectual problems, asking questions such as *How did someone arrive at this result?* and *If I break this information down into its basic form, how could I reconstruct it?*

convert between
forms as appropriate;
and assess the
reasonableness of
answers using mental
computation and
estimation strategies
(NGSS, MS-PS2-1;
MS-PS2-2)

- Explanations of stability
and **change** in natural
or designed systems
can be constructed by
examining the changes
over time and processes
at different scales
(NGSS, MS-PS2-2)

Before: Preparing Students to Transform Forms

Throughout the book, we have presented mental moves for academic skills. Our purpose is to offer a visual model for a thinking process—to make the abstract concrete. When students practice transformation, they sometimes make the abstract concrete, but they also sometimes turn one concrete product into an entirely different concrete product. Consider these differences in how we transform information:

Recycle	Repurpose
Reuse an item by changing its form but not its nature. This involves presenting a concrete product in a different concrete way.	Keep the fundamental elements of an item but change its purpose. This may involve presenting abstract concepts as a concrete product.
Sample Tasks:	*Sample Tasks:*
<ul><li>Present data in a bar graph in a pie chart instead</li><li>Form a thesis statement based on a specific essay question</li><li>Re-create a process as a visual model rather than numbered steps</li></ul>	<ul><li>Turn a scene from a novel into a film or dramatic presentation</li><li>Present a written paper as an oral presentation</li><li>Create a visual model of a concept or unspecified process</li></ul>

It may help your students to consider song or movie remakes and spin-offs. Try listing superhero movies with which your class is familiar—which are examples of recycling the same story and which are examples of repurposing the core ideas of a story to make something new? Is there room for both processes? How are academic tasks similar?

Before you teach students to transform a text, issue, situation, or work, try these four things:

- **Model:** In transforming data or numbers from one form to another, model precisely, using samples like those on which students will work. For transformation from one genre to another, harness students' creativity and open them to possibilities by looking at professional examples or working as a class to brainstorm similar ideas.

- **Define Expectations:** Because transformation can range widely, from acts of creativity to processes of data and numbers, make sure you've explained to students what you expect to see as an outcome. Are you looking for the attempt to transform or a correct answer? Are the process, product, or both part of the grading?

- **Build Content Knowledge:** For processes that involve transformation of data, students need to understand conversion formulas or similar moves. For transformation in the arts or humanities, discuss the elements both of the genre you're transforming from and the one you're transforming to, as well as similarities or differences between them.

- **Practice Mental Moves:** Give students a sample task that involves transforming. Have them work in pairs or groups, using the questions in the sidebar as a guide and to practice the mental moves required for this kind of work. Post these questions and moves on the wall and keep circling back to them as students hone their skills in transforming.

Obstacles to the Moves

When teaching students to transform, watch out for these areas of difficulty:

- **Forgetting the Audience.** Transformation usually involves thinking about how we communicate with an audience; for instance, is information more comprehensible in a graph, chart, or paragraph?

- **Fear of Risks.** Whether it involves presenting data differently or creating a whole new presentation format, changing information often requires students to make leaps of faith; encourage broad thinking and creativity.

Mental Moves

Transform

1. Identify Elements

What are the basic components of the work I will transform? Am I transforming these elements into a simpler and clearer form or synthesizing them into something more complex and nuanced?

2. Choose Elements to Transform

Which of these elements do I wish to convert? Value? Form? Ideas?

3. Consider Processes for Transformation

Which methods could I use to alter this information? What does the assignment require?

4. Envision the Information Reassembled

How can I re-create this information in a new form? What will my product look like?

5. Create a New Product

What do I wish to say and how am I saying it?

During: **Practicing Transforming Texts**

Transformation isn't easy. Even at its simplest level, such as converting numbers from one form into another, students often grapple with the cognitive leaps involved in seeing things in a new way. At more sophisticated levels, attempts to reshape and convert information can leave students frustrated or feeling like failures.

A key step to transformation includes visually representing material in its new form. This might include, for instance,

- Drawing a picture or **storyboard**
- Acting out a scene
- Making a physical model
- Constructing a metaphor or analogy for an idea
- Making a visual model or flowchart
- Creating a concept map or idea web

Incorporate specific steps into your tasks as you model that include creating visuals. If you are dealing with a process, such as revising a piece of writing, reading a text, testing a hypothesis, practicing a speech, learning a new way of solving a math problem, or researching a historical event, try presenting several visual models such as those below (see Appendix VIII for full-page versions) to your class and asking them to discuss which best represents the process and why (these are only examples—students may come up with variations or new images that better represent the process, so stay open to new ideas).

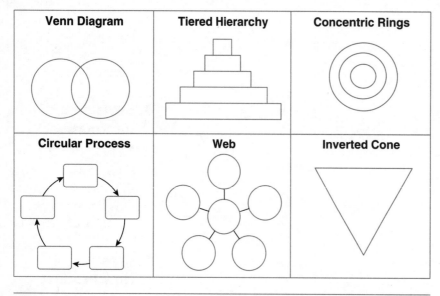

Post models or visuals your students create on anchor charts to remind them of processes and ideas. Keep in mind that both abstract tasks and concrete tasks can use visuals— a student can draw a picture to represent a potential set for a Shakespeare play or make a model such as those shown here that teaches another student how to read a Shakespearean sonnet.

ELL Focus: Do This One Thing to Help

Try allowing ELL students to transform material into their own language (and back, if necessary) as a step in the process—or as a

 Available for download from **www.resources.corwin.com/burkeacademicmoves**

final step. Quite often, transformation from one language into another brings out new ways of examining ideas, new metaphors and phrases, and even new ways of approaching genres and their components.

Discussion, Presentation, Technology, and Multimedia

- **Discuss.** Transformations produced by your own students or by artists, writers, or other professionals provide some of the best discussion starters available. Consider such transformations as a place to derive essential questions with your class through discussion. In particular, the Next Generation Science Standards use the word *change* again and again, because so many scientific phenomena involve fascinating transformations of material, energy, or process, while social studies standards often focus on changes over time in historical events. Students will wish to discuss such changes, along with causes and consequences.

- **Create.** Use technology to transform material studied in your class by having students make graphs in Excel, videos, or web pages to represent information you are studying.

- **Surf.** Find interesting examples of transformed data online and ask students to discuss what they understand from different forms of presentation. For instance,

  → Look at population pyramids at populationpyramid.net, in which raw data about population growth is translated into dynamic charts

  → Google "interesting maps" or "unusual maps" and look for the many sites that show data transformed into visual maps online; your students will be fascinated by these

  → Google "flowcharts" and look at images; then, find a few to discuss. How does this visual tool help make sense of complicated processes? Can your students imagine a process within your class or school that could be captured in a flowchart?

YouTube Moment: One of the most interesting historical examples of transformation—in our perceptions, in the use of data, and in its historical ramifications—lies in the changes to maps of the world over time. As an attempt to transform measurements into visual charts and graphs, maps face the problem of distortion (due to the Earth's shape). You can demonstrate this to students and discuss the difficulties of transforming data from one form to another by simply projecting different versions of maps, including the Mercator, Peters, and Robinson projections (look at Greenland as an example of how landmasses change on these maps). For a fun introduction to the concept, search YouTube for "West Wing Maps Are Wrong" to see a scene in which White House staffers encounter new projections of the world for the first time.

After: Producing Works That Transform

The Task

Find a painting or photograph you like (there are a number of examples posted on our class website). Study this work of art. Then, write a poem, vignette, or monologue from the point of view of the artist, a character or object in the work of art, or a viewer of the work reflecting on its message. In your writing, try to transform the feeling or ideas of the piece into your own feelings and ideas in writing.

Student Example 1: Art and Poetry

The creative writing assignment Katy's teacher gave seemed simple, and Katy was so drawn to Monet's (1899) painting of his bridge at Giverny, *Bridge Over a Pond of Water Lilies*, that she barely looked at any other work. Still, the blank page in front of her was intimidating. There was no character in the painting, and how was she to know what Monet was thinking when he painted it?

"I decided on a metaphor," she said. "When you're crossing a bridge, you're usually just thinking about getting to the other side. People don't stop to enjoy the view from the bridge enough, the way Monet does with the water lilies."

Katy thus did not just transform the work of art into a text; she transformed the ideas of the piece into her own ideas.

Bridge Over a Pond of Water Lilies

You are walking towards your goal
　　but you never think
　　　　about what you've walked past.
You have walked past people
　　you could have helped;
They were reaching
　　towards the sky
　　　　and trying to reach out to you.
You could have helped them grow
　　to be as wise as you
　　　　but instead you kept on walking.
You trampled all the things
　　that could have been without looking back.
Now
　　opportunities that you could
　　　　have had are wasted
You did not even bother
　　to look underneath
　　　　the beautiful bridge
　　　　　　that you walk on,

And you did not even pause

to wonder who these people

you are walking by

could be.

You only want what's ahead of you.

You don't care

about the beauty

of your journey to get there.

When Katy finished the poem, she read it to her class and her teachers, made a few changes, and then posted it in her classroom. At her teacher's instruction, she wrote a reflection on the process:

Katy's Reflection

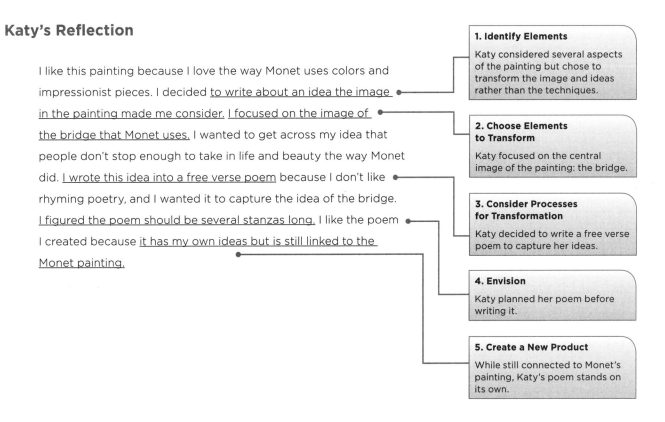

I like this painting because I love the way Monet uses colors and impressionist pieces. I decided <u>to write about an idea the image in the painting made me consider.</u> <u>I focused on the image of the bridge that Monet uses.</u> I wanted to get across my idea that people don't stop enough to take in life and beauty the way Monet did. <u>I wrote this idea into a free verse poem</u> because I don't like rhyming poetry, and I wanted it to capture the idea of the bridge. <u>I figured the poem should be several stanzas long.</u> I like the poem I created because <u>it has my own ideas but is still linked to the Monet painting.</u>

1. Identify Elements

Katy considered several aspects of the painting but chose to transform the image and ideas rather than the techniques.

2. Choose Elements to Transform

Katy focused on the central image of the painting: the bridge.

3. Consider Processes for Transformation

Katy decided to write a free verse poem to capture her ideas.

4. Envision

Katy planned her poem before writing it.

5. Create a New Product

While still connected to Monet's painting, Katy's poem stands on its own.

Student Example 2: Transforming Data in Science and Math

As an early exercise in seventh grade life science class aimed at teaching students to collect and organize data, students in Becky Deehr's class participated in a measurement activity, though Ms. Deehr did not explain the entire activity at the beginning. First, Ms. Deehr put students in pairs and prepared them for the activity: She explained that they were going to measure their partners from fingertip to fingertip with their arms spread using tape measures Ms. Deehr had provided. Then, they would go to a measuring strip on the wall and measure one another's height.

"Before you begin," Ms. Deehr told them, "I want you to write down your height in your science notebooks." All of the students knew their height well enough to write it down or to make a close guess. "I also want you to estimate your wingspan in centimeters and write your estimate in your science notebooks. Why do we estimate?"

"To get a rough idea of what to expect," answered a student. "But why in centimeters?"

"Look at your tape measures," Ms. Deehr answered.

Everyone looked. The tape measures were, in fact, marked in centimeters. Ms. Deehr explained that the metric system is an international system and useful to scientists as they communicate with one another. She also reinforced the value of estimation as a starting place for scientific inquiry. Then she set the students to work.

Quinn and Madison measure wingspan.

Transformation 1: Converting Measurements

Madison and Quinn worked together and quickly discovered that their estimates of their own wingspan were a bit high. They recorded their actual measurements and then went to the wall to check their height, only to encounter a surprise.

"This measurement is in feet and inches, not centimeters," Madison said.

Ms. Deehr stopped the class and discussed Madison's comments. She pointed out that when the students wrote down their height, they all wrote it in feet and inches, not centimeters.

"So how are we going to compare these data?" she asked. "If your height is around 64 inches but your wingspan is around 160 centimeters, is that useful?"

"Not really," Madison answered. "We need to convert it."

"Convert what?" Ms. Deehr prompted. "Which numbers should we convert?"

After a brief discussion of whether they should convert centimeters into inches or inches into centimeters, the class decided on the latter, because Ms. Deehr had already explained the value of the metric system in science.

"So how do we convert inches to centimeters?" Ms. Deehr asked. "What's the mathematical process?"

One of the students knew there were "about two and a half" centimeters in an inch and recommended dividing by two and a half, since "centimeters are smaller, so you divide to make it smaller." Another suggested they had to multiply, so they'd have more centimeters than inches when they finished. Ms. Deehr let them think about the problem for a moment and then explained the actual formula, modeling it both as a simple formula (inches multiplied by 2.54 equals centimeters) and as a ratio.

Quinn's notes during the measurement activity. Because Barry was observing the activity, the girls also gathered his measurements and included them for comparison (Quinn identified Barry as "Dr. G.").

"Now," Ms. Deehr said, once the students had copied the formula into their notebooks, "convert your height to centimeters and write it on our class chart on the board. Be sure to fill in all of the columns, including the difference between height and wingspan."

The class chart.

Transformation 2: Data Chart Into Graph

The class had collected its data, but the chart itself did not allow students an easy way to compare the information or regard it as a whole.

"We're going to transform these data so that we can visualize what it tells us more easily," Ms. Deehr told the students at the start of the next class period. Over the next half hour, she reminded the class about what they'd learned in sixth grade regarding graphs: how they worked, how each axis could be labeled, the scale the graph should or could use, and how to plot data points. Then, she set the students to work graphing the class data while she circulated to assist.

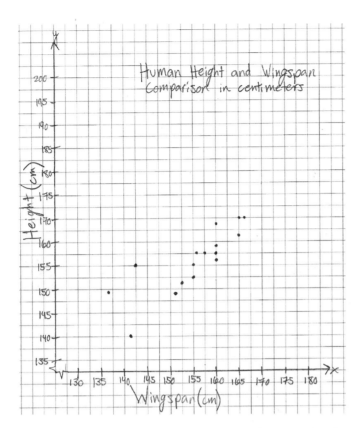

A student graph of wingspan and height measurements for the class.

"What do you notice about our findings?" Ms. Deehr asked when each student had completed his or her graph.

"They make, like, a diagonal line," someone answered.

"Why do you think that is?"

A girl raised her hand. "Because your wingspan is always close to your height, I guess. So the measurement is always somewhere in this general area." She pointed to an imaginary line on her graph.

Once the class had discussed the graphs, Ms. Deehr collected a few questions they might investigate further. One boy wanted to know if good basketball players had longer or shorter wingspans than other people. A girl wanted to know if the difference was passed down from your parents. Another girl asked if the measurements were different for girls and boys. Ms. Deehr recorded the questions in a "parking lot" for future student research and discussion.

Work Cited

Monet, C. (1899). Bridge over a pond of water lilies [painting]. New York, NY: Metropolitan Museum of Art.

Scaffolding Transformation With Webb's DOK

HOW MADISON AND QUINN WORKED

Level One (Recall)

- *Sample Task:* Tell the formula for converting inches to centimeters.

- *What the Girls Did:* Recalled that they had already learned the crucial number 2.54 in a previous class.

Level Two (Skills)

- *Sample Task:* Estimate your own wingspan before you measure it.

- *What the Girls Did:* Constructed an estimate, thus applying prior knowledge and critical thinking to the task before they even began the main part of the assignment.

Level Three (Strategic Thinking)

- *Sample Task:* Transform the measurements of the class into graph form.

- *What the Girls Did:* Used their understanding of range and how graphs work to envision the axes and scales for a graph and then created one.

Level Four (Extended Thinking)

- *Sample Task:* Research and present to the class the scientific reasons behind a correlation between wingspan and height.

- *What the Girls Might Have Done:* Drawn on their knowledge of research processes and human evolution to construct possible explanations for a scientific phenomenon, and then transformed that understanding into a presentation for the class.

Rubric for Transformative Tasks

SCORE	IDEAS AND CONTENT	TRANSFORMATION	ORGANIZATION	STYLE, VOICE, AND CLARITY	CONVENTIONS AND MECHANICS
5 Outstanding	Focus is evident; topic is exceptionally well developed and suited to the audience and purpose	Material has been transformed or converted using appropriate and compelling processes or ideas	Clear and consistent organization with well-executed transitions excellently supports the transformation	The response is clear and original and employs appropriate stylistic elements for effect in an exceptional manner	Syntax, grammar, and conventions are correct and add to the effectiveness of the response
4 Exceeds Expectations	Focus is evident; topic is well developed and suited to the audience and purpose	Material has been transformed or converted using appropriate processes or ideas	The organization is clear and supports the transformation	The response is clear and employs appropriate stylistic elements for effect	Few or no errors are present in usage or syntax
3 Meets Expectations	Focus is evident but possibly inconsistent; topic is somewhat developed and suited to the audience and purpose	Material has been transformed or converted using mostly appropriate processes or ideas; some inconsistencies may exist	The organization is adequate to support the transformation	The response is mostly clear and adequately employs stylistic elements	Minor errors in usage or syntax may be present, but without repetition or undermining overall effectiveness
2 Approaching Expectations	Focus is inconsistent or the topic is underdeveloped or not suited to the audience and purpose	Transformation or conversion of material may depend on inaccurate processes or ideas or be insufficient to convince	Some flaws in organization or lack of clarity and transitions weaken the transformation	The response may be unclear or misuses stylistic elements in ways that interfere with voice and meaning	Patterns of errors in usage or syntax undermine the effectiveness of the response
1 Well Below Expectations	Response lacks focus, and the topic is underdeveloped or unsuited to the task	Transformation or conversion of material is incorrectly completed or absent	The organization lacks focus and clarity; transitions may be unclear	The response is vague or lacks clarity; stylistic choices may confuse rather than enhance meaning	Significant errors in usage or syntax obscure the meaning and effectiveness of the response

Planning Page: Transform

Transform: change in form, function, or nature in order to reveal or emphasize something; convert data from one form into another; alter something through a process

Learning Goal
What will your students transform? What learning outcomes or assessments do you wish to see?

Before	During	After
How will you prepare students to transform texts, issues, situations, or works?	What activities will you use to model, scaffold, and engage students in transforming material?	How will you measure the effectiveness of your lesson?

Notes From This Chapter
What ideas or activities from this chapter do you wish to remember as you teach students to transform?

Appendix I

The fifteen Academic Moves presented in this book were carefully drawn from a wide variety of sources that teachers and students encounter regularly. They are skills students need to complete specific assignments across the disciplines.

But every teacher knows that academic success relies on more than the skills that are named explicitly in an assignment. As we worked on this book, it became clear to us that there was a need for another list of words. Call them attitudes, propensities, or habits. They're the skills today's students will need for true success,

the approaches every student who is *truly* college or career ready must add to academic knowledge and an understanding of particular tasks. They're verbs that one can see in the student examples throughout this book; they undergird the work that good students do.

On the following pages, we present these twenty *other* verbs. Each of these could be explored in its own chapter or book, but we believe that presented in this brief format, these words will help you consider the kind of work you want students to undertake as they apply the Academic Moves.

ADAPT

- adjust
- modify
- tailor

Adapt

apply a process or activity to new circumstances, altering it when necessary

Classroom examples:

- Recognizing the need to apply a formula from math in a science experiment
- Being able to switch sides or positions during a class debate
- Preparing for a test without knowing the format of the test in advance

Students connect to the Academic Moves by

- Determining the best avenue to complete each new task
- Integrating learning from one subject area into other subject areas
- Transforming how knowledge is expressed to apply it to new situations

CHALLENGE

- **confront**
- **investigate**
- **test**

Challenge

question or dispute an idea or process, demanding to know how, why, or whether something works

Classroom examples:

- Debating an idea proposed by an author
- Considering whether an alternate method of completing a lab would produce better results
- Investigating the reliability of a website

Students connect to the Academic Moves by

- Evaluating processes and ideas rather than accepting them at face value
- Comparing and contrasting multiple avenues for completing a task
- Imagining innovative approaches or solutions to problems that go beyond the conventional

CHOOSE

- **decide**
- **determine**
- **select**

Choose

use autonomy to make individual selections related to materials, approaches, or products

Classroom examples:

- Choosing a novel to study in a literature circle
- Selecting between giving a presentation, making a video, or writing a paper on a social studies assessment
- Deciding whether to work alone or with a partner on a major project

Students connect to the Academic Moves by

- Determining which of multiple possibilities they prefer
- Evaluating approaches to decide which works best for them
- Supporting choices to defend why they were made and what the benefits might be

Collaborate

work with a partner or team on a project or activity in order to produce something

Classroom examples:

- Preparing and delivering a joint presentation
- Working on a science lab with a team of students
- Working on a math problem with a partner and then jointly explaining the solution to the class

Students connect to the Academic Moves by

- Evaluating their own ideas and the ideas of others
- Explaining their opinions, ideas, and work to others
- Integrating the work of multiple people into a seamless whole

- **cooperate**
- **interact**
- **team**

Communicate

convey ideas through writing, visuals, oral presentation, or discussion

Classroom examples:

- Teaching the class how to solve a math problem
- Explaining the process of a lab in science to a peer
- Discussing the meaning of a poem in English
- Giving an oral presentation in social studies

Students connect to the Academic Moves by

- Arguing to express an opinion and back it up with evidence
- Describing how or why a process works
- Explaining a text, issue, or problem to someone else
- Interpreting ideas or issues in oral form

- **convey**
- **present**
- **speak**

CONNECT

Connect

establish links between ideas, processes, or people in person or through technology

Classroom examples:

- Commenting on a blog to which students from another school also contribute
- Discussing how material learned in math builds on material learned in science
- Contributing to a class twitter account viewed by parents and other teachers in the school

Students connect to the Academic Moves by

- Determining how ideas can be associated with one another
- Explaining ideas to others
- Integrating ideas from multiple sources into one discussion or presentation

- **bridge**
- **interact**
- **relate**

DESIGN

Design

conceive of and plan an approach, product, or process

Classroom examples:

- Outlining a science fair experiment from start to finish
- Creating a class newspaper
- Constructing a scale model in math

Students connect to the Academic Moves by

- Developing a basic need or idea into a fully formed plan
- Imagining how something could be different or better for a user or audience
- Transforming an idea into a drawing, product, written composition, or outline

- **create**
- **invent**
- **form**

EMPATHIZE

- **comprehend**
- **understand**
- **share**

Empathize

identifying and experiencing the thoughts, feelings, or attitudes of others

Classroom examples:

- Considering the effects of language on an audience when preparing a speech
- Discussing how a scientific phenomenon might affect people in another part of the world
- Writing from the point of view of a historical figure in social studies

Students connect to the Academic Moves by

- Analyzing how an event or work might affect others
- Evaluating the importance or effectiveness of something
- Imagining the feelings of others
- Interpreting cultural and historical norms and attitudes to understand them better

GENERATE

- **brainstorm**
- **create**
- **develop**

Generate

create, especially ideas or possibilities

Classroom examples:

- Listing ideas for possible essay topics
- Working in groups to brainstorm science project ideas
- Creating a list of sources that might be helpful in a history project

Students connect to the Academic Moves by

- Developing ideas in their basic and more complete forms
- Imagining multiple possibilities for how something could work or be
- Integrating ideas and points to come up with new approaches or works

INFLUENCE

- **affect**
- **guide**
- **persuade**

Influence

persuade or compel a change in something or someone

Classroom examples:

- Making a point in a speech or discussion that might change opinions of the audience
- Writing a persuasive essay or opinion piece
- Making changes in an experiment to determine how different substances change an outcome

Students connect to the Academic Moves by

- Arguing a position or point of view
- Evaluating arguments to come to the best conclusion and convincing others of its validity
- Supporting positions with appropriate evidence and reasoning

INITIATE

- **launch**
- **introduce**
- **pioneer**

Initiate

introduce or begin a process or idea

Classroom examples:

- Taking charge in a group project by helping to set a direction and plan for study
- Leading a class discussion with prepared questions or prompts
- Asking unprompted questions in or out of class

Students connect to the Academic Moves by

- Developing a plan of action or course for thinking or discussion
- Explaining a direction or plan to help bring others along
- Imagining possible directions and outcomes for a task or group

INNOVATE

- **discover**
- **invent**
- **reimagine**

Innovate

introduce or change a process or work into something new

Classroom examples:

- Creating a better vehicle for exploring the moon in a science class
- Changing a text into a performance with music, words, and sets
- Introducing a new technology into a project or assignment that allows creativity and new forms of expression

Students connect to the Academic Moves by

- Developing unconventional ideas and approaches
- Imagining new ways of completing tasks
- Transforming prior processes or products in creative and unexpected fashions

INVESTIGATE

- **explore**
- **research**
- **study**

Investigate

inquire into or examine a topic or process in detail, including research and critical questionings

Classroom examples:

- Researching an open-ended question or topic to develop more ideas for inquiry
- Conducting well-planned experiments on a substance in a science lab to determine possible lines of study
- Interviewing a person to find out more about a topic or issue before discussing it in class

Students connect to the Academic Moves by

- Analyzing how something works, including an examination of its components
- Evaluating possible processes or outcomes to determine further lines of study
- Organizing findings into comprehensible forms that allow for an understanding of the issue

LEARN

- **discover**
- **master**
- **understand**

Learn

gain understanding by deep study and by overcoming failures and setbacks

Classroom examples:

- Rewriting an essay after a peer editing session or teacher conference to incorporate suggestions
- Correcting mistakes on a math test and explaining the new answers to a partner
- Studying information by posing and answering questions

Students connect to the Academic Moves by

- Analyzing class material and one's own failures to better understand that material
- Evaluating one's progress through reflection and goal setting
- Explaining how something works, especially something not previously understood

PERSEVERE

- **continue**
- **endure**
- **persist**

Persevere

continue to work toward achievement despite obstacles and setbacks

Classroom examples:

- Completing a long-term project despite fatigue with the topic
- Seeking help from a teacher multiple times until one masters a concept
- Finishing reading an assigned text one does not enjoy

Students connect to the Academic Moves by

- Determining possible benefits and outcomes of continued work
- Imagining alternate means or approaches that might help get work done
- Supporting arguments for continuing to learn and study rather than giving up

QUESTION

- **ask**
- **challenge**
- **inquire**

Question

formulate interrogatives that challenge, probe, or examine material

Classroom examples:

- Participating in discussion by asking questions rather than merely expressing opinions
- Brainstorming possible questions that could be answered or explored in a science lab before the lab begins
- Beginning a group project by agreeing on a driving (open-ended) question that the group will explore

Students connect to the Academic Moves by

- Analyzing material to determine what might be asked
- Developing lists of questions
- Integrating prior knowledge with unknowns in order to pose thoughtful inquiries

REBOUND

- **overcome**
- **rally**
- **revisit**

Rebound

return to a topic, process, or area of study after a clear failure

Classroom examples:

- Studying for and retaking a test after a previous failure
- Outlining an essay for a second time after a conference in which it becomes clear the original thesis is flawed
- Explaining why one did not solve a problem correctly in order to gain understanding about how to solve it the next time

Students connect to the Academic Moves by

- Analyzing their own weaknesses and areas for growth
- Determining ways to improve or change
- Imagining themselves being successful in a task or process

REFLECT

- **consider**
- **examine**
- **self-evaluate**

Reflect

examine one's own progress, learning, or achievement in order to set goals for future improvement

Classroom examples:

- Writing a self-examination of one's learning at the end of a unit or activity
- Giving a presentation to explain how a lab was completed and what could be done differently in the future
- Explaining to a teacher how one solved a problem on a test or assignment

Students connect to the Academic Moves by

- Analyzing one's own successes and failures
- Explaining how tasks were completed and how they could be completed
- Summarizing a process or approach in order to ponder its effectiveness

SOLVE

- **deduce**
- **reason**
- **unravel**

Solve

find an answer or explain something previously not understood

Classroom examples:

- Completing a math problem using a process learned in class
- Working with a group to explore and create answers for a self-posed problem
- Creating a model or flowchart to explain a difficult process or event in history

Students connect to the Academic Moves by

- Analyzing situations or issues to pose and answer questions
- Developing lines of inquiry and research in order to answer questions
- Interpreting information or data in an effort to apply it to new questions or problems

WONDER

- **inquire**
- **question**
- **speculate**

Wonder

speculate about how something functions or about possible causes or outcomes

Classroom examples:

- Generating possible questions that a science class could answer at the start of the year
- Discussing possible background stories or predict outcomes when reading a novel
- Asking how a process or product came into being

Students connect to the Academic Moves by

- Describing unknowns in order to generate possible lines of inquiry
- Imagining possible causes or effects
- Integrating prior knowledge and new information to form questions or speculate about possible outcomes

 Available for download from **www.resources.corwin.com/burkeacademicmoves**

Appendix II

The following "moves" are designed to help students write more effective analytical sentences and paragraphs. While many of these examples complement each other (e.g., you could organize a paragraph around an analogy in order to define something), they often work fine or even best on their own. The goal here is to help students arrange their ideas and paragraphs as they draft and revise in light of their purpose.

TYPE AND DESCRIPTION	SAMPLE EXPOSITORY SENTENCE FRAMES
Analogy Connects things or ideas based on common elements such as structure or qualities to illustrate or emphasize similarities and/or differences.	• Despite their relationship, they were more like enemies than allies . . . • His mind, by this point, resembled a pinball machine as ideas bounced . . . • Like a game of chess, the plot advanced, guided not by x but y.
Cause and Effect Examines and reveals causes, effects—or both. Explaining **why** focuses on causes; focusing on **what** did, will, or could happen involves effects.	• It was x, not y, that explained his decision to do z. • Doing x caused y, which ultimately led to z, an outcome that shows . . . • True, x stemmed from y, but z did not; rather, z was caused by a and b.
Chronological Emphasizes time sequences to show when things happened, the order in which they occurred. Used to describe events, processes, experiences.	• After x happened, y began, which led to z, the final phase of . . . • First, they did x, after which they did y, all of which culminated in z. • They tried x; then they attempted y; finally, they turned to z.
Classification Breaks down or links subjects and processes, based on differences (divisions) or similarities (classes).	• X belonged to a class of people who . . . • Among them there were differences which at first were not apparent . . . • X and Y rejected z; however, Y, as a member of the ___ class, accepted . . .
Comparison and Contrast Focuses on the similarities to compare; examines the differences to contrast. It's possible, even wise, to look, compare, and contrast.	• X and Y were both z, while A and B were c . . . • X shared the sentiments of Y but not Z, believing . . . • Though X and Y agreed that . . . , Y alone argued that . . .
Definition Explains what something means, what it is, in order to define; clarifies how it is similar to or different from other ideas, subjects—to define it by classifying, or comparing/contrasting.	• By any measure, by any criteria, x was . . . • X was y but not z, a but not b . . . • According to X, Y was . . . as well as . . .
Illustration Shows what we mean, what something looks like in order to illustrate our point by using examples to clarify or define.	• One example x appears early on when Y does z . . . • X proves this when he does y, a gesture that clearly shows z . . . • In case we doubted that X was y, we need only remember that he . . .
List Provides a string of reasons, examples, ideas, features, or other factors; we list, try to make a point by repetition, quantity of example, or force of multiples.	• X was many things. It was y but also z. It was a and b. It was also c and d. • Everyone had a theory about x. Y thought . . . Z argued . . . A believed . . . • At this point, he offered a string of reasons for his actions. He said he did it because of x. He then said he did it for y. Then he said it was really z . . .
Narration Uses stories and anecdotes to illustrate ideas or make a point. Narrative power stems from its ability to inspire, move people.	• One time, X left for y, heading off to discover z, an experience that . . . • He had, in the past, done x but only when he began to suffer from . . . • They were different from others; they would run away and be happy . . .

TYPE AND DESCRIPTION	SAMPLE EXPOSITORY SENTENCE FRAMES
Pros and Cons Considers the pros and cons (ad-/disadvantages) in order to allow/force readers to consider a subject or choice from multiple perspectives.	• Of course *x* offered advantages, chief among them being *y*, which . . . • One could not consider *x* without realizing *y*, which was unacceptable . . . • True, *x* was . . . ; however, *y* offered an alternative, one that promised . . .
Problem and Solution Emphasizes the problem(s) or identifies solution(s) by way of framing the subject, process, or argument.	• *X* lacks *y*, which means *z* will have to happen. • The cause of *x* is most often *y*; however, *x* can be solved by doing *z*. • Many argue that X undermines Y, causing it to . . . ; however, Z addresses . .
Process Focuses on the steps or causes that led to the result or current situation; emphasizes the causes and effects; can be mental, physical, or structural.	• Such a problem does not happen all at once, but in a series of stages . . . • While he seems to have suddenly become *x*, the truth is that it was the culmination of many such small decisions, each of which led to . . . • *X* slowly begins to reveal *y*, which leads to *z* and, eventually, *a* and even *b*.
Spatial Emphasizes the location, arrangement, or direction of elements, people, or processes; helps reader visualize what it looks like or how *x* relates to *y* within a space.	• Upon entering *x* you see *y* near *z*; look to the left of *z* to find *a* . . . • *X* appears between *y* and *z*, which results in *a* further down the page. • In the first quatrain, the poet does *x*; in the next two, however, he . . .
Agree Refers to another's point and explains why you agree with or support the idea. May involve a brief summary of the other's idea to create context for your agreement.	• *X* argues . . . , a point I agree with since it suggests . . . • In her article, *X* states that . . . , which confirms my assertion that . . . • *X* could only be *y*, something Jones verifies in her article, saying . . .
Disagree Refers to another's point and explains why you disagree or oppose it. May involve a brief summary of the other's idea to create context for your opposition or rejection.	• While *X* says . . . , this makes little sense in light of . . . • True, *x* is . . . , but *Y* forgets . . . , which undermines her argument by . . . • Several (Jones, 2007; Smith, 2002) argue that *x* is . . . ; however, I disagree as it is clear that . . .
Agree *and* Disagree Refers to another's point and explains why you both agree and disagree. May involve a brief summary of the other's idea to create context for your position(s).	• Yes, *x* is . . . , a point clearly established by *Y* early on; however, this same point comes into question later, when *Z* demonstrates . . . • It is not difficult to see that both are correct: *X* is, as Jones (2007) says, crazy; *X* is also, however, as Smith (2002) shows . . . • I agree that *X* is . . . but reject the notion that *X* could be . . .
Acknowledge Alternatives Recognizes that academic writing makes a claim of some sort; inevitably, others will accept or reject this claim; anticipates and discusses these "naysayers," using their counterarguments to further clarify and emphasize your own argument.	• Some will argue that *x* is, in fact, *y*, a point many (Jones, 2007; Smith, 2002) bring up when considering *z*. • Indeed, as many have noted, *x* is *y*, and even, in some cases, *z*. • Not everyone agrees, however. Jones (2007) contends . . . Others, including Smith (2002), go so far as to argue . . .
Alternative Strategies Recognizes that strategies exist in addition to other strategies that are equally useful but fall between the tidy definitions offered above.	• *Element-by-Element*: Each focuses on a different element of the subject. • *Text-by-Text*: Each focuses on a different text in relation to the subject. • *Idea-by-Idea*: Each focuses on a different idea within the text. • *Character-by-Character*: Each focuses on character A or B (or C and D). • *Event-by-Event*: Each focuses on a different event and its relationship to those that came before it (e.g., the relationship between each of Hamlet's soliloquies and how they evolve and build on each other).

Source: © 2013 by Jim Burke from *The English Teacher's Companion,* fourth edition. Portsmouth, NH: Heinemann. Reprinted by permission.

 Available for download from **www.resources.corwin.com/burkeacademicmoves**

Appendix III

Throughout this book, we've noted that the Academic Moves apply differently in different subject areas. Here, we offer sample tasks for various disciplines for each move. Note that these are not the only tasks you might use to teach each move. We hope these sample activities offer material for discussion in teams and departments about how students learn these skills and how teachers can work together to enhance one another's curriculum.

	ELA	SOCIAL STUDIES	SCIENCE	MATH
Analyze	• The elements and themes of a text, such as a poem, article, story, novel, or video, including structure, characterization, plot, word choice, and tone	• The steps, causes, or consequences of a historical or current event • The elements and ideas of a primary document	• The procedures of an experiment or exploration • Similarities and differences in findings	• The steps used to solve a problem • The purpose or steps used in a math concept
Argue	• An evidence-based interpretation of a text (argument) • A position on a topic or issue (persuasive)	• An evidence-based interpretation of a text (argument) • A position on a topic or issue (persuasive)	• A position on a topic or issue in science or on the quality of a model for a phenomenon or solution to a problem	• The merits of possible alternate solutions to a problem • The results of data
Compare / Contrast	• Two texts that are similar in some aspect of theme, style, or form • Two versions of a text in different media	• Decisions or steps made in two similar historical events • texts that are similar in theme, style, or form	• Methods or approaches to studying a text or topic • The design of two processes or prototypes • Patterns in sets of data	• Alternate approaches to solving a problem • Patterns in data or processes • Expressions of numbers and equations
Describe	• A scene, character, or plot (narrative) • An event or process (informational) • How a text presents information	• The steps, causes, or consequences of a historical or current event • How a text presents information • Trends in graphs or charts	• Procedures or methods used in an experiment or exploration • Patterns in the natural world for further study	• Possible solutions or approaches to a problem • Trends in data • The context in which a math process might be applied
Determine	• Word meanings • Central themes or ideas of a text • Elements related to how authors construct texts (e.g., point of view)	• Word meanings • Central themes or ideas of a text • Possible causes or relationships in historical events	• Possible causes of scientific phenomena • Findings of data	• Most effective methods of solving problems • Findings or significance of data • How one math concept relies upon another

	ELA	SOCIAL STUDIES	SCIENCE	MATH
Develop	• Analysis and arguments related to texts or ideas • narrative elements, such as plot or characterization	• Understanding and presentation of nuanced historical or current events or topics	• Design elements for products or prototypes • ideas related to experiment design such as science fair projects	• Knowledge of multiple ways of solving problems • Models or representations of problem-solving techniques
Evaluate	• Claims of a text • Credibility of digital or print source material • Quantitative information within a text • Speaker's point of view and reasoning	• Claims of a text • Credibility of digital or print source material • Quantitative information within a text • Speaker's point of view and reasoning	• Credibility of digital or print source material • Validity and reliability of multiple claims • Quantitative information and data	• Potential approaches to a particular process or problem
Explain	• How an author creates effects such as tone • How characters or ideas interact over the course of a text or between texts • How ideas in a discussion clarify understanding	• How events unfold, including causes and consequences • How ideas and events interrelate over time and culture	• How processes and phenomena work in the natural world and in the laboratory • How an experiment was conducted	• How a problem was or could be solved • Why a particular process leads to a particular outcome
Imagine	• Narratives of a variety of kinds, including poems, stories, and personal reflections • Predictions for a story outcome • Possible counterclaims in argument writing	• Narratives (written or otherwise) relating to historical periods and other cultures that demonstrate empathy • Possible links, causes, or explanations for events • Methods of research and historical exploration	• Experimental procedures to explain phenomena • Hypotheses within experiments • Ways of managing and interpreting data	• How mathematical knowledge could be or is applied to real-world situations and problems • Alternate ways of portraying or solving data or equations
Integrate	• Material from research, reading, or diverse media for papers or presentations	• Material from research, reading, or diverse media for papers or presentations	• Material from research or reading with quantitative data in order to determine findings	• A variety of math processes into solving a real-world problem, such as a design challenge
Interpret	• Words and phrases as they relate to a text • Information presented in diverse media and formats as it contributes to a topic, text, or issue • The meaning and artistry of poems or other writing	• Words and phrases as they relate to a text • Information presented in diverse media and formats as it contributes to a topic, text, or issue • Events in history as presented through diverse sources	• Data, to provide evidence for phenomena	• Models and statements of value (such as equations) • Graphs and data

	ELA	SOCIAL STUDIES	SCIENCE	MATH
Organize	• Claims, concepts, ideas, and evidence in papers and presentations • Sequences in linear or nonlinear fashion for narratives	• Claims, concepts, ideas, and evidence in papers and presentations • Historical sequences and events, including major eras and movements	• Data and information into findings that can be related to an audience • scientific processes and events, including eras of Earth's history	• Data and numbers into meaningful and useful patterns or representations
Summarize	• Key details, sequences, and points and counterpoints in a text	• Key details, sequences, and points and counterpoints in a text or historical event	• Findings revealed by data or experiments	• The trends revealed by data
Support	• Written and oral arguments or information using specific evidence drawn from texts, research, or experiences	• Written and oral arguments or information using specific evidence drawn from texts, research, or experiences	• An argument about scientific phenomena with evidence, models, or data	• Methods or lines of reasoning used to solve a problem
Transform	• One story into another or reality into fictionalized accounts (in order to understand how authors do the same)	• One story into another or reality into fictionalized accounts (in order to understand how authors do the same)	• Numbers and data from one form to another, including visual representations of value	• Numbers and data from one form to another, including visual representations of value

Appendix IV

Part of engaging students in rich word study involves teaching them to look at the roots of words to draw out nuances of meaning and connections to other topics. Use the etymological information here both to spur your own thinking about the academic moves and also to introduce students to the concepts these verbs entail.

Analyze

Late 16th century, from Latin and Greek roots meaning "to loosen up, break, or release" or "to loose a ship from its moorings"

What to ask students:

- How is analyzing a text or other work like breaking it into pieces?

Argue

From Latin arguere, "to prove, make clear, assert, demonstrate" (ca. 1300, meaning "to dispute, oppose")

What to ask students:

- What is the difference between arguing to win a dispute and arguing to prove or demonstrate a point?

Compare/Contrast

From Latin comparare, "to put together, match" and Latin contra- and stare, "to stand against"

What to ask students:

- What is the benefit of combining these two terms so that we both bring works together and place them in opposition within the same academic task?

Describe

From Latin describere (de + scribere), "to write down, sketch"

What to ask students:

- How has the idea of description evolved from its original meaning of merely writing these down?

Determine

From Latin determinare (de + terminare), "to mark an end or boundary, to limit"

What to ask students:

- In what way is making an academic determination like marking a boundary or a limit?

Develop

From French, ca. 1600, developer, "to unwrap, unveil, reveal the meaning of"

What to ask students:

- How is developing a topic or idea like unwrapping or unveiling something hidden?

Evaluate

From French, ca. mid-1800s, evaluer, "to find the value of," applied to mathematics

What to ask students:

- When we evaluate an idea, text, or issue, how is the process similar to or different from solving a mathematical equation?

Explain

From Latin explanare, "to make clear" or "to smooth out, lay on a flat surface"

What to ask students:

- In what ways is explaining something similar to smoothing it out or making it literally clearer in substance?

Imagine

From Latin imaginari, "to make a mental picture of, create an image"

What to ask students:

- What is the role of images and pictures in using our imagination?

Integrate

From Latin integrare, "to renew, restore" ca. 1600s "to make whole," ca. 1800 "to put pieces together to make something into a whole"

What to ask students:

- Is integrating always about renewing or restoring something? What other meanings does the term have in an academic setting?

Interpret

From Latin interpretari, "explain, understand" and interpres, "translator"

What to ask students:

- How are interpretations and explanations similar and different? How does interpreting a language compare to interpreting a text, work of art, or set of data?

Organize

From Latin organum, "organ," and Medieval Latin organizare, "to construct, arrange, contrive"

What to ask students:

- Is organizing the same thing as arranging, or does it involve different skills? If so, what are they?

Summarize

From Latin summa, "whole, total," and Medieval Latin summarius, "having to do with the total," ca. 1400s "brief, containing the sum of"

What to ask students:

- How is the idea of the whole or total of a work related to the idea of summary?

Support

From Medieval Latin supportare, "to endure, convey," based on Latin verb portare, "to carry, to bear"

What to ask students:

- Notice that a part of support involves the idea of carrying something. How does academic support carry or bear the weight of a response?

Transform

From Latin transformare, "to change in shape" (trans-, "across," + formare, "to form")

What to ask students:

- In an academic setting, what else can transformation involve besides simply changing the shape of a response?

Appendix V

These pages offer you a quick-reference guide to using Norman Webb's Depth of Knowledge (DOK) model when you are developing instructional units, assessment tasks, or specific assignments in your content area. Two central concepts in the DOK model are the **cognitive demands** the learning or assessment tasks make on students and the **depth of knowledge or understanding** a given task or question requires to complete or learn it. The assigned DOK level reflects the degree of cognitive processing a task, topic, text, or test demands. Bloom's taxonomy assumed certain verbs required a level of cognitive processing; in his DOK model, however, Webb, argues that it is what *follows* the verb that determines the complexity of the task. Thus, a word like *describe* could appear at any of the four DOK levels, depending on what one was asked to describe.

RECALL AND REPRODUCE: We know but do not transform facts, details, terms, or principles.		
DESCRIPTION: LEVEL ONE	**REPRESENTATIVE ACTIONS**	**ASSIGNMENT and ASSESSMENT TASKS**
Asks students to *remember, list, locate, retell, identify, define*, or use similar skills on assignments or assessments to show that they know certain target knowledge or skills. At this level, the cognitive demands are basic, requiring knowledge and skills that students either do or do not know; that is, Level One questions or tasks do not ask students to use the facts or other details to solve any problems or figure out additional questions.	• *Identify* all metaphors used in a passage. • *List* three examples of irony from the text. • *Retell* what happens to _____ in the text. • *Define* the word _____ using a dictionary. • *Locate* all details to include in works cited. • *Label* each of the types of sentences in a paragraph. • *Memorize* a passage or a complete poem. • *Recall* the questions to ask about a poem. • Find the key facts about _____ in a text. • Search online using the terms provided.	• Which definition is more accurate for the word _____ as it is used in line 4? • What does the author say is the most memorable quality of _____ in his essay? • What are the elements of a Shakespearean sonnet? • In his second soliloquy, Hamlet describes himself as: a. _____ b. _____ c. _____ . • What different definitions does the dictionary offer for the word _____ ?

LEVEL ONE

LEVEL TWO

SKILLS AND CONCEPTS: We process/transform specified knowledge—and then *use* or *apply* it.

DESCRIPTION: LEVEL TWO

Asks students to *infer, organize, predict, compare, classify, show cause-effect, solve simple problems,* or complete similar processes that require students to determine what a word or concept means—based on any available context or background information—and then go beyond the obvious meaning of the word or concept, using it to *estimate, classify, summarize, revise, translate,* or *modify* something to show they understand it.

REPRESENTATIVE ACTIONS

- *Organize* details in order of importance.
- *Compare* how X is similar to Y.
- *Predict* what X will do next based on_____.
- *Display* data as a table or graph.
- *Summarize* an author's argument.
- *Translate* a table or graph into a paragraph.
- *Paraphrase* a specified portion of the text.
- *Distinguish* the effect of X from Y.
- *Define* based on context clues in text.
- *Represent* the story using a plot diagram.

ASSIGNMENT and ASSESSMENT TASKS

- How would you visually represent the relationship between X and Y?
- What other words could you use to describe X based on what you know?
- What question is the author trying to answer in this essay or presentation?
- What other defendable claims could you make about this text?
- Which of the following sentences makes the clearest, most effective claim?

LEVEL THREE

STRATEGIC THINKING AND REASONING: We integrate in-depth knowledge and skills to solve/produce.

DESCRIPTION: LEVEL THREE

Asks students to *assess, develop, draw conclusions, explain events/ processes in terms of concepts, solve complicated problems,* and engage in similar higher order thinking skills that require planning, reasoning, analysis, and evaluation. Students combine their deepening conceptual knowledge and growing array of skills to think strategically about how to solve and create. Level Three emphasizes deep understanding of *one* text or source.

REPRESENTATIVE ACTIONS

- State the reasoning behind a position and provide relevant evidence that supports it.
- *Investigate* a problem or question, *explaining* its origins and how it has evolved over time as a result of human intervention.
- *Develop a logical argument* about how a literary character changes over the course of a story and how they contribute to the meaning of the text as a whole; *provide textual evidence* to support any claims.

ASSIGNMENT and ASSESSMENT TASKS

- What tone is most appropriate given your task, audience, occasion, or purpose?
- What logic informs the sequence of information in this text, and how does it relate to the author's (or your own) purpose?
- How could you revise your paper to improve the logic or cohesion of your ideas?
- Explain how this poem honors *and* departs from the sonnet form and how that departure affects the poem's meaning.

LEVEL FOUR

EXTENDED THINKING: We extend our knowledge to address complex, real problems or questions.

DESCRIPTION: LEVEL FOUR

Asks students to *extend, integrate, reflect, adjust, design, conduct,* and *initiate* or *monitor* authentic problems that have no obvious or predictable solution, drawing on a range of sources, texts of different types and perspectives, often in collaboration with others and over an extended period of time. Level Four thinking demands we extend our thinking across sources, disciplines, and perspectives to solve a problem or create a final product.

REPRESENTATIVE ACTIONS

- *Design* a multimedia slide presentation that *documents* the civil rights movement from different perspectives, *analyzing* key moments and *explaining* their effect on the movement and the people involved.
- *Investigate* a substantive topic for an extended time from multiple perspectives that results in a 10-page formal paper presented in a 3- to 5-minute multimedia TED-Talk format to parents and peers.

ASSIGNMENT and ASSESSMENT TASKS

- Identify themes that are common to the different texts provided, explaining how these themes are treated and developed.
- Analyze how identity contributes to the meaning of each text, choosing a metaphor that effectively captures what these various sources are saying about identity.
- Write an analysis of two (or more) sonnets, constructing and supporting with evidence a claim about what each says about a subject they have in common.

Available for download from **www.resources.corwin.com/burkeacademicmoves**

Appendix VI

These lists, available at **www.resources.corwin.com/burkeacademicmoves,** are meant to be representative, not comprehensive. When similar standards are repeated through the grade levels, we have condensed them into one entry, trying to preserve the intent of the standards in a summary statement. Note that Florida has standards that cover reading and writing in science, social studies, and technical subjects in addition to ELA.

Ultimately, the preponderance of A-List words throughout all state standards confirms that *Academic Moves* will be an invaluable resource no matter where you teach.

Access the Standards Correlation Chart at
www.resources.corwin.com/burkeacademicmoves

Appendix VII

Compare and Contrast

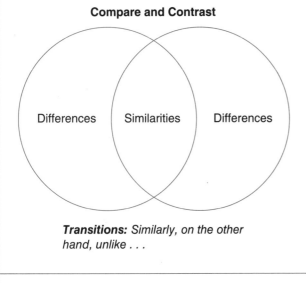

Transitions: *Similarly, on the other hand, unlike . . .*

Cause and Effect

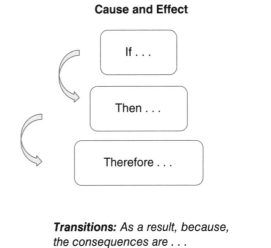

Transitions: *As a result, because, the consequences are . . .*

Concept Definition

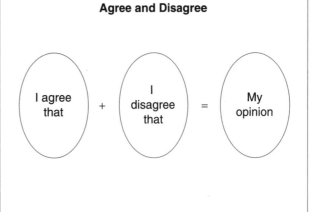

Transitions: *For example, in addition, another characteristic is . . .*

Agree and Disagree

| I agree that | + | I disagree that | = | My opinion |

Transitions: *However, on the other hand, my conclusion is . . .*

Compare and Contrast

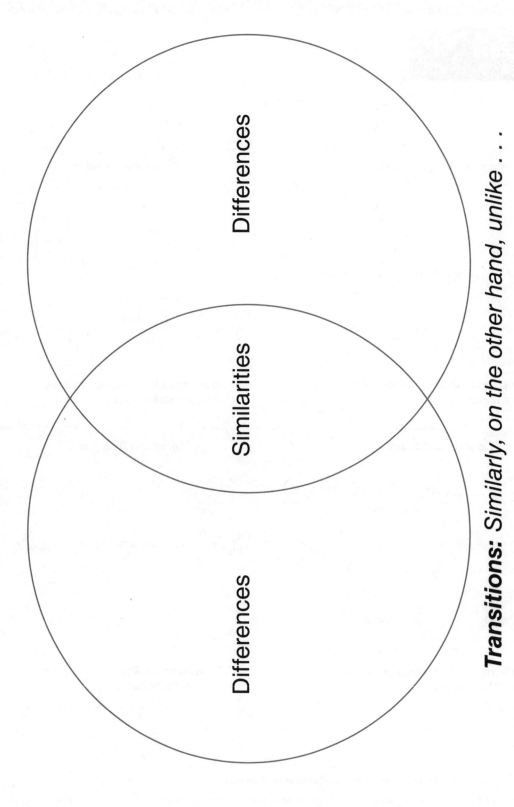

Differences

Similarities

Differences

Transitions: *Similarly, on the other hand, unlike . . .*

Cause and Effect

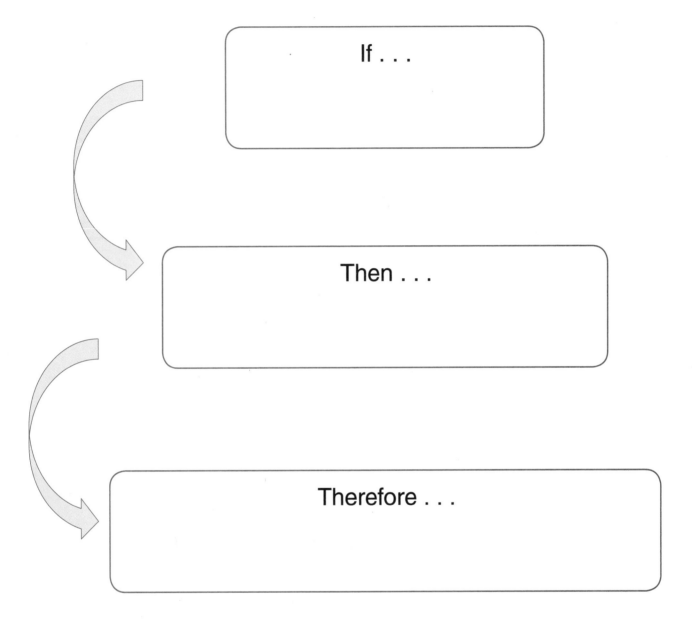

If . . .

Then . . .

Therefore . . .

Transitions: *As a result, because, the consequences are . . .*

Concept Definition

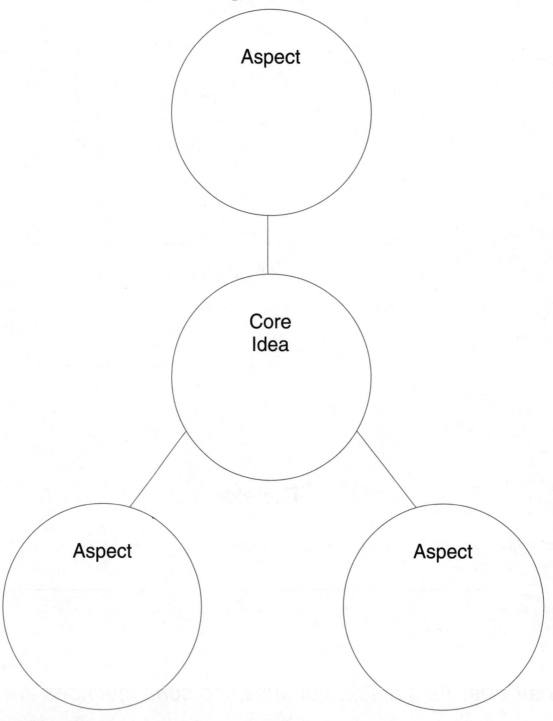

Transitions: *For example, in addition, another characteristic is . . .*

Agree and Disagree

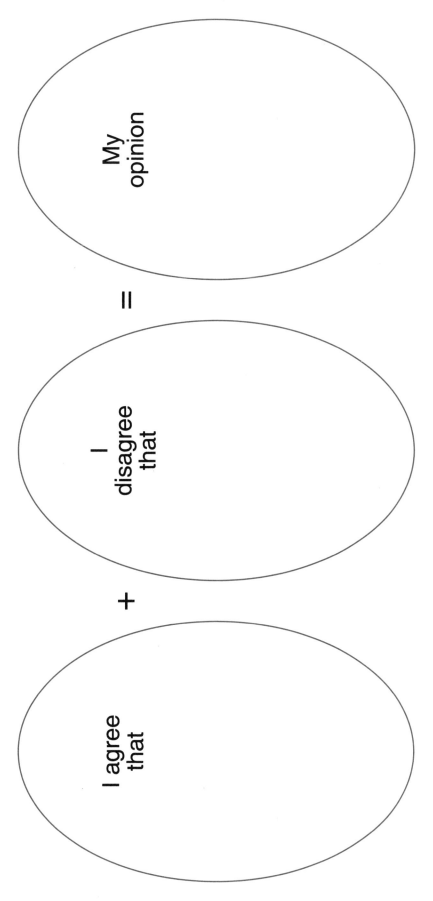

I agree that

+

I disagree that

=

My opinion

Transitions: *However, on the other hand, my conclusion is . . .*

Appendix VIII

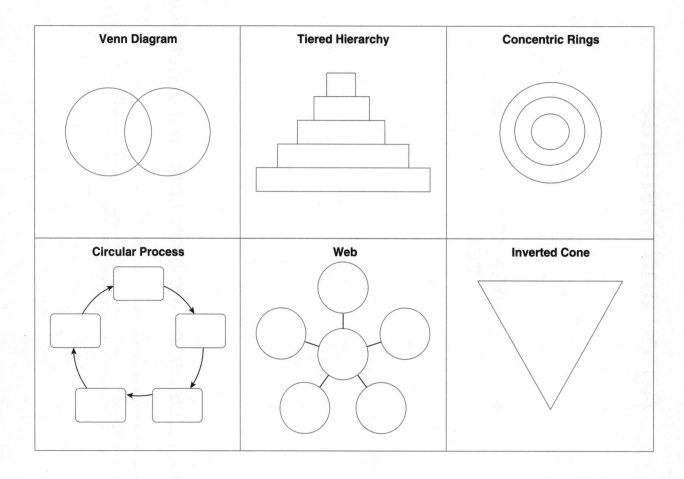

Venn Diagram

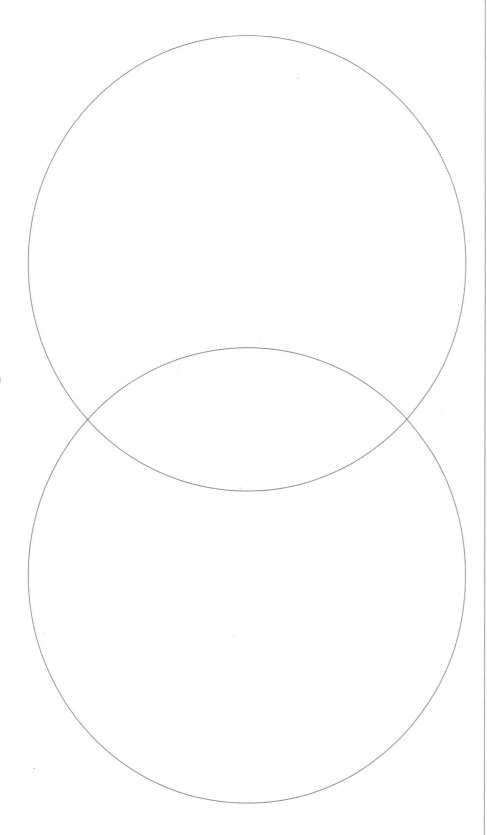

Tiered Hierarchy

Concentric Rings

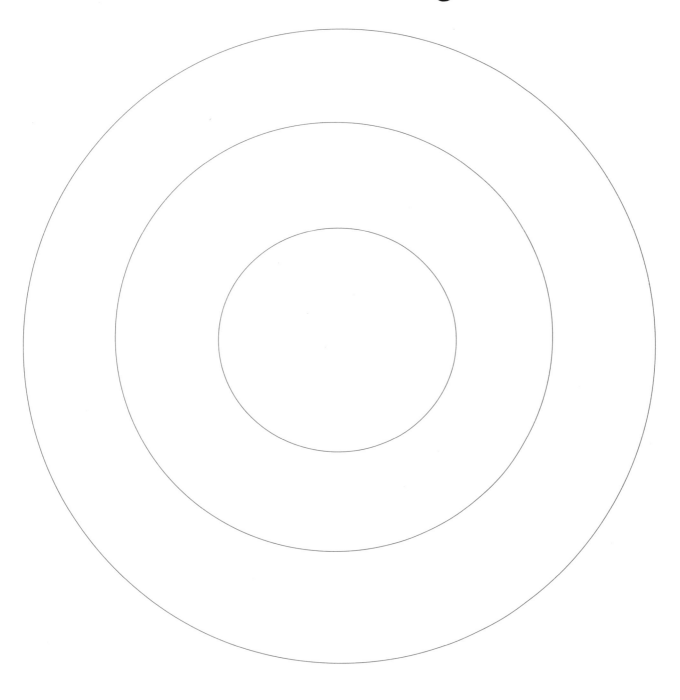

Circular Process

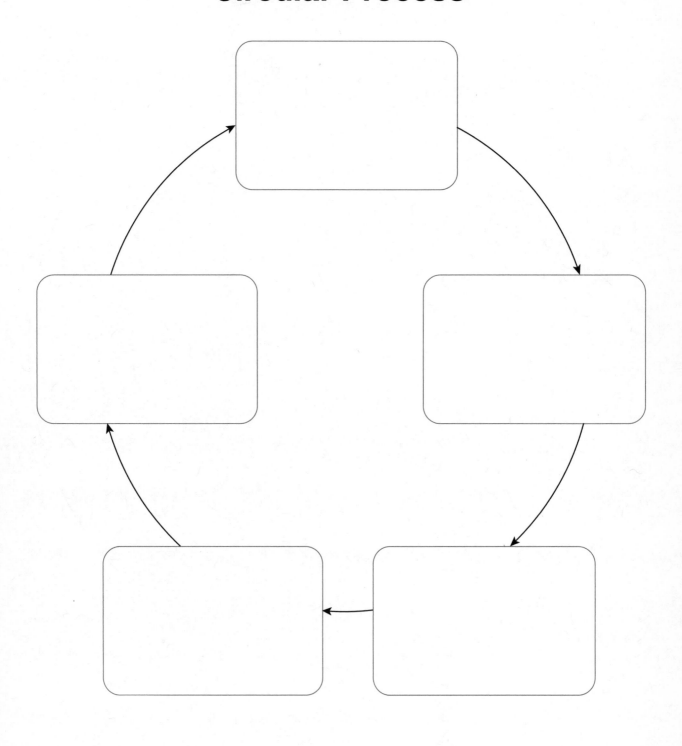

Web

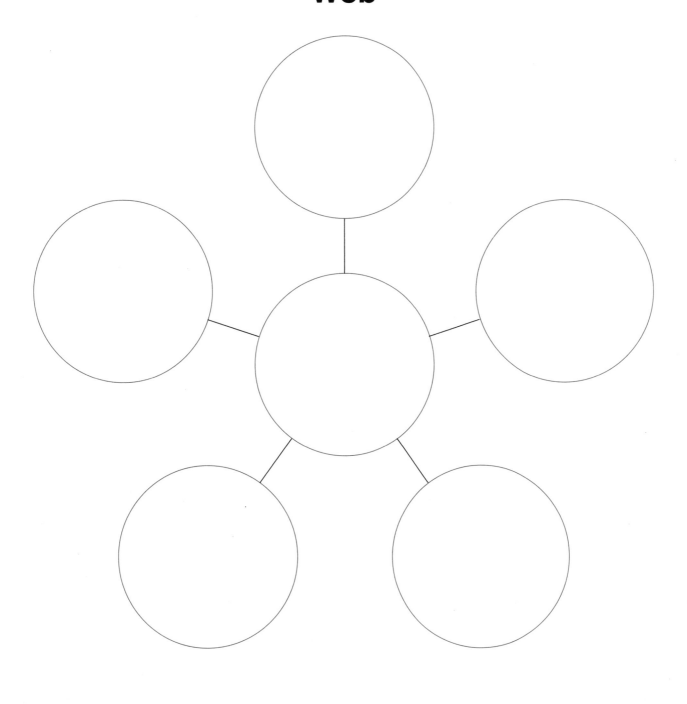

Inverted Cone

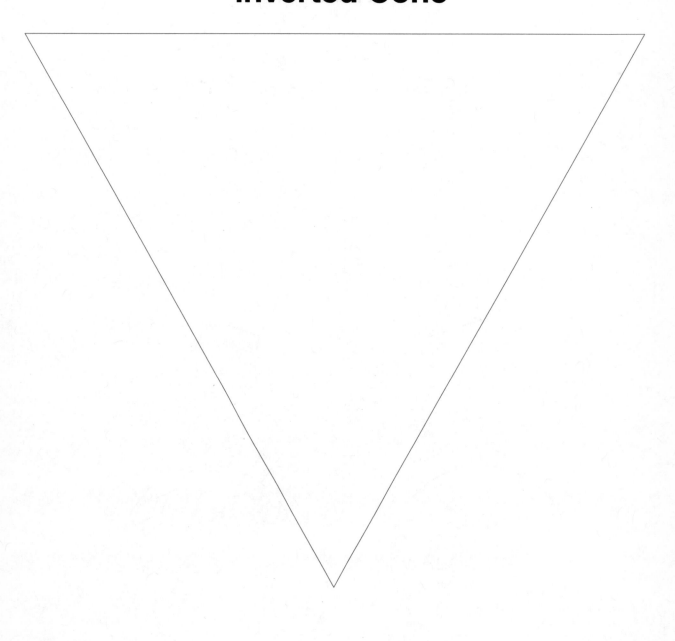

Glossary

anchor chart: a poster-sized list of guidelines, rules, procedures, or reminders about an academic task. Teachers usually collect ideas about rules or guidelines from the class first and then make an anchor chart to post on the wall as a reference for future assignments and class work.

argument: a position on a text, topic, situation, or work that includes an evidence-based claim, recognition of a counterclaim, and persuasive elements. Along with narrative and informational writing, argument is one of three genres of writing presented in the Common Core standards.

Bloom's taxonomy: a six-level interpretation of the levels of cognition students bring to academic tasks. Bloom's taxonomy is typically used to design assessments, activities, and questions that require students to think in a variety of ways. The taxonomy was slightly revised in 2001.

book talk: A short, introductory "teaser" talk designed to attract students to read a book. These can be delivered by a teacher, librarian, other student, or online video.

brainstorming: the process of collecting a wide range of ideas from a group for use in activities or discussion. Recent research shows that some discrimination among ideas as they are collected can be useful, but brainstorming typically involves suspending judgment about the quality of ideas in order to collect the most possible.

claim and counterclaim: a position or stance on a topic, text, or issue that can be argued or supported using evidence (claim). The *counterclaim* is the opposite position; it is usually acknowledged and disavowed (based on evidence or logic) in the course of proving the claim.

close reading: the act of engaging with a text, work, or artifact (such as a video or website) at the level of its key elements or components; close reading involves the examination of individual elements of a text in order to better understand its larger meaning.

concept maps (web): a visual method for organizing ideas. Usually, a concept map begins with one core idea in the center of the page that is connected by lines to several subordinate or relevant ideas; those secondary ideas are in turn connected by lines to yet more concepts or ideas.

content knowledge: information students must learn within a specific discipline in order to apply academic moves successfully in that discipline. Examples might include specific rhetorical elements in literacy or mathematical terminology and formulas in math or science.

decision tree: a graphic organizer that begins with a central question or decision and splits into two or more possible choices with each successive step. A decision tree often resembles a sports tournament bracket, with two spaces opening up for each previous space.

dialectical journal: a tool for readers to note interesting or noteworthy passages while studying a text. A dialectical journal usually involves at least two columns, one for recording the actual passage and one for annotating, or recording, ideas, questions, or thoughts about meaning. A dialectical journal aims to promote a "conversation" between the reader and the text.

evidence: information used to support an argument, claim, or position. Evidence may take the form of specific elements taken from a text or work (such as quotations from a novel or data from a larger set), anecdotes, personal observations and experiences, references to current or historical events, or scientific findings, for instance.

formative assessment: an assessment (including formal tests, discussions, presentations, or a wide range of other activities) that allows a teacher to gather information about student knowledge *before* a concept is fully taught. Formative assessment allows teachers to better tailor learning to the needs of actual students.

graphic organizer: a visual tool that helps students organize thinking, learning, or information.

inference (inferential thinking): understanding of material in a text, work, or artifact that is based on intuitive understanding, the examination of subtext or context, or prior knowledge combined with contextual examination.

informational writing (informative explanatory writing): writing that seeks to inform the reader and convey knowledge accurately. Informational writing may appear as a summary, a process, or a report, for instance. Along with narrative and argument, one of three genres of writing in the Common Core standards.

jigsaw activities: any class activity that allows students to work on material first alone or in a group and then move to other pairings or groups to share what they have learned or developed.

looping: in writing or class activities, the process of drafting a piece of writing or other work and then revisiting it to dig deeper into individual ideas or elements, homing in on new and deeper ideas as one works (not to be confused with the educational term *looping* that refers to the process of teaching the same students over multiple years).

mentor texts: texts or artifacts specifically chosen to demonstrate particular elements or aspects of a discipline. For instance, a page of a novel might serve as a mentor text to teach students how authors use dialogue in actual published writing.

narrative writing: fiction or nonfiction that relates steps over time (a story) using elements of language to communicate not just information but also tone, mood, and concept. Narrative writing may include poetry, fiction, dramatizations, or personal reflections, for instance. Along with informative/ explanatory writing and argument, it is one of three genres of writing presented in the Common Core standards.

paraphrase: an expression of a writer's words in different words or terms, usually in order to achieve clarity or to be more efficient in expression.

prior knowledge: often referred to as *schema*, knowledge that students bring with them to the study of a text, work, or issue.

scaffold: a process or activity that guides learning by breaking it down into distinct steps, making specific information available as learning unfolds, or teaching skills needed to perform a task during the process of performing a task. Ideally, scaffolding allows students to feel appropriately challenged without becoming frustrated at the inability to complete a task.

self-efficacy: the sense that one *can* accomplish a task or learning goal. Struggling or reluctant learners are often subject to a low sense of self-efficacy, which further impedes their ability to learn.

storyboard: a visual tool for planning a plot or story, usually made up of visual panels or drawings that show how a story will unfold.

summative assessment: a measure of learning that comes at the end of a unit of study. Summative assessments may appear as formal tests, presentations, discussions, or a wide variety of other products.

synthesis: the process of bringing together similar or dissimilar works, texts, situations, or issues in order to make greater sense out of the whole.

T chart: a two-column graphic organizer designed to help students compare and contrast or otherwise organize dichotomous ideas. A T chart might be used to list pros and cons, similarities and differences, or before and after thinking, for instance.

text: a piece of writing, speech, video, or other artifact in its original format. It is important to note that in its current usage, "text" is not limited to printed words; it may include visuals, digital information, or material presented in a variety of other manners.

transfer: the act of applying learning of one kind to another task, realm, discipline, or process. For example, a student who learns the formula for area by studying a textbook would have to demonstrate the ability to transfer that formula to another task if asked to construct a bookshelf.

Venn diagram: a set of two overlapping circles used to organize information or thinking. The purpose of using a Venn diagram is to examine the areas where information falls into distinct categories or overlaps those categories.

verisimilitude: the quality of seeming real or true; even stories that are fantastical in nature may possess verisimilitude as they offer a level of believability to the reader.

Webb's Depth of Knowledge: a four-tier system used to describe the level of abstraction and cognitive demand (over time) required of academic tasks and assessments.

wiki: a website that allows multiple users to contribute and access information. Wikipedia is the most famous example.

writing on demand: writing tasks that require an answer to a specific prompt written in a timed setting.

zoom in (and zoom out): the process of examining a work, text, or idea by looking at the big picture or whole piece (zooming out) and also at the constituent parts of the piece (zooming in) in order to understand the whole more clearly.

Index

Distinguish, 27. *See also* Comparison/
contrast
Document-based questions (DBQs),
128–129
DOK (Depth of Knowledge).
See Depth of Knowledge
Dombek, K., xiii
Drawing, 106
Dystopian literature, 112–114

ELA (English language arts), using
Academic Moves in, 209–211 (chart)
ELLs (English language learners)
and analysis, 4
and argument, 16
challenges to, xii
and comparison/contrast, 29
and description, 42
and determination, 53
and development, 64
and evaluation, 81
and explanation, 96
and inference, 4
and interpretation, 136–137
and organization, 148–149
and summarizing, 162
and support, 173
and synthesis, 121
and transformation, 186–187
Empathize, 201
Endings, imagining, 104 (box)
Engineering, development of ideas in,
70–72, 70 (figure)
English language arts (ELA),
using Academic Moves in,
209–211 (chart)
English language learners (ELLs).
See ELLs
Essays, analytical. *See* Analytical essays
Essays, digital, 107
Essays, personal, 97–98
Ethos, 16, 16 (figure), 17
Etymology, of Academic Moves, 212–213
Evaluation
and answers, 78 (box)
defined, 76
and discussion, 81
and ELLs, differentiating instruction
for, 81
and evidence, 78 (box)
mental moves for, 79, 84–86
and multimedia, 82
obstacles to mental moves for, 79
vs. opinion, 80–81

and personal connections, 78 (box)
planning page for, 91
practicing, 80–82
preparing students for, 78–79
and presentation, 81
rubric for, 90
scaffolding with DOK, 89
in standards, 76–77
student examples of, 83–88
tasks for, 83 (box), 87 (box),
89, 210 (chart)
and technology, 82
underlying skills for, 77
YouTube moment, 82
See also Academic Moves
Evidence
evaluating, 78 (box)
and interpretation, 134
Expectations, xiii
Explanation, 93 (box)
defined, 92
and ELLs, differentiating instruction
for, 96
mental moves for, 94, 97–98
obstacles to mental moves for, 94
vs. opinions, 94
planning page for, 102
practicing, 95–96
preparing students for, 93–94
producing, 97–99
rubric for, 101
scaffolding with DOK, 100
and self-efficacy, 95
in standards, 92–93
student examples of, 97–99
tasks for, 97 (box), 98 (box),
100, 210 (chart)
underlying skills for, 92
value of, 93, 95, 98–99
writing about math, 98–99
YouTube moment for, 96
See also Academic Moves
Explanatory writing. *See* Informational
writing
Extended thinking, 215 (chart).
See also Depth of Knowledge

Failure, 103, 105, 106, 110
Faulkner, William, 6–7
The Fault in Our Stars (Green),
83–86
Ferlazzo, L., 16
Fishbowl discussion, 18
Food deserts/food insecurity, 43–44

Generate, 201
Gilman, Charlotte Perkins, 31–32
Gilmor, B., xiii
Goleman, Daniel, xiv
Graff, G., xii, xiii
Graphic novels, interpretation of,
138–139
Graphic organizers
circular process, 186 (figure),
226 (figure)
concentric rings, 186 (figure),
225 (figure)
concept maps, 42, 65, 112, 112 (figure),
173, 173 (figure), 186 (figure),
222 (figure), 227 (figure)
inverted cone, 186 (figure), 228 (figure)
and support, 173, 173 (figure),
177, 177 (figure)
T charts, 17, 29
tiered hierarchy, 186 (figure),
224 (figure)
for transformation, 186, 186 (figure)
Venn diagram, 16, 16 (figure),
26, 29, 186 (figure), 223 (figure)
The Great Gatsby (Fitzgerald),
52, 55–56
Green, John, 83–86, 96

Hamlet (Shakespeare), 150–153, 160
Hand washing station, 70–72, 70 (figure),
71 (figure), 72 (figure)
Heritage, M., xii
Herland (Gilman), 31–32
Herndon, S., xiii
Historical writing, 33–34
"How and Why We Read"
(Green), 96
Hull-Sypnieski, K., 16
Hypothesis. *See* Imagination

Ideas
developing. *See* Development
generating, 106. *See also* Imagination/
imaginative tasks
supporting. *See* Support
transformation of. *See* Transformation
IDEO, 107
Imagery, in description, 39 (box)
Imagination/imaginative tasks
defined, 103
and discussion, 106–107
and failure, 103, 105, 106, 110
imagining beginnings, 104 (box)
imagining endings, 104 (box)

CORWIN
A SAGE Company

Corwin is committed to improving education for all learners by publishing books and other professional development resources for those serving the field of PreK–12 education. By providing practical, hands-on materials, Corwin continues to carry out the promise of its motto: **"Helping Educators Do Their Work Better."**